A TO Z
OF
ASTROLOGY

Indian Astrology has stood the test of time ever since the sage Bhrigu revealed his mastery of this ancient wisdom of forecasting the influence of the stars on human affairs. After 40 years of his studies in Astrology, Mahan Vir Tulli has penned this encyclopaedia based on the characteristics and behaviour patterns of Ascendants and planetary configurations which shape the course of events.

Diplomacy and Astrology may make strange companions, but Tulli brought them together professionally during his chequered career in the Indian Foreign Service. He has travelled to over 100 countries, where he lectured in several languages and held discussions on Astro sciences, meditation and para psychology. He has met world celebrities from all walks of life and predicted historic events with great precision. In the process, he has earned the sobriquet "the Oracle of Delhi".

Tulli is currently promoting this knowledge through his Mahan Astrological Research Centre established in Delhi after his retirement from the IFS.

A to Z
of
ASTROLOGY

MAHAN VIR TULLI

S. Abdul Majeed & Co.
In Association with
Sterling Publishers (P) Ltd

Published in Malaysia by:
S. Abdul Majeed & Co.
2210 Malayan Mansion
Jalan Masjid India
50100 Kuala Lumpur
MALAYSIA
1995

© *Mahan vir Tulli*

ISBN NO: 81207-1647-7

Printed by:
Percetakan Sooriya
(wholly owned by S. Abdul Majeed & Co)

PREFACE

An attempt has been made in this book to bring to you in a capsule the wider influences and impact of ancient Hindu Astrology in a fairly exhaustive manner, as also the significance of planetary configurations and their impact on human life. The fundamental principles of astrology lay greater emphasis on the predictive part. These have been clearly brought out.

It is hoped that it will help amateurs as also savants of astrology to derive full benefit and appreciate its usefulness in day-to-day life, more particularly with a view to counteracting the adverse planetary configurations. If the natives are well aware of their personal and other astrological indicators, and have an insight into day-to-day planetary movements, they can predict through the right choice of alternatives of the principles explained in this book. These fronts are :

(1) Finance,
(2) Health,
(3) Career,
(4) Hobbies and Pastimes,
(5) Marital life and Social Relationships, and
(6) Honours and Awards.

It is hoped that this book will help the reader to achieve personal choices and overcome the barriers/speed breakers that occur at the crucial junctures of life. The forces beyond send across their own good and not so good signals, and wise men act accordingly. The purpose of life on this planet is to find greater peace of mind and happiness and I hope that the book will surely prove to be a comprehensive guide to all — from the common man to the occult lover — in their noble quest for peace, harmony and happiness.

The basic tenets and principles explained in the several chapters of the book have been tested and tried, and I sincerely hope that these general guidelines contained in the book would be found useful and helpful by one and all.

Life on this planet as well as human behaviour is greatly influenced by planetary configurations and the transits, which highly influence the lives of the natives in all spheres of human activity, particularly health, position and prestige, happiness, including marital bliss, financial gains, business acumen and, most important of all, personal relations and love life.

One must have the right type of astro-guidance. He should always consult experienced and competent astrologers, as it is only with proper and right astro-guidance, and with timely remedial measures that many vexing and intricate problems can be solved.

Life on this planet is a continuous struggle. The moment a child is born, a book containing his fate is opened. He may face good times and not so good times. He has to put in effort and struggle, meet with obstacles and failures as also accept the successes and defeats coming his way. Our long voyage in the sea of life is conditioned by some mystic and hidden forces. A most beautiful and highly accomplished girl does not get the comfort and joy of marital bliss, whereas an ugly woman, with no talents and qualifications, meets a handsome millionaire, entices him in seconds and becomes his consort for life time. This is what the *karmik* influences are all about.

The first six houses of a natal chart speak about the *karmik* influences, whereas the later six houses reflect effort and struggle. Just as a right medicine can cure a patient, similarly the right type of astrological guidance can solve many a problem. The adverse planetary transits cause hassles, inconveniences, discomforts, pain and morbidity and sometimes major health problems while the benefic transits make life smooth, comfortable and enjoyable.

Proper astro-guidance can help in the diagnosis of serious problems of health, love and life and can assist one and all in meeting the challenges faced by the medical and social scientists. Often the remedial measures suggested to ward off the adverse planetary influences can avoid serious mishaps, financial losses and make life more meaningful and pleasant, provided they are undertaken with the required degree of care and devotion.

I would like to express grateful thanks to Sh. B.S. Rangachari, noted Astrologer and Sh. N. Kumar, the renowned Astro-Numerologist from Kurukshetra, for their valuable advice and help in clearing many doubts. My thanks are also due to Mr. S.K. Ghai, Managing Director, Sterling Publishers Pvt. Ltd., for having agreed to publish this book entitled *A to Z of Astrology*. I will be failing in my duty if I do not thank my wife, Indu Bala, for putting up with my late hours of work in writing this book.

I hope that the book will be found useful by all those who have interest in this science.

Mahan Vir Tulli
I.F.S. (Retd.)

CONTENTS

1

INTRODUCTION TO ASTROLOGY

We are on the threshold of entering the 21st Century, which implies a greater thrust of super-technology, a jet-set life style. Our lives will be increasingly determined by what the super computers are fed with and perhaps soon enough we may be relying on robots who would be at our beck and call. For all we know, we might be heading for an almost mechanical life where sophisticated gadgets would have a stronger role to play, almost overtaking our lives.

Yet, notwithstanding the growing significance and impact of the scientific temperament, one essential fact remains undisputed and that is the ability of the human mind to see and perceive beyond what meets the eye only at the surface.

It has been established over the ages that the planets right up there in the solar system have a formidable influence on human life, the thinking and behaviour patterns of human beings, and that the turn of events in his/her life are largely shaped by the stars in our galaxy. The Sun and the planets have the greatest and most immediate influence on the Earth's atmosphere and environment because the Earth is a part of the solar system.

Seasonal changes on Earth, the occurrences of natural calamities, the rhythmic life pattern of plants and animals, tidal waves and weather patterns are synonymous with the movements of the planets in relation to the Earth's movements. Due to this changing pattern, the lives of men are also continuously in a state of flux. The science which can analyse and interpret the results of these influences is called "astrology"

Now we are stepping into a field of knowledge and interest which is highly debatable. The redeeming factor is that this debate too in itself is highly scientific.

Astrology is a combination of Science and Metaphysics. To make a map and erect a horoscope from the birth particulars is a scientific process requiring considerable expertise, skill and application.

There are five basic elements in the human system which directly co-relate to parallel elements in the solar system and this is precisely where the crux of the issue lies. Hence, going in for an extensive and intensive astrological study can be a pretty arduous task because each movement of each planet owing to its position in the respective birth chart has to be closely monitored which is a complex and intricate task. So, you can vouch for a fair amount of accuracy only when its finer nuances have been meticulously researched. So by no means should it give us a superstitious outlook because astrology is only an attempt to have a glimpse of the future stream of life and foresee the likely trend of events which would consequently help us to manage our affairs in a more sagacious and expeditious manner.

Just as we can decipher the impact of astrological science on an individual's life pattern, it is similarly analysed for a nation and country, as also for a town or a city or an organisation at large. Even the plants and animal life are influenced by the planetary configurations. By the action of the Moon, flow-tides and ebb-tides occur on Earth.

Similarly, the water balance in human body is influenced by the Moon. This water-balance, on the other hand, controls our bodies and mind.

Similarly many ailments are caused by the adverse planetary impact of the Moon, e.g., Influenza, Chronic Coughs and Colds, Bronchitis, Tuberculosis, Asthma, Nervous Tensions, Gout, Sciatica etc. A weak Moon in a birth chart can also create lunatics. Mental disorders are caused by an adverse or weak Moon and it has been observed that the problems of mental patients get accentuated on new moon days and full moon days.

The Moon influences the mind and emotional reactions. Similarly, the evil spell of each of the planets causes serious ailments. Whether a particular planet is auspicious or otherwise for a native requires detailed analytical study of the birth chart and other parameters.

A planet, when in an exalted position, is fairly strong and if unafflicted by any malefic planet is good and blesses the native with favourable results.

Similarly a Planet in a *moolatrikone* (a positive sign owned by a planet) position is also considered to be auspicious to cause good results provided, of course, if it is not aspected by any acrimonious planet. A planet in its own house, i.e., *swakhetra* position is also good, if it does not receive the aspect or association of any malefic or enemy planet.

A planet in an enemy-house or in a house conjoined with an enemy or in a debilitating position is quite an inimical planet. We should look at the 27 Constellations (Asterisms) and their Lords.

The Zodiac consists of 360 degrees of an arc which is divided into 27 Constellations. We have also to judge the good or evil relations of the planets with the constellations and their Lords. These Constellation Divisions come in handy while analysing the results of transits of planets through these constellations. But the entire calculation is carried out on the basis of scientific principles and time tested theories.

India is accepted as the leading country in the field of astro-sciences by world renowned astrologers. The ancient Indian *Atharva Veda* is the starting point of Indian Astrology, in which it is clearly indicated that all sciences of the world may have defects or flaws but astrology is an Absolute Science which is amply proved by the movement and actions of the Sun and the Moon and other planets, and the cycles within which the events repeat themselves.

The great Indian Astrologer, Bhrigu, in his most ancient treatise *Bhrigu Samhita* propounded the results of his study on an astrological basis (regarding any man or woman with a particular Birth Chart or Horoscope), so lucidly that even today after a considerable lapse of time, whatever the ancient Indian philosopher propounded on astrology is relevant with full force. So the fact that Astrology is at par with other natural sciences cannot be doubted. The works of the great Indian Astrologers, like "Parashar", "Jaimini", "Arya Bhatta", "Varaha-Mihir" etc. are valuable landmarks in the history of Indian Astrology.

The astounding action of astrological science is manifested by the   diseases that are caused by the action of evil planets on a particular native. From a correct horoscope, we can decipher, in advance, what ailments may afflict a particular native. For that matter, even in medical science, no matter how brilliant a specialist is, his diagnosis can go wrong in certain cases. Some of the finer engineering brains behind the construction of bridges fail when they predict that the bridges will last for 200 years but they collapse in two months.

So, somewhere along the line, calculations may go wrong. To err is human. Besides, let us not forget that there are always certain forces at work which go beyond human calculations and subsequent perceptions and predictions. The lattice structure of astronomy and astrology is based on the movement of the heavenly bodies. It is imperative to understand the complexity of this movement. Since at no two points in time and space can all the parameters coincide, hence the significance of each and every moment, in its entirety, cannot be underrated. The movement of the planet's rotation on its own axis, the planet's revolution around the centre of the universe, the Sun and the cosmic displacement or drifting of the whole universe. The third movement is as imperceptible as that of a glacier, yet it is there. This may well explicate the "errors" and factors of chance in astro-predictions as the third cosmic movement is slightly beyond human comprehension.

Now it is time to talk about the co-relation between astrology and numerology, i.e., astro-numerology. This science of numbers also makes a very fascinating study while making predictions. It is undisputed that there is *karmik* influence. The Hindu system bears a direct impact on one's birth, death, marriage, children etc. Surely, there is an element of truth in the contention that such acts are pre-determined and in a way pre-destined.

The astro-sciences, like a doctor, guide you. Say, if your birth chart has been correctly drawn and carefully analysed and interpreted. It can fairly reveal what would be your basic characteristics, likes and dislikes, marital harmony or discord, your level of intellect and many such related matters including love life, professional achievements, honours and distinctions. A systematic study of astro-science goes a long way in getting the best out of one's life and helping one to sail through turbulent times. Numerology is so lucid that even a non-expert can gain from this study. It is not as transcendental and mystical as the occult sciences are usually thought to be.

Astro-numerology can efficaciously build a better character and add to your success especially for a person who has developed a feeling of insecurity, loneliness or fear of the unknown. He/she can be brought back to life with more confidence under its guidance. Such a person can override unfounded apprehensions empirically. The predictions, when made with the utmost accuracy, can extend a guiding hand.

The Hindu system of astrology, as also other branches of the occult, including astro-numerology, are based on perception, observation and experiment. And the criterion of truth, as an observed phenomenon, can be carefully analysed and sifted in a scientific manner. This ancient scientific heritage is sound one and we should feel proud of. So modern science should not dismiss our achievements in the occult.

Astrology is growing in importance. Just as the right medicine can cure a patient, similarly proper and timely astro-guidance can solve one's problems in life. Our achievements in the study and research of Astrology and other astro-sciences have been remarkable. This is a continuous process and more research is needed. All this is based on the concept that human life is inseparable and intimately allied to the multifarious movements in the cosmos. To reiterate the human effort and will power, spiritual evolution and other remedial measures can change the fate of an individual or nation and, therefore, by studying and applying the science of astrology, one can contribute a lot for the well being of human beings.

The right use of names, colours, dress, dates, partners, business associates, through astrological assistance or guidance gives life a smooth run. For that you need a harmonious application of cosmic energy. Our astrological knowledge is based on past experiences extending over thousands of years which have gone into the making of the science of Hindu Astrology.

Everyone is happy to possess wealth and riches. It is not enough to simply possess wealth but one should be able to use this wealth for one's benefit and happiness. The astro-sciences which are India's rich heritage should be properly understood and made use of in day-to-day life and in predicting major events such as earthquakes, natural calamities, so that man can take effective and timely measures to counteract these adversities and make life more pleasant and enjoyable on this planet.

2

THE ZODIAC AND THE SOLAR SYSTEM

GENERAL

Time Limit

A day	=	24 hours
An hour	=	60 minutes
A minute	=	60 seconds
1 day	=	86, 400 seconds.

The Timetable

A day	=	60 *ghatikas*
A *ghatika*	=	60 *vighatikas*
A *vighatika*	=	60 *viliptas*
A *lipta*	=	60 *viliptas*
A *lipta*	=	60 *paras*
A *para*	=	60 *tatparas*
∴ 1 day	=	46,656,000,000 *tatparas*.

Time is eternal. It cannot be measured. But a change may happen in a thing, as mud becomes a pot through the labour of a potter. This new form may be said to have started at a certain particular time and its destruction by being broken etc. may also be indicated by a certain time. This duration or interim period when it existed as a pot, is the limitation of time for the object.

Astrology may be divided into seven divisions :

(1) Vegetable Horoscope.

(2) Animal Horoscope.
(3) Human Natal Astrology.
(4) Mundane Astrology [Political Astrology].
(5) Horary Astrology [Prasna Tantra].
(6) Electional or Muhurta Astrology.
(7) Commercial Astrology.

No. 1. Indicates the seasons and mostly relates to crops and weather conditions.

No. 2. Indicates animals, their increase, decrease, etc.

The Solar year has twelve months called :

Chittarai	*Adi*	*Alpisi*	*Thai*
Vykasi	*Avani*	*Karthikai*	*Masi*
Ani	*Perattasi*	*Margali*	*Panguni*

These months are calculated according to the entry of the Sun into each Sign from Aries.

The Hindu Cycle of Sixty Years

Prabhava	1987-1988	*Sarvajit*	2007-2008
Vibhaca	1988-1989	*Sarvadhari*	2008-2009
Sukla	1989-1990	*Virodhi*	2009-2010
Pramoduta	1990-1991	*Vidruti*	2010-2011
Prajotpatty	1991-1992	*Khara*	2011-2012
Angirasa	1992-1993	*Nandana*	2012-2013
Srimukha	1993-1994	*Vijaya*	2013-2014
Bhava	1994-1995	*Jaya*	2014-2015
Yuva	1995-1996	*Manmatha*	2015-2016
Dhatu	1996-1997	*Durmukhi*	2016-2017
Iswara	1997-1998	*Hevilambi*	2017-2018
Bahudhanya	1998-1999	*Vilabmi*	2018-2019
Pramadhi	1999-2000	*Vikary*	2019-2020
Vikrama	2000-2001	*Sarwari*	2020-2021
Vishu	2001-2002	*Plava*	2021-2022
Chitrabhanu	2002-2003	*Subhakrit*	2022-2023
Swabhanu	2003-2004	*Subhakrit*	2023-2024
Tarana	2004-2005	*Krodhi*	2024-2025
Parthiva	2005-2006	*Viswavasu*	2025-2026
Vyaya	2006-2007	*Parabhava*	2026-2027

Plavanga	2027-2028	*Pingala*	2037-2038
Keelaka	2028-2029	*Kalayukti*	2038-2039
Soumya	2029-2030	*Siddhadri*	2039-2040
Sadharana	2030-2031	*Rowdri*	2040-2041
Virodhikrit	2031-2032	*Durmati*	2041-2042
Paridhavi	2032-2033	*Dumdubi*	2042-2043
Pramadeecha	2033-2034	*Rudrotggari*	2043-2044
Ananada	2034-2035	*Raktakshi*	2044-2045
Rakshasa	2035-2036	*Krodhana*	2045-2046
Nala	2036-2037	*Akshaya*	2046-2047

Each year is said to produce certain effects independently on its own and that refers not to any individual but has a distinct bearing on mundane horoscopy with particular reference to the common people.

Name of Planet			*Time taken to move in a Sign or Rashi*
Sun	—	*Surya*	About 1 month
Moon	—	*Chandra*	2-1/4 days
Mars	—	*Mangal*	45 days
		or Kuja	
Mercury	—	*Budha*	About a month
Jupiter	—	*Guru*	A year
Venus	—	*Sukra*	A month
Saturn	—	*Sani*	2-1/4 years
Dragon's Head	—	*Rahu*	1-1/2 years
Dragon's Tail	—	*Ketu*	1-1/2 years

The Sun and the Moon **never** have a retrograde motion but may have an accelerated or retarded motion.

Rahu and Ketu always have a retrograde motion.

All the other planets have direct, retrograde, accelerated or retarded motions.

THE ZODIAC

The Zodiac is an imaginary belt stretching about 9° north and 9° south of the eclipse within which the planets and the Moon remain in the course of their movement. In case of the Moon, the deviation from the ecliptic is about + 5°. This belt is divided into 12 equal parts each of 30° and each part is called a sign. According to the western system of Astrology, the first sign, i.e., Aries starts from the point of intersection of the ecliptic and the equator. There are 12 signs., in both the systems, the first being Aries, followed by Taurus. The twelfth sign of the Zodiac is Pisces.

Signs or Rashis

There are twelve signs in the Zodiac, namely, Aries, Taurus, Gemini, Cancer, Leo, Virgo, Libra, Scorpio, Sagittarius, Capricorn, Aquarius, and Pisces. Each of these signs has a stretch of 30° in the Zodiac.

PLANETS

The planets which, according to astrology, have the most powerful influence on the Earth are nine in number, namely, Sun, Moon, Mars, Mercury, Jupiter, Venus, Saturn, Rahu and Ketu. The last two are called the shadowy planets as they do not have physical or celestial bodies like the other planets. Of the two places where the Moon crosses the ecliptic (that is, the path of the Sun), the north point is known as Rahu and the corresponding south point which is exactly 180° away from the former is called Ketu. In spite of the fact that they are not celestial bodies like other planets, they are very sensitive and effective points and it is on account of their powerful influence on the Earth, that our ancient savants of astrology have termed them as planets.

In western astrology, though some importance is now being given to Rahu and Ketu, these planets find little importance in their predictive system. On the other hand, the western astrologers have given significant place to the newly discovered planets Uranus (also called Herschel), Neptune and Pluto. Each planet exercises its influence on the Earth according to its strength, position and dignity etc., in the Zodiac at the time of birth of an individual, or even in day-to-day affairs.

Movements and Motions of Planets

All the planets (Rahu and Ketu excepted) perform the double function of not only revolving on their own axes (from West to

East), but also round the Sun. Saturn is the most distant from the Earth. Jupiter, Mars, the Sun, Venus, Mercury and the Moon come next in order of their distance from the terrestial globe. The velocity of each planet diminshes as its distance from the Earth increases.

Although, in Western astrology not much significance is attached to the two shadowy planets, Rahu and Ketu in the Indian system these planets which are called *karmic* planets are given great importance.

While Rahu is associated with power and affluence, Ketu is considered more spiritual, helping the Hindus to develop their nobler and spiritual interests and to facilitate attainment of *moksha* or Salvation. The extra Saturnine planets, Uranus, Neptune and Pluto do not find much prominence in the Indian System though, of late, more and more Indian Astrolgers are blending the Eastern and Western Systems to derive the full benefits from the researches made by the Western Scholars.

The planets exercise their influence on the life on this planet, according to their placement, strength and dignity in the Zodiac at the time of birth.

The Sun is the centre of Solar System and radiates solar energy towards the Earth from its distance of 92 millions of miles. In spite of its great distance from Earth, solar energy regulates life on this planet. Similarly other planets like Saturn, Jupiter, Mars, Venus, Mercury, the Moon who have varying orbits and are part of the Solar System also exercise influence on life on this globe. The newly discovered planets, Uranus, Neptune and Pluto are extra Saturnian planets, as their orbits are far away from that of Saturn. Mercury and the Moon are closer to the Earth and are fast moving. These are termed as inferior planets, as their orbits lie within the Earth's orbit round the Sun. On the other hand, Mars, Jupiter, Saturn, etc. are termed as superior planets.

The planets do not have uniform motions. At certain times they are faster in their speed, while at other times they slow down or become stationary for a few days. Their irregular movement is of interest to us.

On certain days the actual motions are slightly less or more. This is due to the fact that the planets while revolving round the Sun, owing to cosmic influences, become somewhat irregular in their movements. A planet's revolution is the time taken by a planet to conplete its orbit across the Zodiac. The planets and the time taken by them to complete the revolution is indicated against each.

Planets	Time taken
Moon	27.32 days
Sun	365.2422 days (12 months approx.)
Mercury	87.97 days
Venus	224.70 days
Mars	1.9 years
Jupiter	11.86 years
Saturn	29.46 years
Uranus	84.02 years
Neptune	164.77 years
Pluto	248.42 years

These planets move in orbits, which are elliptical. The planets are at certain times farther from the Sun, when they are stated to be in their aphelion. The point of the orbit when they are nearest to the Sun is called the perihelion. At aphelion, the planets have slower motions, while at perihelion, their movement is faster than their average speed.

Mercury, which is fast moving, is very close to the Sun. It often becomes retrograde and its movement very unsteady. Mercury moves within a range of 28° from the Sun.

Rahu and Ketu invariably move in reverse direction. This movement is called retrogression. The Sun and the Moon are never retrograde. They have only direct motions. The Moon is the nearest to the Earth and exercises considerable influence on life on this planet.

The Earth revolves around the Sun in roughly one year. The Earth rotates on its own axis in 24 hours. The Moon moves around the Earth in 28 days and it takes 2-1/2 days to move in one sign.

Characteristics and Description of Planets

Sun

The Sun is the king of planets and represents the soul. He is cruel in nature, masculine by instinct and Kshatriya by caste.The Sun should never be mistaken to be a malefic. He has broad shoulders. He is tall and majestic, has few hairs, possesses strong bones and eyes of yellow colour and is of bilious disposition. The body is both real and mixed black and is broad, loves war, is strong during day. He is lean, likes bitter and pungent things, loves truth, is charitable, righteous, God-fearing, loving and helps others. He is dignified, honourable, generous, punctual and has good and serious manners. He is industrious, entertains noble thoughts. He has a strong will power, which bestows power, authority, dignity, resolution, self reliance and is a source of all vital energy. The Sun causes diseases of the heart, eyes, arteries, lungs and vital organs. He wanders through forests. He looks in appearance as around fifty years (Earth). Wears cloth of thick thread. The Sun represents the soul in man. A well placed Sun in the natal chart bestows an aggressive individuality.

Moon

She is the queen among planets and is next to Sun. She represents the mind as Sun represents the soul in any living organism. It also represents, personality, feeling, emotions, passions, pleasure and pain. She is waxing or waning accordingly as manifested in the brighter or darker half. The former is called the *Shukla Paksha* and the latter, *krishna paksha*, on Earth (apparent observation).

The waxing Moon is benefic, whereas the waning would be malefic. Some perceive the Moon to be benefic from fifth of *Shukla Paksha* to the fifth of *krishna paksha* and malefic afterwards. Moon is female and *Vaisya* by the caste according to the Manu Samhita. She influences more strongly during the night as compared to the Sun's activity during the day.

She is fair, attractive in appearance, capable of knowing things, related to aesthetics, white in colour as observed on Earth, fickle-minded, wavering, breezy, and phlegmatic in constitution, and possesses more blood, speaks sweet words and is kind-hearted. She has a round and tall body. She is a friend, is of the *satvik* temperament, mild, truthful, charitable, God-fearing, righteous, loving, optimistic and helps others. Her physique comprises of short arms, thick hands and feet, grey eyes and a round face. A malefic Moon causes venereal diseases and nose inflammation. She always wears new clothes and shows an appetite for salty things.

The Moon is a satellite of the Earth and nearest to the Earth, having vital implications on the life of this planet. The Moon has a significant effect over mind, emotions, sentiments and human activity of all sort. In Indian astrology, monthly forecasts are often made on the basis of the transits of planets from the natal Moon. The Moon thus occupies a pivotal position in the Indian system of astrology. The placement of Moon in the Natal Chart reveals the basic likes and dislikes of man and flaws which can make or mar individual's life and standing.

The Moon revolves around the Earth. It is 238840 miles away from the Earth and goes round the Earth in roughly 28 days. The Moon is a feminine planet and signifies fair complexion, young and attractive features and well-shaped body.

In the Ist house, the Moon gives attractive appearance and in the 2nd house blesses the native with a reasonable accumulation of wealth. In the 3rd house, he gets ample love and affection from his brothers and sisters. He will also get enough strength and courage to face problems in life. In the 4th house, it bestows moderate happiness through vehicles, landed properties and mother's affection. It also makes him happy and gives enjoyment of the life. In the 5th house, the Moon endows the native with creative intelligence and one of his children becomes famous. In the 6th house, it causes some adversaries and stomach ailments and adversely affects his compatibility with his life partner. In other words, in conjugal happiness, there could be some strains and hassles. But if the native is born on the full Moon, its location in the 6th house is quite comfortable. In the 7th house, the Moon attracts him to the members of the opposite sex and blesses him with an attractive spouse. The placement of the Moon in the 8th house causes some ailments besides adverse effects on the longevity angle. If the birth be during night and in the *shukla paksha*, i.e., brighter half, it is not quite favourable for conferring long life for the native. It also makes him suffer through mental tensions. The Moon in the 9th, 10th and 11th houses is considered quite favourable for position, prestige, wealth, happiness etc., whereas in the 12th house it causes some setbacks. It can also affect the eyesight of the native and make society question his unethical acts. Such natives should be very cautious of the company they keep and avoid the temptations of life and should remember the Almighty and offer alms to the poor.

Mars

It is a planet of dynamic energy, practical action, impulse, creative force, heat and activation. Mars represents expanding force, awakening desire and an outgoing temperament. It is a male, a dry planet and significator of stamina, courage, ambition, desire, weapons and immovable property. He is the commander-in-chief. In human beings, he represents physical strength. He is cruel, malefic and masculine as these traits belong to the Kshatriya caste. He is of a tyrannic temper and wickedness. However he is slightly tall, and always young. But he has bad habits and an unsteady temperament. He possesses the lustre of the end of a lotus leaf. He is of extremely astringent taste. He has sparkling eyes with a fiery complexion. He is steady, brave, strong, bony, bellicose but can be generous also. He is treacherous, cruel, possesses a fighting spirit, is confident, rash, angry, violent and commanding. His constitution is healthy, responsible for quarrels, laziness, cruelty, deceit, passions and desires. Diseases of fever, small-pox, carbuncle, swelling in the scrotum, boils, diseases caused by mal-nutrition, headache, jaundice, diseases in the private parts, stones in the bladder, phlegm, wounds, hurts and gun-shots come under this planet. He acts as a soldier, doctor, barber, blacksmith and a mechanic. Mars has four feet and inhabits mountains or forests. He is fond of wearing a partly burnt cloth and prefers bitter and sour tasting edibles.

Mercury

He is the heir-apparent or prince. He is a messenger of the Sun and represents the mind and the intellect. He represents speech in human being. He would be benefic when associated with benefics, malefic combined with malefics. He is Shudra by caste and impotent not virile. Some ascribe him to be a female eunuch. He is of middle stature, has visible hollow nerves and is shrewd in business. He has a thick skin. He is always happy and joyous, *Rajasik* in temperament. He emits green radiation in the spectrum of light. He is well-informed, courageous, luxurious and loves romantic enterprises since he is fond of women. He is either masculine or feminine, lucky or unlucky according to his position in a horoscope. He is of a tender age and has a vigorous and active mind with a good memory and intellect. By nature he is cold, dry and melancholic with short stature.

If strong, he makes the native changeable, clean, excitable, strong and nervous, versed with the dynamics of cosmic vibration, and the subjects of philosophy, mathematics, poetry, science and merchandise. He is well educated and ingenious.

If badly placed, he would make the native mean, cunning, a thief. messenger or a servant. He is anxious to please and oblige others. He is open-hearted and talkative. He would have command over messages, communication networks and editorial assignments. He is familiar with law, excels as an orator with powers of persuasion but can also cause affliction of brain, madness, lethargy, stammering, dry cough, nervous disorders in hands and feet. He wears a wet cloth.

The most unique character of the fast-moving Mercury is its power of commanding other planets and imbibing their qualities and characteristics. If associated with the Sun, it wi.ll gain in dignity, position, prestige, and comprehensiveness. Its association with the Moon will enhance the native's interest in the occult, and parapsychology. It will activate their urge for action with a greater amount of interest in love and life, as also accelerate a fertile imagination and intuition. In association with the energy giver, Mars, it will bestow the natives with a higher social image and energy, initiative and drive. With Venus, it will accentuate their social and emotional urges and enhance the personal image with the opposite sex. Its association with Jupiter will enhance the nobler qualities in a man, giving him sound judgement, as also depth of vision. Its association with Saturn will enhance sobriety and a profound outlook making the best of writers, lawyers, preachers, authors, publishers and printers. It is exalted in Virgo, debilitated in Pisces, rules over Gemini and is weak in Sagittarius.

Jupiter

As a Prime Minister in the solar system, Jupiter is the largest planet. He represents wisdom and happiness. He is benefic and masculine by instinct, Brahmin by caste and has eyes of the colour of honey. He has a stout body, is phlegmatic in nature, white in colour, and possesses gold coloured hair. He has a strong constitution and is shorter in stature. He is *satvik* by temperament. As an earthly planet, he is of golden yellow colour. He prefers sweet things. He is mild, lover of truth, charitable, righteous, God-fearing, loves and helps others. He is benevolent, merciful, sacrificing, philanthropic, jovial, honest and emotional. He is associated with immense good fortune and cheer, harmony and equanimity. He is very intelligent and clever, but has pure motives. He is bestowed with an upright body, a high forehead, brown and ruddy complexion and long legs and feet.

If Jupiter is strong in one's horoscope, it makes the native jovial, religious and honest. If aspected by Saturn or Mars, he would be a jolly good fellow, and have no enemy of his own. His mental qualities are mirth, religiousness, honour, magnanimity, benevolence and hope. He is the planet of joy and hope, sympathy, and true generosity. He makes a person conservative, catholic, orthodox and formal.

Professionally, Jupiter manifests as the minister, judge, lawyer and priest and is also connected with educational and religious and charitable institutions, even shipping and marriage and has an even temperament. He is youthful and makes and possesses strong flesh. He is responsible for the disorders of the liver, spleen, lungs, heart, fever, impurity of blood and indigestion. He prefers a used cloth and in his routine, he has a cycle or 12 years in solar system. It rules over Sagittarius and Pisces. It is exalted in Cancer and debilitated in Capricorn.

Venus

Venus too manifests itself as a parallel Prime Minister. She represents lust and passion among living organisms. She is a benefic planet and a Brahmin by caste, with feminine instincts. She has a slightly dark colour, broad joints and black hair. She likes enjoyment and pleasure and has an attractive personality. She is windy, and phlegmatic by nature, pleasant in speech with plenty of vital fluid, *rajasik* by temperament, watery, with dull vibrations of neither white nor black in colour. Venus gives a symmetrical body, has a liking for sour taste, and makes one a person of high tastes, passionate, loving, romantic, well-informed and enterprising. She is fond of women or feminine animals, who are courageous and leads a luxurious life. She is called a morning or an evening star. If powerful in one's natal chart, she would make the native beautiful with sparkling eyes, ruddy lips, smooth hair, amorous looks and a charming countenance. She has sonorous voice, is fond of perfumes and scents, showers love and affection and shows a refined taste in the finer things of life, like music, art and culture, dance and drama, ornaments and jewels. She enhances her social image and has an urge for socialising. She bestows her warmth and affection particularly on the opposite sex. She has artistic skills and displays harmony and balance which make her amiable. If afflicted and ill placed, Venus would lead to voluptuousness, making the native profligate, careless, amorous, indiscriminate with an inclination for unhealthy company. She is responsible for sore throat, venereal diseases or those connected with urine, genitals, loins, spleen, kidneys, diabetes and impotency. She knows the dynamics of science and has kind looks. Being a watery planet, she prefers to speak softly and loves sexual enjoyment. She would lead a comfortable life, and wears a strong blended cloth. It rules over Taurus and Libra. It is weak in Leo and Sagittarius and is exalted in Pisces.

Saturn

Saturn is a servant by nature. He represents discipline, system, order, diligence, prudence, discretion, persistence, obedience and faithfulness. He is malefic and impotent by behaviour. However, he is the weakest of all the planets. From the worldly point of view he belongs to a low or mixed caste. He is lean and tall with eyes of *kapila* colour, a delicate body and a slow gait. He has hollow nerves and is of a very suspicious disposition. He is an earthly planet and likes bitter things. He can be a gossip monger, quarrelsome, stubborn, lazy and cruel by instinct but a hard task master. The greatest malignant planet, Saturn (*shani*) is called the star of sorrow and is a associated with darkness, grief, misfortune, delays, difficulties and sufferings. He likes pungent things, looks the oldest in age. If Saturn is strong in one's horoscope, he would make the native shy, averse to society, careful of his affairs and family, austere, averse to sudden changes, stubborn, morose, fanciful, and subtle for his own ends. He takes the subjects over longer journeys, gives steady results which commensurate with labour, brings in endurance, calmness, consideration for the welfare of the society, interest in the occult and spiritualism. It causes diseases from cold, melancholy, epilepsy, leprosy, fistula, pain in limbs and joints, gout, deafness, rheumatism, stammering, dumbness. By occupation, he is a servant, agriculturist, miner, potter, brick-manufacturer, scavenger, carter, property dealer, occultist and a seasoned politician, gardener, caretaker for livestocks and domesticated animals. He is responsible for re-marriage, is old and has owl's eyes, rotten nails, unattractive hair. He's gluttonous and loves the species of the underworld. He is a male eunuch of *tamasic* temperament and wears torn clothes. Saturn in exalted in Libra, inauspicious in Leo in powerful in Capricorn and Aquarius, the two houses it owns.

The role of Saturn in life has often been misunderstood as most people consider it to be a planet of adversity, harshness, sorrow, pain, suffering, loss and ill-luck. People dread Saturn so much that its transit in the various natal houses of the horoscope leaves an important mark over the houses and the planets it interacts within its transits. Its transit over the natal Moon is popularly known as Saturn's averse period (*sade sati*). Saturn, when placed in Gemini, Virgo and Taurus and Libra is considered friendly and auspicious for the natives, but in other signs the results are interdependent. Saturn is friendly to Venus and

Mercury, netural in its relations with Jupiter and unfriendly with the Sun, Moon and Mars. Saturn, if not afflicted or debilitated, can add strength to the natal chart. An exalted Saturn magnifies the beneficial results of the houses. It sometimes enhances the thinking capacity of the natives. It also adds mental strength, courage and endurance and interest to probe deep into the mysteries of nature as also interest in subjects like parapsychology, the occult, *Yoga*, meditation, religion and philosophy. World renowned religious leaders, philosophers and reformers have had the benefic effect of well placed Saturn in their natal charts. No doubt, Saturn calls for trials and tribulations. But it is a plain truth that life without struggle is no life and human beings cannot progress without overcoming obstacles. It is Saturn that imbues in the natives the will to undergo hardship and come up in life through dint of hard labour. Natives governed by a well-placed Saturn would be serious minded and devoted to nobler causes. It is, therefore, incorrect to say that Saturn is only a malefic planet.

Rahu (Dragon's Head)

Rahu is a shadowy planet, fisher-man by caste, a female, a Mlechchha, i.e., of wicked disposition, moves in *apasavya* direction, is courageous, malefic, inhabits mountains and forests, and causes epilepsy, pox, worms, suicide, leprosy.

Like other planets in the planetary system, Rahu also exerts its formidable influence on a man's destiny. The image of a demon with a very big and protruding head — the head being completely severed from the rest of the body — symbolizes Rahu's insatiable lust for life and endless desires which are unlikely to materialize. The Dragon's Head is dark and shadowy in colour and it molests the two vital luminaries viz., the Sun and the Moon. It has lordship over the house of Virgo. It gets exalted in Gemini and gets debilitated in Sagittarius.

Rahu is an accelerator and a catalyst. It magnifies the noble qualities of a house provided, of course, that it is strongly placed and free from blemishes, in order to obtain the optimum benefits from such a placement. Taurus, Gemini, Virgo, Libra, Capricorn and Aquarius are considered favourable placements of Rahu. Its favourable relationship with Mercury or Venus in the natal chart is also a positive factor to be given due consideration in this regard. And its placement in an angle or a trine undoubtedly accentuates its positive influence on the native. Saturn usually interferes with its intrinsic ability to magnify the result of the house where it is located.

Rahu is malefic, very similar influence to Saturn. If a planet by virtue of its position and lordship is capable of producing good results, Rahu involved with a close relationship with that particular planet would magnify beneficial results in important sectors such as politics and public life. Rahu generally gives good results if placed in the third, sixth, tenth or eleventh angles.

Ketu (Dragon's Tail)

Ketu is also a shadowy planet, catches snakes and is a *sanyasin* by profession. She lives on alms, belongs to a mixed caste and knows *mantras*. She is a medical practitioner, grateful but clever, and dexterous, makes pilgrimages, practises *Yoga*, has divine and supernatural strength and helps in salvation of man from the cycle of birth and rebirth. Ketu, the dragon's tail is an enunch *karmik* planet. It is a planet of secrets and mysteries. The position of Ketu in a native chart shows the qualities and characteristics developed during past lives. A planet in conjunction with *Rahu* has a special significance in relation to the results signified by Ketu's association with the other planet. Ketu's placement in the first half of the natal chart is considered to be highly auspicious for one's steady rise. While his childhood may be difficult, he will make progress as the years advance and will become more prosperous with age. The case would be reverse if Ketu is placed in the second half of the native's chart. A well-positioned Ketu with good associations and aspects would facilitate the native to rise to great heights and bestows name, fame and social esteem. Afflicated nodes (Ketu and Rahu) often cause setbacks and difficulties, tensions and turmoils. But mostly after undergoing some trying phases in life, the natives have chances of subsequent improvements including interest in spiritual aspects of life, as also in parapsychology and the occult. Ketu has the influence of Mars conjuncting Saturn. Ketu is exalted in Sagittarius, ruler in Pisces, harmonious in Aries, debilitated in Gemini, detrimental in Virgo and inharmonious in Libra.

3

PLANETS — EXALTATION AND DEBILITATION

Planets, the houses they own, exaltation and debilitation position and calculation of Dasha periods.

If a planet is posted in his own sign he is said to be in his own house. If he is in the sign of exaltation, he is considered to be in a state of exaltation. If he is in his debilitation sign, he is said to be in a state of debilitation. In between a planet's own house and exaltation position, there is another point of astrological importance for any planet. This position is attained when he is in his *Moolatrikona* sign.

The various planets and their respective positions of ownership, strength and weakness are tabulated in Table 1.

Mercury is well placed in Libra and Aquarius, Venus is fairly effective in Cancer, a watery sign, Sun in Sagittarius, a fiery sign, Mars in Leo and Sagittarius are also comparatively more effective, but the Moon is detrimental in Pisces as the dignities of the planet and the sign are at considerable variance.

The seventh sign from the house of exaltation is the debilitation sign. Exaltation means strength of a planet and debilitation means weakness. Planets in retrograde motion are always strong, but planets in exaltation when retrograde, give inauspicious or inadequate results. Planets in debilitation are strong. They give corresponding results.

Table 1

Planet	Own Sign	Moola Trikona	Exaltation Sign	Debilitation Sign
1. Sun	Leo [20° - 30°]	Leo [1 - 20°]	Aries 10°	Libra 10°
2. Moon	Cancer	Taurus 3°	Taurus 3°	Scorpio 3°
3. Mars	Aries & Scorpio	Aries	Capricorn 28°	Cancer 28°
4. Mercury	Gemini & [15° - 20°] Virgo [20° - 30°]	Virgo [15° - 20°]	Virgo [15° - 20°]	Pisces [15° - 20°]
5. Jupiter	Sagittarius & Pisces [13° - 30°]	Sagittarius [0° - 13°]	Cancer 5°	Capricorn 5°
6. Venus	Taurus and Libra [10° - 30°]	Libra [0° - 10°]	Pisces 27°	Virgo 27°
7. Saturn	Capricorn & Aquarius [20° - 30°]	Aquarius [0° - 20°]	Libra 20°	Aries 20°
8. Rahu [Dragon's head]	Virgo		Taurus	Scorpio
9. Ketu [Dragon's tail]	Pisces		Sagittarius	Taurus

Navamsa

When a sign is divided into nine parts, each part is called a *navamsa*. Each *navamsa* is a *pada* or one-fourth constellation. Each sign has 2-1/4 constellations. Each constellation has four parts. The *navamsa* for Aries will be from Aries to Sagittarius and for Taurus will be from Capricorn to Virgo, and so on.

If a planet is in the same *rashi* and *navamsa*, it is called *vargottama*, meaning it has gained additional strength, to show good or inauspicious portents. Here it should not be mistaken as good only. It may be good or otherwise according to the plant's placement being good or otherwise from the Ascendant etc.

Lords of Navamsas

For Aries, Leo and Sagittarius

1.	Mars	6.	Mercury
2.	Venus	7.	Venus
3.	Mercury	8.	Mars
4.	Moon	9.	Jupiter.
5.	Sun		

For Taurus, Virgo and Capricorn

1.	Saturn	6.	Merucry
2.	Saturn	7.	Moon
3.	Jupiter	8.	Sun
4.	Mars	9.	Mercury
5.	Venus		

For Gemini, Libra and Aquarius

1.	Moon	6.	Jupiter
2.	Sun	7.	Saturn
3.	Mercury	8.	Venus
4.	Venus	9.	Mercury
5.	Mars		

For Cancer, Scorpio and Pisces

1.	Moon	5.	Mars
2.	Sun	6.	Jupiter
3.	Mercury	7.	Saturn
4.	Venus		

Vargottama

1st *Navamsa* in Aries, Cancer, Libra, Capricorn.

5th *Navamsa* in Taurus, Leo, Scorpio, Capricorn.

9th *Navamsa* in Gemini, Virgo, Sagittarius, Pisces.

There are 27 stars = *yoga-taras*. (*Abhijit* is between *Uttarashada* & *Shravana*.)

Aswini, Makha and *Moola* start with Ketu's Major period, running for 7 years.

Bharani, Poorvaphalguni and *Poorvashadha* start with Venus' Major period running for 20 years.

Krittika, Uttaraphalguni and *Uttarashadha* start with the Sun's Major period for 6 years.

Rohini, Hasta and *Shravana* start with the Moon's Major period for 10 years.

Mrigashira, Chitra & Dhanishta start with Mar's Major period for 7 years.

Ardra, Swati and *Satabhisha* start with Rahu's Major period for 19 years.

Punarvasu, Vishakha and *Poorvabharapada* start with Jupiter's Major period for 18 years.

Pushyami, Anuradha and *Uttarabhadrapada* start with Saturn's Major period for 19 years.

Aslesha, Jyestha and *Revati* start with Mercury's Major period for 17 years.

Calculation of Dashas (Major periods)

From a *Panchanga*, find out the *nakshatra* ruling on the day and see if the same *nakshatra* is ruling at the time of birth. If the next *nakshatra* has begun, find out the duration of this on the day in question and on the following day. The net magnitude is called *Adyanta* or total duration. Find out the unexpired period of the *nakshatra* at the time of birth. Suppose the total number of *ghatikas* is 65. After birth, the balance of *nakshatra* is only 5 gh. If the *nakshatra* should be *krittika*, the balance of Sun's dasha at birth will be 1/13th of 6 years period or 5 months, 16 days, 9 ghatis.

Then the sequence of *dashas* will follow, Sun, Moon, Mars, Rahu, Juptier, Saturn, Mercury, Ketu, Venus, according to *Vimshothari* Major Period system on the presumption of planetary influence on living organisms as 120 years by taking Earth as the reference object in the Solar system.

In every Major period, its own Sub-period starts first. In the Sun's Major-period, the first Sub-period will be that of the Sun followed by those of, the Moon, Mars, Rahu, Jupiter, Saturn, Mercury, Ketu and Venus.

4

PLANETARY *PHASES (AVASTHAS)*

The Planets are given technical names according to their placement as follows :

(1) Exaltation (*Deeptha*)
(2) Own House (*Swastha*)
(3) *Athimithra* House (*Mudita*)
(4) Friend's House (*Shanta*) — The Friend Being Benefic
(5) Neutral House (*Hina*)
(6) Enemy's House (*Dhukha* or *Dhukhitha*)
(7) Associated with Malefics (*Vikala*)
(8) Being defeated in Planetary War (*Khala*)
(9) Eclipsed in association with Sun (*Kopi*)
(10) In Accelerated Motion (*Bheeta*)

Results of Phases (*Avasthas*)

In *Deeptha dasha* : In the major-period of an exalted planet, the results will be success, prosperity, purchase of land, joy, happiness, respect from relations, presents and honours from high dignitaries, acquisition of luxuries, pleasant position in society.

In *Swastha dasha* : Wealth, happiness, learning, fame, respect, happiness from spouse and family.

In *Mudita dasha* : Good dress, lands, perfumes, jewellery and general happiness are indicated.

In Shanta dasha : Patience, help from relations, courage, fruitful vocation, job satisfaction, learning, wealth and recreation, pleasant trips are indicated.

In Hina dasha : Change of residence, strained relations with kith and kin, living by unfair means and being disowned by people, all round tensions, health hassles are indicated.

In Dhukha dasha : Living in a foreign country, being miserable, loss of relations, fear from thieves, fire and fear of punishment from the Government are strong possibilities.

In Vikala dasha : Difficulties, mental uneasiness, death of parents, theft of clothes, ornaments and valuables belonging to spouse and children and sometimes danger from accidents/traffic hazards are to be faced.

In Khala dasha : Quarrels, separation from or death of spouse and family, and of parents, loss of wealth and property through inimical activities and being suspected by his own people are found.

In Kopi dasha : Being prone to many sins, loss of fame, loss of spouse, loss of wealth, loss of property through the Government or agencies are indicated.

In Bheeta dasha : Unfavourable results and untoward happenings occur.

The above are generalised statements. These may be useful when taken into consideration with other conditions and factors.

There are other *Avasthas* which deserve to be mentioned and are as follows:

1. Bathing
2. Dressing
3. Sweet scent
4. Preparation for worship
5. Prayer
6. Worship
7. Preparing for sacrifice
8. Meditation
9. Kneeling
10. Going round the altar
11. Contemplation
12. Receiving guests
13. Dining
14. Drinking water
15. Anger
16. Chewing betal

17. Court entry
18. Crowning
19. Private consultation
20. Delay
21. Sleeping
22. Drinking alcohol
23. Drinking sweet drinks
24. Acquiring wealth
25. Removing the crown
26. Profound sleep
27. Sexual union or matters pertaining to conjugal happiness

To find out the condition of a planet in a horoscope at the time of birth, the following method should be adopted. Find out the number of houses from Aries or the Ascendant, both inclusive.

Add the two numbers and multiply the sum by two.

Multiply this sum again by the number of years given for the planetary Major-Period of the planet, according to the *Vimshottari dasha* system.

Divide the result by 27 and note the remainder. This number shows the condition of the planet in the above rule.

The conditions in numbers 1, 2, 3, 4, 6, 8, 9, 11, 12, 16, 17, 18, 19, 23, and 25 give auspicious and favourable results.

The conditions in the remaining numbers may cause considerable effort and difficulties, as one has to face several challenges in these unfavourable periods.

These difficulties can be effectively tackled with timely and suitable measures.

5

CASTING A HOROSCOPE

There are elaborate methods of casting a horoscope. The following method can be conveniently used with some advantage for a rough and ready reckoning. For this purpose, one has to follow the *Nirayana* (ex-precession) position of planets.

One must have an Ephemeris (*Panchanga*) meaning the five *Angas* (an Almanac) before one begins. These five *Angas* are Lunar day (*Tithi*), Day (*Vara*), Constellation (*Nakshatra*), *Yoga* and *Karana*.

Every *Panchanga* (*Nirayana*) has been computed according to the conception of *Ayanamsha* degrees. The following *Nirayana* has been found to be a popular and acceptable system.

One has to find the *Udaya* Ascendant or the sign which the Sun is moving through at the time of local sunrise on the date followed by the number of *ghatikas* to be traversed by the Sun in that house. Divide the number of *ghatikas* appropriate to the sign occupied by the Sun by the number of days of the solar month and multiply the result by the remaining number of days of the solar month. The remaining *ghatikas* of the Sun's *rashi* has been arrived at. Add to these, the *ghatika* measure of the next *Rashi* or *Rashis* as may be necessary to arrive at the total time represented by "*Ishta*", i.e., the period lapsed between the· sun rise and the moment of birth (or "*Prashna*" etc.). The last *Rashi* by the addition of which the *Ishta* is arrived at will be the

Ascendant. You will then have to place the planets in the twelve houses and this can be done by referring to the Ephemeris (*Panchanga*), which will indicate the positions of the planets for any given date.

The duration of each Sign (*rashi*) differs according to the latitude. For example, Madras gets for Aries/*Mesha* 4 *ghatis* and 28 *vighatis*, whereas Bombay gets for Aries/*Mesha* 4 *ghatis* and 17 *vighatis*, and so on.

The next step will be to find out the *Navamsa* (the ninth division) which means that each Sign is split into 9 parts. This is useful in finding out what part of the house a planet is located in and whether it is a benefic or a malefic portion, or the portion of a friend or an enemy. This has also to be taken into consideration when predictions are made. This is calculated thus, for Aries (*Mesha*), the first *Navamsa* will begin with Aries (*Mesha*) itself and end with Sagittarius (*Dhanus*). For Taurus, the first *Navamsa* will be of Capricorn because in Aries the last is Sagittarius and after Sagittarius we have Capricorn and so on. For easy calculation, for Aries, Leo and Sagittarius, count from Aries; for Taurus, Virgo and Capricorn, count from Libra; for Cancer, Scorpio, and Pisces, count from Cancer. There is a *Drekkana* or the 3 divisions of each house. Here these are divided opinions :

(1) The lord of the first *drekkana* of any house will be the lord himself; for the 2nd *drekkana*, the lord of the 5th house; the lord of the 3rd *drekkana* will be the lord of the 9th house; e.g., for Aries,the lord of the three *drekkanas* will be Mars, Sun and Jupiter, respectively.

(2) Another school of thought : The rashis are divided into *Chara*, *Sthira* and *Ubhaya*, i.e., movable, fixed and dual. The lord of the three *drekkanas* for movable signs will be the lords of the 1st, 5th and 9th house from that house. For fixed *rashis* the lord of the three *drekkanas* will be the lords of the 9th house, the 1st house and the 5th house respectively; the *drekkanas* for the dual houses will be that of the lord of the 5th house, the 9th house and the 1st house respectively. For Aries — *Chara rashi*, the lord of the three *drekkanas* will be Mars, Sun and Jupiter, for Taurus

— a fixed sign, the lord of the three *drekkanas* will be Saturn, Venus and Mercury, and for Gemini a dual sign, the lord of the three *drekkanas* will be Venus, Saturn and Mercury respectively.

Besides the *Navamsas* and the *Drekkanas,* the Hindu Astrology contains elaborate considerations of other divisions or *vargas,* viz., *Hora* (two divisions), *Saptamamsa* (seven divisions), *Ashtamamsa* (eight divisions), *Dashamamsa* (ten divisions), *Dwadashamsa* (twelve divisions), *Shodashamsa* (sixteen divisions), *Trimshamsa* (thirty divisions) and *Shashtyamsha* (sixty divisions).

6

THE SIGNIFICANCE OF ASCENDANTS AND OTHER HOUSES

The Ascendant (*Lagna*) or First House : fundamentally signifies body, besides fame, limbs, appearance, disposition, life, soul, character, wisdom, habits, birth, inclination, mood, activity, age, strength, stature, health, happiness, complexion, beauty, high life, colour, hair, weakness, politics, knowledge, splendour, place of birth, and head.

The Second House : fundamentally signifies *face, family,* wealth, domestic happiness, eyes, speech, thoughts, prosperity, memory, pleasure, loss or gain, food, ear, learning, intelligence, cunning, savings, anger, pecuniary affairs, personal property (i.e., of exclusive use to one's own self), fortunes, relations, fixed temperament, jewels, inauguration, metals, observation, right eye, persons under protection, tongue, nails, silver, gold, precious gems, passion, modesty, miserliness, comfort and taste, financial position, in-laws.

The Third House : fundamentally signifies *courage, brothers,* besides anger, ears, neck, meals, skill, patience, sisters, friends, neighbours, travels, cousins, ornaments, improvement, enterprise, clothing, steadiness, war, difficulty in getting food, power, instruction, help, medicine, right arm, voice, servants, subordinates, power of hearing, diseases in the ear, gold and silver vessels, heroic deeds, capacity, ability, courage, battle, meekness, skill and longevity of life, speech, writing, correspondence, family.

The Fourth House : fundamentally signifies *Mother, land, houses,* education, relations, happiness, conveyance besides tanks, wells, cows, cattle, gardens, agriculture, comfort, lineage, residence, inheritance, water, travels, milk, palace, clothes, falsehood, true words, distant relatives, property, fields, benevolence, art, stores, fort, *mandap,* flower gardens, heart, friends, things in the bottom, nectar, mental qualities, the end of life and the end of things, reputation, popularity, love of work, scents, perspiration, oil bath, ornaments.

The Fifth House : fundamentally signifies *sons, daughters, intellect, creative intelligence, Poorva Punya,* i.e., the *Karma* of a previous birth besides manthras, success in speculation, lottery and gambling, pleasures, enterprise, investments, mind, discrimination, reasoning, father, honour, religion, precepts, joy, worship of household deities, modesty, belly, stomach, charity, hearing, feeding, merry making, drinking, eating, firm disposition, inheritance, father's generosity, geneology, ministership, advice, skill, care and caution, memory, secrecy, pride, good conduct, cooking, bathing and physical pleasures, love affairs.

The Sixth House : fundamentally signifies *enemies, disease, debts,* imprisonment besides relations, servants, inferiors, small pets, wounds, troubles, obstacles, difficulty in getting food, sorrow, misery, poverty, maternal relations, fear, boils, step-mother, fear of shame, good food, theft, superstition, injuries by weapons, cousins from paternal side, calamities through women, intimidation, vengeance, bad habits and diabetes, recovery from illness, benefit through servants.

The Seventh House : fundamentally signifies *marriage-description of wife or husband,* besides generosity, respect, lust, partnership, enjoyment, lawsuits, adultery, death, public enemies, holy places, speculation, love affairs, desires, immorality, sunset, trade, forgetfulness, voyage, loss in livelihood or occupation, dealings with women, love of betel, opponents, public affairs, obstacles to travelling, losing the way, private parts, sexual conduct, marital discord, music, dance, patronage from ruling circles, duration of wife's life, freedom, character, daily earnings, litigation.

The **Eighth House** fundamentally signifies *life (longevity)*, *sin*, sorrow, hell, rebirth *besides legacies*, personal property of marriage partner, nature of death, happiness in food, venereal diseases, trouble, dowry, suddenly acquired wealth, lotteries, loss, occultism, danger, chronic diseases, obstacles, uneasiness, loss of money, loss of limb, enmity, cruelty, dwelling houses as opposed to agricultural lands and hidden wealth, legacies and windfalls, gains through insurance and strangers, sexual organs.

The **Ninth House** fundamentally signifies *Guru, Father, virtuous deeds, dharma, prosperity, tapasaya* besides faith, medicine, kindness, benevolence, bathing in holy rivers, morality, purity of mind, honour, credit, ceremonies, father's possession, luck and spiritual learning, good company, good conduct, fame, public beneficence, meritorious acts, wealth, irrigation, fertile fields and desires, happiness which wealth can buy, divine favours, brother and sister-in-law, grand-children, future; *in short, general welfare, long journeys,* foreign travels, *study of philosophy & art*, religious and legal affairs, intuition and interest in occult.

The **Tenth House** fundamentally signifies *profession, karma, living, kingdom, authority besides fame, trade, clothes*, employment, honour, credit, reputation, activity, charity, meals, deeds, persons in power and authority, cultivation, medicine, loss of honour, punishment, prices, treasure, titles, preferment, business and success, gifts, presents, athletes, pride, public good, mercy, wisdom, mendicancy, fortitude, worship, concentration, living in foreign lands and countries, knowledge, rank and status, treasure-trove, adopted son, mother-in-law, service, renunciation and spiritual acts, profession, success in life, honour, position, prestige, promotion for those in services, moral standards, long distance journeys.

The **Eleventh House** fundamentally signifies *Gains, Profits, Earnings by self*, elder brother besides friends, hopes, wishes, mother's prosperity, sisters, miserliness, income, cooking, left ear, slandering, acquisitions, legs, worship, son-in-law, paternal uncle, patrimony, dependence, insight, vehicles, power of overwhelming, obstacles, loss of wealth, total income, clothes, *friends and business partnership, success in business.*

The Twelfth House fundamentally signifies *losses, expenditure and Moksha* besides bad deeds, travels, secret, enemies, sorrow, imprisonment, sin, spending, giving physical troubles, difficulties, defamation, mental anxiety, misfortunes, loss of sleep, misery, dignity, deep occultism, sacrifice, left eye, prosperity in profession, self-destination, tribulation, affliction, defect in organs, derangement of brain or mind, sale of carriages and houses, distress, back-biters, assassination, treason, suicide, journey, settling abroad, disputes, waste of money, adultery, bed comforts, and luxuries generosity and real happiness, gains through adversaries, gains through religious, charitable and public institutions.

It will be seen that the same effects have been mentioned as being signified by more than one house. It means that the two houses are inter-allied in giving effects; or it will be found that one house is Bhavath-Bhavam to the other, e.g., 5th house is 3rd from 3rd and therefore the 5th house also will have to be considered along with the 3rd house, so far as the indications relating to the 3rd house are concerned.

7

PLANETS, SIGNS AND THEIR PROPERTIES

The Direction of Planets

The Sun is the Lord of the East
Venus is the Lord of the South East
Mars is the Lord of the South
Rahu is the Lord of the South West
Saturn is the Lord of the West
Moon is the Lord of the North West
Mercury is the Lord of the North
Jupiter is the Lord of the North East

Caste

Jupiter and Venus are Brahmins
The Sun and Mars are Kshatriyas
The Moon is a Vaisya
Mercury is a Sudra
Saturn is an Outcaste.

Sex

The Sun, Mars, Jupiter and Ketu are males.
Venus and the Moon are females.
Saturn, Mercury and Rahu are eunuch.
Mercury is a female eunuch.
Rahu is a male eunuch.

Every odd sign viz., Aries, Gemini etc. is masculine and every even sign viz., Taurus, Cancer etc. is feminine.

The influence of these planets determines the sex of the children as well as brothers and sisters. They are also very useful in determining the sexual potency of a person, possibility of a love marriage and companionship as also the ability to look after family and children.

Temporary Friends

Any planet which occupies the 2nd, 3rd, 4th, 10th, 11th and 12th houses from that of any given planet, becomes the temporary friend of the given planet. The rest are his enemies.

Planets which are both permanent and temporary friends give very good results.

Planets which are permanent and temporary enemies do not give satisfactory results.

Planets which are permanent friends and temporary enemies or vice versa, give medium results.

The 1st, 4th, 7th, 10th houses from the Ascendant are Kendras (angular).

1st, 5th, 9th houses from the Ascendant are Konas or Trines.

Note : The Ascendant is both a *Kendra* (Angle) and *Konam* (Trine). That is why the placement of any planet in it is considered to be good.

Panaparas or succeeding houses are 2nd, 5th, 8th, and 11th houses from Ascendant. But 5th house is a *Kona* (Trine) and therefire may be excluded.

Apoklimas (the cadent houses) or the next houses to these are 3rd, 6th, 9th and 12th. But here the 9th house may not be included as it has been taken as a *Kona* (Trine).

Opachayas or Improving houses : These are the 3rd, 6th, 10th and 11th houses from Ascendant.

Aspects

All planets aspect the 3rd and 10th houses with a quarter sight.

All planets aspect 5th and 9th houses with half sight.

All planets aspect 4th and 8th houses with *three-fourth sight.*

All planets aspect the 7th house in full. This aspect is considered to be very powerful.

Saturn aspects the 3rd and 10th houses in full.

Jupiter aspects the 3rd and 9th houses in full.

Mars aspects 4th and 8th houses in full.

The Sun, Moon, Mercury and Venus give full results by their aspect.

Mars gives three-fourth result by his aspect.

Jupiter gives half results.

Saturn gives quarter results.

Planets have Shad-Balas

The strength attained by the aspect is called the Drig-Bala.

By strength of position, Sthan-Bala.

By natural strength, Naisargik-Bala.

By the strength of motion, Cheshta-Bala.

By the strength of direction, Dik-Bala.

By the strength according to time, Kala-Bala.

Planets have *Sthanabala* when they occupy the *Vaisheshika Vargas* produced by the combination of any three or more of the following conditions :

1. Planets in their exaltation
2. In moola thrikona
3. In a friend's house
4. In own drekkana
5. In own house
6. In own navamsha
7. Being in the Ascendant (*Lagna*) and possessing not less than 5 points in the *Ashtaka Varga*.

Planets do not have much strength —

when they have no aspect of natural benefic planets or other such good influences,

when they are in depression or associated with or aspected by inimical or malefic planets, or

if they occupy the *Vargas* of inimical or malefic planets, or

possess few points in their *Ashtaka Varga* (less than five), or

when they occupy the bad portions of a *Rashi* (sign), or

when they are eclipsed by Sun, or

when they are defeated in the planetary war.

Mercury and Jupiter have *Digbala* in Ascendant or in an Eastern house. Venus and Moon have *Digbala* in the 4th house or a Northern House. Saturn has *Digbala* in the 7th house or in a Western House. The Sun and Mars have *Digbala* in the 10th house or a Southern house.

The Sun, Mercury, Jupiter and Venus have Kalabala during day. The Moon, Saturn and Mars have *Kalabala* at night. In his hour, day, month and year, each planet is strong.

Benefic planets have strength in the bright half and the malefics in the dark half of a lunar month. Mercury is always strong.

Venus, Mercury, Mars and Jupiter have *Cheshtabala* when they are retrograde and victorious in the planetary war. The Sun and the Moon have *Cheshtabala* in *Uttarayana*.

Naisargikabala is in the following order :

The Sun is of the highest strength and Saturn of the lowest.

Sun	—	7
Moon	—	6
Venus	—	5
Jupiter	—	4
Mercury	—	3
Mars	—	2
Saturn	-	1

Shadbala is measured thus :

Drigbala	—	1
Cheshtabala	—	5
Sthanabala	—	5
Digbala	—	1
Naisargikabala	—	1
Kalabala	—	7

Planets do harm by virtue of their position.

The Lords of the movable houses occupying the 11th house, the Lords of fixed houses occupying the 9th house and the Lords of dual houses occupying the 7th house from their houses, do harm. The houses they occupy also become harmful, if these planets own at the same time the houses occupied by the dragon's head, i.e., Rahu.

Mercury, Jupiter and Venus become harmful if they occupy the 4th, 5th, and 7th houses respectively from the Ascendant.

Saturn if he occupies the 8th house, gives good and happy results. Some hold that he may cause early death.

Planetary Wars

> The Sun defeats Saturn
> Saturn defeats Mars
> Mars defeats Jupiter
> Jupiter defeats the Moon
> The Moon defeats Venus
> Venus defeats Mercury
> Mercury defeats the Moon

Planets are successful in war when they occupy the star subsequent to the star which Mars occupies or when they occupy the subsequent house, or Asma, i.e., to say if Mars is behind and the planet in question be in advance.

If Mercury, Jupiter, Venus and Saturn are associated with Mars, they are defeated in war. The planet that is situated previous to the star in which Mars is situated, is a planet that is defeated in war.

Karakatwams

Sun is the *Karaka* or indicator of the 1st housae or Ascendant.

Jupiter is the *Karaka* or indicator of the 2nd house.

Mars is the *Karaka* or indicator of the 3rd house.

The Moon and Mercury are the *Karakas* or indicators of the 4th house. Jupiter is the *Karaka* or indicator of the 5th house.

Mars and Saturn are the *Karakas* or indiçators of the 6th house.

Venus is the *Karaka* or indicator of the 7th house.

Sautrn is the *Karaka* or indicator of the 8th house.

The Sun and Jupiter are *Karakas* or indicators of the 9th house.

Mercury, Saturn, Jupiter and Sun are the *Karakas* or indicators of the 10th house.

Jupiter is the *Karaka* or indicator of the 11th house.

Saturn is the *Karaka* or indicator of the 12th house.

The Sun is the *Karaka* or indicator of the father, eyes, body and general prosperity.

The Moon is the *Karaka* or indicator of the mother and happiness and general prosperity.

The Moon is the *Karaka* or indicator of brothers, lands, and courage.

Mercury is the *Karaka* or indicator of intelligence, knowledge and trade.

Jupiter is the *Karaka* or indicator of children and wealth.

Venus is the *Karaka* or indicator of marriage, spouse, fame, eyes and conveyance.

Saturn is the *Karaka* or indicator of Longevity.

Rahu is the *Karaka* or indicator of the maternal grandfather and foreign languages.

Ketu is the *Karaka* or indicator of the paternal grandfather, slavation, bath in holy waters and spiritual attainments, mantras etc.

Aspects and Their Significance

While analysing a horoscope, certain important elements have to be considered, and combined together with logical judgement. Once the fundamentals, namely, the characteristics of the planets, the nature of the twelve Zodiacal signs, the matters governed by the different Houses (*Bhavas*), the quality of the aspects etc., have been well understood, then the proper analysis and application will be facilitated.

The aspecting planet often indicates the changes/ modifications in the nature of the result; and the cause for such a change and the source which brings about such a change. The planet receiving the aspect produces such results which it may indicate.

An aspect is an angle formed on the Earth by the beams of two planets. The term is employed, in astrology, to refer to angular distance measured in degrees and minutes of celestial longitude between two points in the Zodiac. According to Western Astrologers, aspects are formed between two planets or between a planet and a point in the horoscope as for instance the cusp of a house (*Bhava*), say Ascendant M.C., etc. 'Cusp' may be defined as the edge of a house, i.e., the exact beginning of a house (which is also the end of the previous house) reckoned in degrees and minutes of celestial longitude. It is beyond any doubt that some angular distances do produce varied results which are significant in the lives of natives as well as nations.

A planet is considered to be in aspect with another planet or a sensitive point in the Zodiac only when it is placed from the planet or the sensitive point by a certain longitudinal distance.

Planets are ever moving in their known orbits in the Zodiac and so aspects may be formed between the two planets and the difference in their longitudes will form a particular aspect. That is, at any given time, in some part of the Zodiac, two planets may be transiting at a particular distance from each other and certain angles are formed upon the earth by such relationships. In has been found that these angles exert significant impact on those natives, animaters or vibrations by reason of the fact that at their birth, cosmic vibrations of similar nature were in existence.

According to the ancient Hindu sages and seers, the aspects (drishities) should be counted from sign to sign, irrespective of the position of the planet in the sign and the relative distance between two planets. Further, the aspects themselves are neither decided as favourable nor unfavourable considering the longitudinal distance between them. They depend mainly upon the natural relationship between the planets in aspect. It must also be considered whether the aspect or planet and the aspectee planet is said to be inauspicious and the aspect of a benefic planet is invariably good and stimulating.

Suppose a planet is located in any degree in the sign Mesha (Aries), then *Vrishaba* (Taurus) is said to be the second from that planet, *Mithuna* (the Gemini) the third, etc., in that order. If a birth falls, say, in the *Simha* (Leo) Ascendant then *Kanya* (Virgo) is the second house to that native, *Tula* (Libra) is the third and so on.

The ancient Hindu sages said that all planets aspect the 7th sign counted from the sign occupied by them to a full extent. Suppose two planets are placed in opposite signs of the Zodiac, as, for example, Jupiter in *Mithuna* (Gemini) and Mercury in *Dhanus* (Sagittarius). They are in the 7th aspect to each other, no matter what the actual distance may be between the two planets.

Besides the 7th aspect, all planets are said to cast a quarter aspect over the the 3rd and 10th houses from the one occupied by them, but Saturn's 3rd and 10th house aspects are stronger and more forceful than even its 7th aspect. Similarly, Jupiter is dominant with its bright and optimistic rays over the 5th and 9th houses from the house occupied by it, and these aspects are more powerful than its 7th house aspect. The other planets also view the 5th house aspect. Mars, in addition to its 7th aspect, powerfully aspects the 4th and 8th houses from the sign in which it is placed.

Mantreswara mentions in "Phaladeepika" (*sloka* 9, *Adhyaya* IV) that the 7th aspect is the only one that should be declared as most effective in all cases and not so the rest, but other ancient scholars of astrology are of the view that the special aspects of Saturn, Mars and Jupiter are equally and powerfully effective, as these major planets play significant roles in the lives of the natives and reveal most interesting details about various aspects of their life such as family, finances, food habits, friendships, love and romance, health, etc. which are vital for one's progress and achievements.

8

PLANETS—NATURE AND SIGNIFICANCE

If any planet or planets be strong at the time of birth of a person in his horoscope, then the mental qualities represented by the said planets will be equally strong in the person. If the planets are weak, the corresponding mental qualities will also be weak. But in the case of Saturn alone, there is an exception that if Saturn is strong in the horoscope, the pessimism represented by Saturn will be less but if Saturn is weak, then that pessimism is likely to be accelerated.

The Colour and Form of Planets

The Sun has a form with dark red rays.

The Moon has a youthful form with a white body.

Mars is of a pale red colur.

Mercury is of dark green colour of bent grass.

Jupiter has a body of yellow colour.

Venus has a white body and is of variegated colour.

Saturn is dark in colour.

Rahu has a black body.

Ketu has a variegated colour.

Planets — Lustrous, Stars and Dark Planets

The Moon and the Sun are lustrous planets.

Mars, Mercury, Jupiter, Venus and Saturn are star planets.

Ketu and Rahu are dark planets.

Mercury is extremely brilliant when he is 29 degrees away from the Sun.

Venus is extremely brilliant when she is 47 degrees away from the Sun.

First 10 days of a lunar month, the Moon of Moderate Strength

In the 2nd 10 days, the Moon is very auspicious and strong.

In the 3rd 10 days, it has little strength of its own but will be auspicous if aspected by benefic planets.

Rising of the Planets

The Sun, Mars, Rahu and Saturn rise with the hind part first.

Venus, the Moon and Mercury rise with head foremost.

Jupiter rises both ways.

Forms of Planets

The Sun and Mercury have the form of a bird.

The Moon is of the shape of a reptile.

Jupiter and Venus are bipeds.

Saturn and Mars are quadrupeds.

Reisdence of Planets

The Moon and Venus rest in water.

Jupiter and Mercury live in places where learned men reside.

Mars, Rahu, Saturn, Ketu and the Sun live in mountains and forests.

Age of Planets

Mars is a child.

Mercury is a boy.

Venus is 16 years old.

Jupiter is 50 years old.

The Moon is 70 years old.

Saturn is 100 years old.

Rahu is 100 years old.

Ketu is 100 years old.

Lords of Material Objects

Jupiter, Venus, Mars, are lords of vegetable kingdom.

Mars and the Sun are lords of minerals.

Venus and Jupiter are lords of the animal kingdom.

Mercury is the lord of all of these put together.

The Planets represent various Gems, Minerals and Stones

Sun	—	Copper
Mars	—	Gold
Jupiter	—	Silver
Saturn	—	Iron
Moon	—	Gems
Mercury	—	Alloy of Metals
Venus	—	Pearls

The Planets represent Precious Gems

The Sun	—	Ruby
The Moon	—	Pearl or Moonstone
Mars	—	Coral
Mercury	—	Emerald
Jupiter	—	Topaz or Yellow Sapphire
Venus	—	Diamond or Zircons .
Saturn	—	Blue Sapphire
Rahu and Ketu	—	Agate

Planets Represent Clothing

Sun	—	. Thick clothes
Moon	—	New fine clothes
Mars	—	Clothes partially burnt by fire
Mercury	—	Laundered clothes
Jupiter	—	Ordinary clothes
Venus	—	Long lasting fabrics
Saturn	—	Ill-attired or dressed

Planets are Lords of Directions

The Sun is Lord of East.

Venus is the lord of the South-East.

Mars is the lord of the South.

Rahu is lord of the South-West.

Saturn is lord of the West.

Moon is lord of the North.

Jupiter is lord of the North-East.

Planets — Lords of Seasons

Venus is Lord of *Vasantha*.

The Sun and Mars are lords of *Greeshma*.

The Moon is lord of *Varsha*.

Mercury is lord of *Sharad*.

Jupiter is lord of *Hemant*.

Saturn is lord of *Shishira*.

Planets own Particular Places

Sun	—	Occupies a shrine temple or holy place.
Moon	—	Shore or river Bund(river bank).
Mars	—	Fireplace hearth.
Mercury	—	Pleasure ground.
Jupiter	—	Treasury locker.
Venus	—	Is the lord of the bed-chamber (river bank)

Saturn	—	Is the lord of heap of rubbish or ruins or kucha (haphazard) terrains.
Rahu and Ketu	—	Corners of House.

Planets — Lords of *Vedas*

Jupiter is the lord of the *Rig Veda*.

Mercury is the lord of the *Atharva Veda*.

Mars is the lord of the *Som Veda*.

Venus is the lord of the *Yajur-Veda*.

Nature of the Planets

Planets	Caste	Nature	Sex	Elements
Sun	Kshatriya	Satvik	Male	Fire
Moon	Vaisya	Satvik	Female	Water
Mars	Kshatriya	Tamasik	Male	Fire
Mercury Eunuch	Shudra	Rajasik	Female	Earth
Jupiter	Brahmin	Satvik	Male	Air
Venus	Brahmin	Rajasik	Female	Water
Saturn Eunuch	Outcaste	Tamasik	Male	Air
Rahu	Boya	Tamasik	Male	Eunuch
Ketu	Sanyasi	Satvik	Male	Eunuch

Note : This naturn should be predicted in individuals after ascertaining the strength of the planets that own, occupy and aspect the ascendant and the house occupied by the moon. Chiefly the planet whose Trimsamsa Sun occupies, gives the prominent characteristics of the native.

Planets are Lords of Internal Substances

Marsis the lord ofMarrow.

Saturn	"	"	"	"	Fat.
Jupiter	"	"	"	"	Bone.
Sun	"	"	"	"	Semen.
Venus	"	"	"	"	Blood.
Moon	"	"	"	"	Skin.

Planets	Taste	Period of influence
Sun	Pungent	6 months
Moon	Saline	2 ghatikas or 48 minutes
Mars	Bitter	1 day
Mercury	Mixed	2 months
Jupiter	Sweet	1 month
Venus	Astringent	15 days
Saturn	Acid	1 year.

Sight of Planets

Sun and Mars look upwards.

Venus and Mercury look sideways.

Moon and Jupiter look evenly.

Rahu and Saturn look downwards.

Planets Have Particular Characters

Sun is steadfast.

The Moon is wandering and unsteady.

Mars is violent.

Mercury is mixture or various qualities.

Jupiter is gentle.

Venus is light or easy.

Saturn is harsh.

Planets — 5 Stages of Life in Each House

In odd houses according to the number of degrees advanced, a planet is said to be (in order) :

(1) in infancy,
(2) in boyhood,
(3) in youth,
(4) in middle age,
(5) in extremely old age.

In even houses, a planet is said to be (in order) :

(1) in extremely old age,
(2) in middle age,
(3) in youth,
(4) in boyhood,
(5) in infancy.

Planets have Awakened and Sleeping States

(1) The portion of the Zodiacal house in which a planet is in exaltation and the Navamsa which is owned by it, is its awakened state.
(2) The Navamsa belonging to a friendly planet is its dreaming state.
(3) The portion where it is in depression and that which is owned by its enemy, is sleeping state.

Planets — 6 Stages of Life. These stages are :

1. Bala   —   Infancy.
2. Kumara   —   Below 7 years of age
3. Tharuna   —   Youth
4. Vridha   —   Old
5. Alasa   —   Slow
6. Mritya   —   Death

Everything in this world has an ego of its own. That which overpowers one's own ego is bad. For instance, the Sun is so overpowering and hence it is considered a malefic.

It is dark, while the former is pleasant. Jupiter and Venus shed an agreeble light, hence they are benefics. Saturn, Rahu and Ketu have dark rays and hence are malefic or unpleasant. Mars a reddish light not so agreeble, hence a malefic. Mercury is colourless and can blend with anything. Therefore a well associated Mercury is a benefic while a badly associated Mercury is a malefic.

9

PLANETS — FRIENDS AND FOES

The following principle may be easily adopted in understanding the planets and to know which are enemies or friends of a particular planet.

Mars

If you have a look at the celestial map of the Heavens, you will find that certain planets are placed in certain positions in relation to each other. For instance, taking Aries as the first sign of which the lord is Mars, we find that Mercury, a natural benefic, has Rashis which are the 3rd and 6th from Aries. Therefore, Mercury becomes an enemy of Mars. Even from Scorpio, which is owned by Mars, Mercury owns the 8th and 11th houses from Scorpio. The 3rd, 6th, 8th and 11th houses are definitely bad. From Gemini, Mars becomes the lord of the 3rd and 8th houses. Therefore, the common position of the 3rd, 6th and 8th, which are all inauspicious, affect the two planets. Therefore, Mars and Mercury are inimical.

From Aries, the Sun becomes the lord of the 5th house, and therefore a friend. From Scorpio, he is the lord of the 10th house. From Leo, Mars becomes the lord of the two benefic houses, 4th and 9th. Therefore, the Sun and Mars are friends.

From Aries, the Moon is the lord of the 4th house and from Scorpio, the Moon is the lord of the 9th house. From Cancer, Mars becomes the lord of the 5th and 10th houses. Therefore, the Moon and Mars are friends.

From Aries, Venus is the lord of the 2nd and 7th houses and from Scorpio, the 7th and 12th houses. From Taurus, Mars becomes the lord of the 7th and 12th houses. From Libra, Mars becomes the lord of the 2nd and 7th houses. Therefore, we may safely count Mars and Venus more as friends than as neutrals.

Jupiter is the lord of the 9th and 12th houses from Aries, from Scorpio of 2nd and 9th houses. From Pisces, Mars is the lord of the 2nd and 9th houses. From Sagittarius, Mars is the lord of the 5th and 12th houses. Mars and Jupiter are therefore friends.

Coming to Saturn, from Aries, Saturn is the lord of the 10th and 11th houses. From Scorpio it is the lord of the 3rd and 4th houses. From Capricorn, Mars happens to be the lord of the 4th and 11th houses, whereas from Aquarius, it is the lord of the 3rd and 10th houses. It can be seen here, one very bad house, the 3rd, is very predominant though in both the cases there is a Kendra also to mitigate the evil. Still Mars and Saturn must be considered to be more inimical than neutrals.

Therefore, we can conclude that for Mars:

Friends: Venus, the Moon, the Sun, Jupiter and Ketu (Dragon's Tail).

Enemies: Mercury, Saturn and Rahu (Dragon's Head).

Venus

Taking a Taurus Ascendant, it can be seen that Mercury is the lord of the 2nd and 5th houses, whereas from Libra it is the lord of the 9th and 12th houses. From Gemini, Venus is the lord of the 5th and 12th houses, whereas from Virgo, she is the lord of the 2nd and 9th houses. Therefore, it will be seen that the 2nd, 5th and 9th houses are an important factor and as such Mercury and Venus are friends.

The Moon is the lord of the 3rd house from Taurus, but from Libra, it is the lord of the 10th house. Still, the 3rd house is playing an important factor. From Cancer, Venus happens to be the lord of the 4th and 11th houses. 3rd and 11th houses are playing an important factor. Hence, for Venus, the Moon is an enemy.

Coming to the Sun, from Taurus, the Sun is no doubt the lord of the 4th house. But from Libra, he happens to be the lord of the 11th house and from Leo itself, Venus happens to be the lord of the 3rd as well as the 10th houses. Therefore, the Sun has to be considered an enemy of Venus and not a friend, because the 3rd and 11th houses are again playing a vital role.

From Taurus, Saturn is the lord of the 9th and 10th houses, whereas from Libra, he happens to be the lord of the 4th and 5th houses. From Capricorn, Venus is the lord of the 5th and 10th houses, whereas from Aquarius, Venus owns the 4th and 9th houses. Therefore, Venus and Saturn are friends.

Jupiter is the lord of the 8th and 11th houses from Taurus. From Libra, it is the lord of the 3rd and 6th houses. From Saggitarius, Venus owns the 6th and 11th houses, while from Pisces, she owns the 3rd and 8th houses. Therefore, here also it can be seen that the 3rd, 6th, 8th and 11th houses are an important factor. Hence, Venus and Jupiter must be considered to be more inimical than neutrals.

Therefore, we can conclude that for Venus :

Friends: Mercury, Venus, Saturn and Rahu (Dragon's Head).

Enemies: The Sun, the Moon, Jupiter and Ketu (Dragon's Tail).

Mercury

From Gemini, the Moon is no doubt the lord of the 2nd house but from Virgo, she owns the 11th house. From the Moon, Mercury owns 12. Therefore, the Moon must be considered to be an enemy of Mercury.

The Sun is the lord of the 3rd house, no doubt it is inauspicious especially as Leo is the 12th house from Virgo. But from the Sun, Mercury owns the 11th. It is also a known fact that Mercury alone is not considered to be eclipsed when it is in conjunction with the Sun. Therefore, the Sun must be considered more as a friend than otherwise.

The relationship of Venus and Mars with Mercury has already been discussed. Venus must be considered to be a friend, but Mars, an adversary. Jupiter owns 7th and 10th from Gemini and 4th and 7th from Virgo. Both of these being Kendras, Mercury and Jupiter must be considered to be more friendly than inimical.

Saturn owns 8th and 9th houses from Gemini, while from Virgo, it is the lord of 5th and 6th.

Mercury owns the 6th and 9th houses from Capricorn and 5th and 8th from Aquarius. Therefore in both cases the 5th, 6th and 8th houses are playing an important factor. Hence Mercury and Saturn are considered to be more neutral than inimical for, while there is one point in favour, the other points are not. However, one thing must be remembered that Mercury is a colourless planet and therefore must be considered as having no enemy at all, for Mercury will blend with any other planet. Hence, Mercury need not be said to have any ememies.

But as a sort of general guideline, we may say that for Mercury :

Friends: The Sun, Venus and Rahu (Dragon's Head).

Enemies: The Moon and Mars.

The Moon

From the Moon, the Sun owns the 2nd house and therefore is a friend. Mercury is the lord of the 3rd and 12th, and therefore this planet has to be considered an enemy. But we have considered Mercury, a friend for the Moon, and the Moon an enemy for Mercury. Venus owns the 4th and 11th. Because from Taurus, the Moon owns the 3rd and from Cancer Venus is the lord of the 11th house. Venus is an enemy of the Moon. Mars is the lord of the 5th and 10th houses and therefore Mars and the Moon are friends. Jupiter is the lord of the 6th and 9th houses, whereas from Sagittarius and Pisces, she owns the 8th and 5th respectively.

6th and 8th must be considered to have cancelled each other and the 5th and 9th are given great importance; therefore Jupiter and the Moon are considered friends.

Saturn owns the 7th and 8th houses and from Capricorn, the Moon is the lord of the 7th house, while from Aquarius, she is the lord of the 6th house. Therefore, 6th and 8th houses play an important role. Therefore, Saturn and the Moon are considered enemies. the Moon, however, is said to be the enemy of no planet.

Therefore, a conclusion may be drawn and it can be said for the Moon :

Friends: Jupiter, the Sun, Mars, Mercury and Ketu (Dragon's tail).

Enemies: Venus, Saturn and Rahu (Dragon's Head)

The Sun

For a Leo Ascendant, Mercury owns the 2nd and 11th houses. For Mercury, the Sun has been considered more a friend because Mercury does not get eclipsed when it is in conjunction with the Sun. In fact, Mercury is in very close degrees of the Sun. Therefore, the Sun and Mercury need not be considered to be enemies, they are more friends.

Venus is the lord of the 3rd and 10th houses. Thus Venus is considered an enemy of the Sun. Mars is the lord of 4th and 9th houses and therefore a friend. Jupiter is the lord of the 5th and 8th houses, whereas from Jupiter, the Sun is the lord of the 6th and 9th houses. Therefore, Jupiter and the Sun are friends. Saturn owns 6th and 7th houses and from Saturn, the Sun is the lord of 7th and. 8th houses, therefore Saturn and the Sun are enemies.

A line may be drawn and said for the Sun :

Friends: The Moon, Mars, Jupiter, Mercury and Ketu (Dragon's Tail).

Enemies: Venus, Saturn and Rahu (Dragon's Head).

Jupiter

Jupiter's relationship with Mars, Venus, Mercury, the Moon and the Sun has been considered previously. From Jupiter, Saturn owns the 2nd, and 3rd and 11th and 12th houses; from Saturn, Jupiter owns the 3rd and 12th, and 2nd and 11th houses. Because the 3rd and 11th houses are playing an important role, Jupiter and Saturn are not considered friends, though not enemies either.

Therefore we can conclude for Jupiter :

Friends: The Sun, the Moon, Mars, Mercury and Ketu (Dragon's Tail).

Enemies: Venus and Rahu (Dragon's Head).

Saturn

The relationship of Saturn with other planets has been examined earlier and therefore we can conclude for Saturn :

Friends: Mercury, Venus, Rahu (Dragon's Head) and Jupiter.

Enemies: The Sun, the Moon, Mars, and Ketu (Dragon's Tail).

10

ALL ABOUT ASCENDANTS

In the following pages, the 12 Ascendants are discussed one by one. A chart has to be made with the planets placed in their own houses. For instance, Mars must be placed both in Aries and in Scorpio and Saturn both in Capricorn and Aquarius. Therefore, Saturn will be aspecting certain signs from Capricorn as well as Aquarius. There will be the aspect of Saturn both on Cancer and Leo. The aim of this explanation is to motivate the aspiring astrologers into learning the method of analyzing scientifically the aspects of planets and secondly to show that even in the heavens, the 12 signs are placed in a particular way and their effects also must necessarily be at variance. For instance, whereas Aries and Scorpio are placed between Jupiter and Venus, two benefic planets, Sagittarius and Pisces are placed between two malefic planets, Saturn and Mars. Aries and Scorpio will have the aspect of Saturn, whereas Taurus will not receive any aspect of Saturn. Therefore, fundamentally there must be a difference in these houses and people born in the different signs must have different characteristics and behaviour patterns in life. This is only a general method of viewing the signs, and the effects discussed here will certainly vary from the actual facts according to the strength of a particular radical horoscope under study.

While the general trend in all cases will be the same either in a male or a female chart, there will be a slight difference in the matter of the 7th house which speaks of the spouse and conjugal happiness. Venus is the indicator of the wife and marital happiness, whereas Jupiter is the indicator for the husband. Therefore when the 7th house is examined in a female horoscope, Jupiter will have to be taken into consideration, just the same way as Venus is considered in a male chart.

Aries

This is the first sign of the Zodiac and its lord is Mars. This house is between Jupiter and Venus, both of them natural benefics, and this house will be having the aspect of Venus, Jupiter and Saturn. Mars by itself is a strong, sturdy planet. Hence the native is generally well-built. Owing to the aspect of Saturn on the Ascendant , generally in their youth, these people have slight ill-health and that always happens during the first major period after birth. This house contains the constellations *aswini*, *bharani* and the first quarter of *krittika*. The benefic planets for this Ascendant are : Venus, the Moon, the Sun, Jupiter, and Saturn; Venus, because she happens to be the lord of the 2nd and 7th houses, the Moon because she happens to be the owner of the 4th house, and the Sun, the lord of the 5th house; Jupiter, the lord of the 9th house; and Saturn the lord of the 10th and 11th houses. All these are very important houses, and excepting Saturn all the others are very friendly with Mars. Hence the native is likely to rise in life though it will not be without obstacles, because Mars and Saturn are not friendly, and temperamentally Mars being a martial planet, these people generally do not go down in life and even if they do, they do so not without putting up a tough fight.

Venus is the lord of the 2nd and 7th houses. The 2nd house is between Mars and Mercury and this house has only the aspect of Mars. Mars and Mercury are friends of Venus. But one is a natural malefic while the other is a doubtful benefic. Mars and Venus being very friendly, they have a fairly good amount of domestic happiness. They are also well placed financially but they are not able to save much. They are rather outspoken and truthful. They come from a good and respectable family because Mars and the Sun are friendly and so also Mars and Venus.

They can be good speakers if they try. Mars, the Sun and Jupiter are friends.

The 3rd house belongs to Mercury and this house is between Venus and the Moon and both of them are friends of Mercury besides being natural benefics. This house has the aspect of Jupiter and Mars. The aspect of Jupiter on the 3rd house must not be considered to be very beneficial. He may have brothers and sisters, but the native himself is likely to be in a better position than his brothers or sisters, and very often it can be noticed that because Mars and Mercury are not friends, there is not much agreement between himself and his brothers and sisters. Owing to the aspect of Mars and Jupiter on this house, they are alternately very rash and thoughtful in their acts. They have frequent short journeys on land and even travel overseas.

The Moon is the lord of the 4th house and this house is between Mercury and the Sun. This house has the aspect of Mars, Saturn and Jupiter. The Moon happens to be not only the lord of the 4th house indicating mother but also the indicator for the mother. Therefore, they have indeed a very respectable and good lady as a mother, but owing to the aspect of two malefic planets, Saturn and Mars, somehow the lady's health is not really good or else she has some sort of mental unhappiness. Their education is very often interrupted because of the aspect of Saturn but with a well-placed Mercury in the horoscope, they may have a very liberal education owing to the aspect of Jupiter on this house. Mars and Saturn being two malefic planets aspecting the 4th house, they may be short-tempered and they may not translate their evil thoughts into action. They will have a number of friends both in high and low society. Because of the aspect of Jupiter and Saturn respectively, somehow they are not able to do much good to their friends in spite of their position in life.

Sun is the Lord of the 5th house, and this house is between the Moon and Mercury, both of them more or less benefic and friends of the Sun. This house has the aspect of the Jupiter and Saturn. The aspect of Jupiter is no doubt positive but the aspect of Saturn cannot be considered to be good at all especially since

Saturn and the Sun are adversaries. This house indicates not only children but also *poorvapunya* and authority as also love affairs and creative intelligence. While owing to the aspect of Jupiter, one will have to say that these people are really lucky in life; still one thing will have to be remembered that owing to the aspect of Saturn, there will be some fluctuations in their fortune in life. These people are generally blessed with children. But, very often, they are indecisive.

The 6th house has Mercury as its Lord and this house is between the Sun and Venus. This house has the aspect of Jupiter. The aspect of Jupiter is necessarily bad because it increases the effects of the 6th house and therefore, these people have a number of enemies. Mars and Mercury themselves are enemies. But one thing, generally the enemies do not get the upper hand. These people very often have overseas travels.

The 7th house has Venus with the aspect of Mars and Saturn. Mars aspecting the 7th house as the lord of theAscendant, must be considered to be bad especially on the 7th house. It has to be noted that this house is between Mercury and Mars, of whom one is a positive malefic and the other is a doubtful benefic. It is also unfortunate that there is no aspect of a benefic Jupiter. But Mars and Venus are friendly planets. Hence they marry well or at least they are able to make their own choice. But the aspect of Saturn is likely to give them more than one wife or in these modern times, very strong chances of a separation or a divorce. These people do not generally enter into public life very much unless they are forced to do so. The health of the wife is fairly good.

The 8th house has the aspect of Mars, Venus, Jupiter and Saturn. Though Mars and Saturn are inimical planets, yet the aspect of two very benefic and powerful planets, Jupiter and Venus, gives them a fairly long life. This house is between Venus and Jupiter, two very benefic planets. But one thing has also to be remembered that owing to the aspect of two very benefic planets on the 8th house, though this may be conducive to a long life, it may also result in suffering and hardship and be the cause of misery and unhappiness in life.

The 9th house has Jupiter as its lord and this house unfortunately is between Mars and Saturn, two natural malefic planets. This house has the aspect of Mercury alone. But Jupiter and the Sun, the indicator for father, are friends. Mars and Jupiter are also friends. The native's father may have some money but somehow that money is lost before it comes to them or at least after it comes. For, it must be noted that the lord of 2nd house, Venus and the Sun are inimical planets. So also Venus and Jupiter. Somehow or other these people do not get the advantage of a father's care or even if they get they manage to lose it.

The 10th house has Saturn as its lord and this house has only the aspect of the Moon. This house is between Jupiter and Saturn himself. Saturn is more a servant than a master. Besides, Mars and Saturn are bitter inimical planets. Therefore, in life, these people will generally have many obstacles thrown in their way. To achieve their goals, they will have to fight every inch of the way. They will not get things easily. As for religion, they would be more catholic than orthodox. They do rise to a position of eminence but only after a bitter struggle.

Saturn again happens to be the lord of the 11th house and this house has the aspect of Mars and the Sun, both of them natural malefics. Mars and Saturn are inimical planets. Here one peculiarity has to be observed. While Saturn and Venus are friendly planets, Jupiter and Venus happen to be inimical. Hence their incomes do not commensurate with the input.

The 12th house has as its lord Jupiter, and it is between Saturn and Mars, two malefics, and this house has also the aspect of Saturn and Mercury. Hence it can be seen that these people are not able to enjoy life as well as their position and income would warrant. They may have the desired object but the enjoyment of it as such would be denied to them.

Taurus

This Ascendant has as its lord Venus and is situated between Mars and Mercury and has the aspect of Mars alone. For Venus, Mars and Mercury are friends, and Venus is said to be the planet responsible for all worldly pleasures. Hence people born in Taurus Ascendant are generally considered to be lucky. But there is one thing. Venus, the Sun and Mercury are generally always very close to each other and as such the conjunction of the Sun and Venus will generally spoil the strength of the horoscope because the Ascendant lord will be eclipsed in spite of the conjunction of the lords of the 1st and 4th houses and therefore for Taurus generally to give a powerful yoga, Venus must be as far away from the Sun as possible—preferably in advance of the Sun rather than being behind the Sun. Of the two ascendants Taurus and Libra, though both of them are owned by the same planet, Taurus must be considered to be slightly better than Libra. Because in the former case Venus, the lord of the Ascendant will happen to be lord of the 6th house, whereas in the latter case, Venus, the lord of the Ascendant will happen to be the lord of the 8th house. Between the two malefic houses, 6th and 8th, 8th is said to be the worse. One interesting point here will be that Venus and Mercury are friendly planets and Mercury for Taurus becomes as a *Yogakarak* becomes a planet conferring beneficial results by virtue of being the lord of the 2nd and 5th houses. Even Jupiter and Mercury are not enemies. These people by virtue of having Venus as the lord of the Ascendant with the aspect of friendly Mars, though a malefic by nature, and also owing to the absence of any malefic aspect on the Ascendant, generally are good-looking, fairly tall and with a certain amount of symmetry about their physique. Generally, since the Sun and Mercury are always together, the conjunction of the Sun and Mercury will be very good, because they happen to be the lords of the 4th and 5th houses.

The 2nd house has Mercury as its lord and this house, it can be observed, is between two benefic planets Venus and the Moon, and this house has the aspect of Mars and Jupiter. These people generally are truthful and honest and earn money fairly well in their lives.

The 3rd house has the Moon as its lord and is between Mercury and the Sun. The 3rd house has the aspect of Saturn as well as Mars and Jupiter. No doubt Mars is a friend of both

Venus and the Moon. They will have brothers and sisters, but the aspect of Saturn may not produce much harmony between them. These people are generally bold, but owing to the aspect of Saturn, sometimes get slightly revengeful and a bit excited. They very often undertake long travels.

The 4th house has the Sun in it and this house is between the Moon and Mercury, and has the aspect of Jupiter and the Saturn. The Moon and the Sun are friends. These people generally will have a very good lady as the mother but owing to the aspect of Saturn, in certain cases, especially where the Moon is badly placed in their horoscopes, an early death of the mother or some sort of trouble about the mother has to be predicted. The Sun and Mercury are friends. They get a fairly good education but owing to the aspect of Saturn, sometimes there may be an interruption/setback in their educational career before completion. It has to be remembered that both, the 3rd house which speaks of the lower mind and the 4th house which speaks of the upper mind, have the aspect of Saturn as well as Jupiter. Only the 4th house does not get the aspect of a malefic Mars. Therefore though they are rather excitable, they are not revengeful by nature. They own lands, properties and more vehicles and this Ascendant is also very favourable for landed property. Mars and the Sun are friends. So also Mars and Venus. Though the Sun and Venus are adversaries, owing to the aspect of Saturn natives go in for built-up property and residential flats and renovate property.

The 5th house has the aspect of Jupiter. This house is not only the house of intelligence and children, but also *Poorvapunya* (Good deeds of the previous birth). Therefore when the 5th house is not in anyway badly afflicted, they are generally lucky in their lives. They have children who are a great solace to their parents in their old age. The native is generally intelligent and understanding. It can be seen that both the 2nd and 5th houses have the aspect of Jupiter. This house is situated between the Sun and Venus.

The 6th house has its lord Venus, and this house has the aspect of Mars and Saturn. The aspect of two malefic planets on the 6th house has a very interesting indication in that it removes debts, disease etc., that are represented by this house. Therefore, one can say that the native has generally freedom from disease, debts etc. Besides, this house is between Mercury, a doubtful benefic and Mars, a malefic planet, which makes the 6th house weak.

The 7th house has as its lord Mars, and this house has the aspect of Saturn, Jupiter, Mars and Venus. Mars and Venus are friends. It will be very interesting to note that this house is between two powerful benefics, Venus and Jupiter. Therefore, they are lucky with regard to marital happiness and with regard to the qualities of their spouse. The aspect of Saturn on this 7th house has to be given serious consideration, so also the fact that Mars and Mercury, the lord of the 2nd house indicating domestic happiness, are adversaries. Therefore, the spouse may not be in such a position as to contribute his/her efforts fully towards family happiness, owing to perhaps ill-health or some such other reason. That the native will have a very charming partner or if it is a woman's horoscope, a very good husband, there is absolutely no doubt.

The 8th house has Jupiter as its lord, and Jupiter and Saturn must be considered to be friends, at least, not enemies. This house is between two malefics, Mars and Saturn, which is really an advantage, in that, this house representing poverty and adversity becomes weak. This house has the aspect of only Mercury and no malefic planet. Hence these people live up to a fairly old age.

The 9th house has its lord Saturn. Saturn and Venus are friendly planets and the Moon is aspecting this house. But the Sun and Saturn are enemies. So also the Sun and Venus. Therefore, one will have to predict that though these people may inherit some paternal property, yet some misunderstanding between the father and son is very likely. This house is between Jupiter and Saturn and Saturn happens to be its own lord and, therefore, need not be given any serious attention as a malefic. Besides, Saturn becomes a perfect benefic for people born in this Ascendant.

One thing may be stated here that some astrologers hold that for Taurus Ascendant, Saturn is not a benefactor though he may be the lord of the 9th and 10th houses. That may perhaps be due to the fact that it is always said that the conjunction of the lords of the 9th and 10th houses is good but in this case, the lords of both the houses being the same it will not be a conjunction of two different planets as lords of the 9th or 10th houses.

The 10th house has Saturn as its lord, and this house is between Saturn and Jupiter. This house has the aspect of Sun as well as Mars. Generally these people get into government service and rise to a fairly high position in life. Many surgeons and medical specialists have been born in this ascendant.

The 11th house has as its lord Jupiter, and this house is between Saturn and Mars. This house has the aspect of Saturn and Mercury. These people generally earn well. But the house being between two malefic planets, indicates that very often their income will not be commensurate with the labour involved. One may also point out that the lord of the 2nd house is not an enemy of the 11th house.

The 12th house has Mars as its lord, and this house has the aspect of Jupiter, Saturn and Venus and is between Jupiter and Venus. They generally spend well and enjoy life very much. But one thing can be said that owing to the aspect of Saturn, there may not be much discretion in the matter of their charity or expenditure.

Gemini

This is the 3rd sign of the Zodiac and is situated between Venus and the Moon, two benefic planets. This house has the aspect of Jupiter, and Mars. Its lord is Mercury. This planet is considered a half benefic for, in conjunction with benefic, it becomes a benefic, and in conjunction with a malefic, it becomes a malefic. This planet is generally very close to the Sun and as such, there is generally a conjunction between the Sun and Mercury the lords of the 3rd and 1st houses, which is not very pleasant for however much the Sun may be a friend of Mercury, it is a cruel planet, besides being the Lord of the 3rd house, which is malefic.

Generally speaking, since Mercury also happens to be the lord of the 4th house, which indicates *Vidya* or education, many lawyers are found born in this Ascendant. To add to it, the 10th house is also owned by Jupiter, who is a spiritual teacher and hence in an extended sense an indicator for justice and legal knowledge. These people have a fairly good health, unless Mercury or ascendant itself is badly afflicted and generally speaking they are not very robust in health.

The 2nd house has the Moon as its lord and this house is between Mercury and the Sun. This house has the aspect of Saturn, Mars and Jupiter. These people are generally truthful but still they have the capacity to make an untruth appear as a great truth, meaning thereby that they can be very diplomatic. Birth during the waning Moon, especially during the last week, is not very conducive to any great domestic happiness and though Jupiter may have an aspect on the 2nd house, the aspect of Saturn and Mars generally indicates some sort of want in their domestic happiness. So far as the question of money is concerned, they are able to save money but they generally manage to lose much of their savings. Jupiter and the Moon are friendly planets, at least not inimical.

The 3rd house has the Sun as its lord and this house is between the Moon and Mercury. The Sun and Mercury are friends, so also the Sun and Mars. This house has the aspect of Jupiter and Saturn. These people generally have a good number of brothers and sisters, but unfortunately owing to the aspect of Saturn, the native thrives much better than the brothers or sisters. The aspect of Saturn especially on this house, makes them a bit vengeful and excitable by nature. Whether they act upon it or not is a different matter, and very often they suffer from a certain amount of vanity. They have frequent small journeys on land.

The 4th house has Mercury as its lord and this house is between the Sun and Venus, and they both are friends of Mercury. This house has the aspect of only Jupiter. The Moon and Mercury must be considered to be friends. So also Jupiter and Mercury. Hence they have a very good and respectable lady as the mother, but if the Moon is badly placed in the horoscope, they lose their mother early in life. They get decent education and have a large circle of friends. The aspect of Jupiter on this house is indeed very welcome, in that they do not translate their negative thoughts into action.

The 5th house has Venus as its lord, with the aspect of Saturn and Mars. Both of them are friendly with Venus and this house is between Mercury on one side and Mars on the other. Owing to the aspect of Mars, they have a very good intellect, but owing to the aspect of Saturn, they do not have an agile mind or sharp perception. No doubt Mercury and Venus are friends but Jupiter and Venus are enemies. The natives have children. They may lose one or two but most of the children survive them. The aspect of Saturn brings them lucky breaks. They are fond of power and authority but somehow they are not able to exercise it properly.

Scorpio, the 6th house, is between two benefics Venus and Jupiter, with the aspect of Saturn, Jupiter, Mars and Venus. This position brings them a number of enemies and it must be remembered also that Mars and Mercury are enemies and their enemies are sometimes life-long. Unless Mars is weakened in the horoscope, and Mercury is comparatively stronger, the enemies keep giving them a lot of trouble in their lives, more or less continuously. They are generally subjected to periodical ill-health but nothing serious. Sometimes they run into debt as well, and very often they are cheated.

The 7th house has Jupiter as its lord, and this house is between Mars and Saturn. However much they may be natural malefics, they are both friends of Jupiter. But Jupiter and Venus are enemies. This house has the aspect of Mercury, hence they marry well but there are very strong indications of plurality of marriage and somehow there is a discount on their domestic happiness.

The 8th house has Saturn as its lord, and this house is situated between Jupiter and Saturn, with the aspect of the Moon. Hence these people live up to a fairly old age. Saturn happens to be the lord of the 8th house with the aspect of the Moon. It may be responsible for the unhappiness which they very often have in their lives.

The 9th house has as its lord Saturn, and this house is between Saturn and Jupiter. There is the aspect of Mars and the Sun. Saturn and the Sun are enemies, so also Saturn and the Mars. The absence of any benefic aspect on this house is very distressing. Somehow there is a definite misunderstanding between the father and the son, and the native rarely inherits paternal property worth the name. The aspect of the Sun on the 9th house as "pitrukaraka" is really not good. They are fairly religious in thought, and they are quite charitable.

The 10th house has as its lord Jupiter, and this house is between Mars and Saturn. This house has the aspect of Mercury. These people will do well in any advisory capacity such as lawyers, secretaries etc. The aspect of Saturn on this house brings them much labour in any work they undertake. They become religious and orthodox as their age advances.

The 11th house has Mars as its lord, with the aspect of Venus, Jupiter and Saturn. They earn very well in their lives, often much more than they deserve.

The 12th house has Venus in it and is situated between Mars and Mercury with the aspect of Mars. They are very liberal in spirit, but many a time they are very eccentric. While sometimes they spend, say a hundred rupees with equanimity, they will on the other hand haggle very seriously for a few paise. Still as Venus is the lord of that house, they know how to enjoy their lives. Mars is a malefic planet but it is a friend of Venus.

The absence of any malefic aspect on this house is indeed good.

Cancer

This Ascendant has as its lord the Moon, which is placed in between Mercury and the Sun. This Ascendant has the aspect of Saturn, Jupiter and Mars and is generally associated with saints, and philosophers or at least people who are greatly spiritually inclined. This is due to the fact that in the cycle of constellations, the first set of nine ends and then Leo begins again with *Makha* with Ketu (Dragon's tail) as its lord just as *Aswini* begins with Ketu in Aries. Therefore, the three Ascendants Cancer, Scorpio and Pisces are generally associated with saintly people and of these three, Cancer and Pisces seem to have been more favoured by them. It can be seen that the cycle ends once again with Scorpio, and Sagittarius begins with *Moola*, whose lord is Ketu, and ends with Pisces. The last constellation there, is *Revati*, which has Mercury as its Lord. Perhaps the reason is, that somehow or the other, the aspect of two malefic planets on the Ascendant (and more so if the native is born during *Krishna Paksha* or the darker half of the Lunar month, when the lord of the Ascendant becomes weak), the malefic planets become stronger and the benefic planets become weaker. Therefore, worldly happiness and riches keep playing truant in their lives but with a spiritual inclination, they generally evolve very well and rise very high. They are fairly healthy during their childhood. Owing to the aspect of Saturn and another malefic Mars, they have strain with regard to their health but still they have a fairly long and happy life. This Ascendant generally becomes less powerful especially when these natives are born very near *amavasya* or immediately after *amavasya*, i.e. (the darkest moonless night), in which they are likely to be affected by many changes, ups and downs in life and experience conditions similar to what is experienced by a farmer in the monsoon weather viz., sometimes too bright, while at other times less bright.

The 2nd house has the Sun in it and this house is between the Moon and Mercury. This house has the aspect of Saturn and Jupiter. Saturn aspecting the 2nd house is always bad, causing some sort of domestic unhappiness in their lives. Very often it can be seen that these people marry more than once. Jupiter and the Sun are friends and Jupiter happens to be the lord of the 9th house. Generally these people inherit paternal property. Here again this Ascendant will suffer from one disability and that is, the Lord of the 2nd house is likely to be in conjunction with Mercury, the lord of the 12th house. This conjunction is definitely bad. That particular conjunction of the Sun with Mercury may be good, but so far as the question of money or wealth is concerned, the question will be whether it is good. One will definitely have to say that it is bad. These people are independent, truthful and honest. Somehow or other, domestic happiness is very often denied to them.

The 3rd house has Mercury as its lord with the aspect of Jupiter. They have brothers and sisters and generally rise well in life. The native generally is very fond of his brothers and sisters and quite often very helpful. But since Mars and Mercury are inimical some death among them is likely. Though they are very thoughtful, they can get excited but since the Sun is the lord of the 2nd house with the aspect of Saturn, they have perfect control over their feelings. Somehow they do not travel much.

The 4th house has Venus as its lord and this house is between Mercury and Mars. Mercury and Venus are friends, so also Venus and Mars. This house has the aspect of Saturn and Mars. There is generally a break in their education or some delay before completion. But still they attain some knowledge. Again, the aspect of two malefic planets on this house shows the lack of happiness and mental peace. Here again there is a trouble. The Sun and Venus are generally together. Venus, a benefic planet by virtue of being the lord of the 4th house being in conjunction with the Sun and hence getting eclipsed, cannot be considered good at all. Therefore, whatever be their position so far as the question of money is concerned somehow or the other mental peace and happiness are often not found upto their minimum expectations. They have a very excellent lady as mother, but the 4th house being badly afflicted by the virtue of the aspect of Saturn and Mars aspecting, very often it has been seen that the mother is afflicted or some sorrow haunts her. There is no dearth or trouble so far as vehicles or conveyance is concerned. They also have a large circle of friends, and are fond of home and family life.

The 5th house has as its lord Mars and this house is between two excellent benefics Jupiter and Venus. This house has the aspect of Jupiter, Mars and Saturn. They are really very intelligent and they have a quickness of perception. They know how to yield power and authority and are generally loved by their kith and kin. The 5th house speaks of *poorva-punya* also and they are generally lucky. They are blessed with children as Jupiter and Mars are friends. All of their children may not survive them.

The 6th house has as its lord Jupiter, and this house has the aspect of Mercury. This house being strong shows that these people have always to meet many troubles in life though they may eventually be able to overcome them because this house is between two malefic planets, Mars and Saturn. They very often run into debts. These people must take care about that aspect. This house, except in exceptional cases, shows that these people have not got much opportunity to travel.

The 7th house has as its lord Saturn, and this house is between Jupiter and Saturn. This house has the aspect of the Moon alone. Saturn and Venus are friends. The Moon and Saturn are more or less friends. Therefore, they marry well in life and they have a very good spouse. But still the Sun, the lord of the 2nd house indicating domestic happiness and Saturn are enemies. So also Venus and the Sun. Hence either they do not get any domestic happiness or they have a plurality of wives. Somehow or other, for no fault of either, one can see in a case of Cancer Ascendant domestic happiness being denied especially if the native happens to be a male.

The 8th the house has as its lord Saturn, and is in between Saturn and Jupiter. This house has the aspect of Mars as well as the Sun. This is very good, in that it removes much of the misfortunes etc., indicated by that house. Since the Moon and Saturn are friendly, they have a fairly long life but it can be seen that these people have more or less a sudden death, i.e., not after a prolonged illness. They get inheritances, but not without sustained efforts.

The 9th house has Jupiter as its lord and the house is between Saturn and Mars. This house has the aspect of Saturn and Mercury. Jupiter, the lord of the 9th house and the Sun, the *Pitrukarak,* are friendly. Hence they generally inherit some paternal property. They generally come from a good and respectable family. They are fairly religious by temperament and their spiritual interests get kindled at a young age.

The 10th house has Mars as its lord with Jupiter and Venus on either side. This house has the aspect of Jupiter, Venus and Saturn. The aspect of two such perfect benefics on this house is very interesting. It shows they are very successful in their business or whatever be their vocation. They are thoroughly honest. In public life, they are highly favoured and attain distinctions and high honours.

The 11th house has as its lord Venus, and this house has the aspect of Mars, and Mars for people born in Cancer is a great *Yogakarak*. Besides, Mars and Venus are friends. Practically Mars is the best benefic for people born in this sign. Venus has the disability of being the lord of the 11th house, Jupiter, the lord of the 6th house, Saturn the lord of the 8th house, Mercury the lord of the 3rd and 12th houses. Hence Mars is the one great benefic that must be strong for natives born in this Ascendant. It does not have the aspect of any malefic planet or conjunction. Even a debilitated Mars in Cancer is much preferable to Mars being in a bad house. Therefore, these people earn fairly well in life.

The 12th house has Mercury in it, with the aspect of Jupiter and Mars. These people spend a lot of money, more so during the middle portion of their lives. But very often there is a danger of their losing at least some of this fortune.

Now it can be seen that somehow or the other, domestic happiness is denied, trouble through the wife or from the wife is foreseen, mental peace is afflicted and if unfortunately the Sun and Mercury are together, money may be lost. But the 12th house from the Ascendant has a benefic aspect of Jupiter and their 5th house again has a benefic aspect of Jupiter as well as Venus. So also the 10th house with the aspect of Jupiter and Venus. Hence these people, if they turn their thoughts towards God, rise much higher spiritually than materially in their lives.

Leo

The lord of this sign is the Sun, the most powerful of all planets. Hence, it is considered that people born in this sign are generally successful and rise in life and overcome any number of obstacles that come in their way. This house is between two more or less benefic planets, the Moon and Mercury on either side and both of them are friends of the Sun. This Ascendant has the aspect of a very benefic Jupiter as well as the aspect of a malefic Saturn. These people owing to the malefic aspect of Saturn, especially if they are born in the *nakshatra* of *Makha* or within the first *Drekkana* of this Ascendant develop a detached outlook early in life unless properly guided and suffer from ill-health during their childhood or youth, but later on they are free from diseases. One peculiarity is that there will generally be a conjunction between the Sun and Mercury which, in this case is indeed very good as they happen to be the lords of the 1st and 2nd houses. Of course much will depend upon the position of these two planets in a horoscope with other aspects. But, generally speaking, the conjunction of the lords of 1st and 2nd houses must be considered to be very good and in this case it almost always happens that more often than not, the native is a self-made man, with only minor fluctuations in financial fortune, but their living and thinking will always be of the royal type.

The second house has as its lord Mercury and the house is between the Sun and Venus. Both of these planets are friends of Mercury and this house has the aspect of Jupiter only. Therefore, these people are truthful and honest and they are generally able to earn well in their lives because this Mercury happens to be not only the lord of the 2nd house but also of the 11th house. Any conjunction between the Lords of the 1st, 2nd, and 11th houses is always considered to be very beneficial. Though these people are generally truthful and honest they are slightly given to flattery. They generally are not much blessed with domestic happiness, for Saturn the lord of the 7th house is an enemy of the Sun, the lord of the Ascendant. It will be more truthful to say that these people though they may marry good spouses; somehow or the other, the understanding between them is not too good or there is a plurality of marriages.

The 3rd house has Venus in it and this house has the aspect of Mars as well as Saturn and is between Mercury and Mars.

Therefore, there will be some deaths of brothers or a want of understanding between the native and his brothers or sisters. He is bold, but owing to the aspect of Saturn, one will have to say that these people are also sometimes a bit obstinate and difficult in personal relations. If once they decide something, they very rarely change their minds. They will not have much travel.

The 4th house has Mars as its lord and this house is between Venus and Jupiter. This house has the aspect of the Mars, Venus, Jupiter and Saturn. The aspect of so many planets on one particular house shows a very good and respectable mother and that can be seen also by the fact that the Moon, the indicator for mother and Mars, the lord of the 4th house are friends. They are successful in their education however much Mars and Mercury may be inimical. But one thing has to be said that these people even treat their enemies generously. All that they generally desire is the credit of having won, no matter at what cost. They generally have good conveyances.

Sagittarius is in the 5th house with Jupiter as its lord having the aspect of Mercury. This house is between Mars and Saturn. Hence these people generally have children. Besides, the Sun and Jupiter are also friends. They are very intelligent and have a sharp intellect. The absence of any malefic aspect on this house is indicative of the fact that they have some luck behind them. They are generally very fond of authority and they also know how to use it successfully. One thing has to be remembered. The position of this house between two malefic planets indicates that their children may suffer from some ill-health or they will not gain much happiness through them.

The 6th house is of Capricorn whose lord is Saturn and is between Jupiter and Saturn. This has the aspect of the Moon only and this shows that they are very susceptible to the influence of women and generally, these people must be careful of their association with women. Whatever be their income, they generally fall into debt.

The 7th house has Saturn as its lord and this house is between Jupiter and Saturn and has the aspect of the Sun and

Mars, both of them malefic planets and also enemies of Saturn. But Venus, the indicator for spouse, is friendly towards Saturn and Mercury the lord of the 2nd house is friendly with Venus. Hence they marry well, and often get a very good wife. But somehow, since the Sun and Saturn are enemies, so also the Sun and Venus, there is lack of perfect understanding between husband and wife.

The 8th house with Jupiter as its lord has also the aspect of Saturn and Mercury. This gives them a fairly long life. Besides, Jupiter and Saturn are friends and this house being placed between Saturn and Mars is indeed very good. For, the 8th house speaks not only of longevity but also of misery and unhappiness. So this house being hemmed in between malefic planets reduces this misery and unhappiness.

The 9th house with Mars as its lord is between Jupiter and Venus, both of them friends of Mars. Mars and the Sun, the indicators of the father, are friends and this house has the aspect of Jupiter, Saturn and Venus. Therefore, they are likely to inherit some paternal property.

The 10th house has Venus as its lord with the aspects of Mars and it lies between the Mars and Mercury. This indicates some sort of an independent profession. These people are not religious, though they aren't atheists either.

The 11th house with its lord Mercury is between Venus and the Moon, with the aspect of Jupiter and Mars. These people earn well in their lives.

The 12th house with the Moon as its lord has the aspect of Saturn and Mars, and this house is between two friendly planets, Mercury and the Sun. These people, therefore, tend to spend and often try living beyond their means — a tendency which they must try to curb because they generally like to show off.

Virgo

This sign is owned by Mercury, who also happens to be the lord of Gemini, the 10th house. This is a weak planet and is considered to be half benefic because in conjunction with benefics, it becomes a benefic and in conjunction with malefics it becomes a malefic.

This house is between the Sun and Venus, both of whom are friends of Mercury. It has the aspect of Jupiter. This Ascendant is best suited for women to be born in, for it is an even sign and women born in even signs especially with the Moon also in an even sign, are said to be very modest and also have all those inexplicable qualities which are a woman's own. But here there is one problem; the Sun and Mercury are often always together, so also are Mercury and Venus. The Sun and Mercury being together must definitely be considered to be bad because the lord of the Ascendant will be in conjunction with the lord of the 12th house and hence it is bad unless this conjunction takes place in one of the malefic houses 6th, 8th or 12th wherein also there must be only the aspect of a malefic planet or at least there must be absence of influence of any benefic planet.

The conjunction of Mercury and Venus is certainly very good, in that, it happens to be a conjunction of the lords of the 1st and 2nd houses. But even here, there is a possibility of the Sun and Venus being together. Therefore, especially for a Virgo Ascendant Mercury and Venus have to be as far away from the Sun as possible so that the strength of the horoscope may not be reduced.

This sign is associated, so also Gemini, with lawyers, religious preachers etc., for the simple reason that Mercury, the indicator for knowledge, happens to be the lord of the 1st and 10th houses for Virgo Ascendant and 1st and 4th houses if the Ascendant happens to be Gemini. The Ascendant has the aspect of Jupiter and generally people born in this sign or in Gemini, are a bit obese and medium statured. They are lovers of art and beauty and enjoy themselves through travels and social contacts and retain the vigour of youth even in old age.

The 2nd house has Venus as its lord with the aspect of Saturn and Mars. This house is between Mercury and Mars. The aspect of these two malefic planets on this house, is indeed very bad. These people are prone to be a bit untruthful and somehow domestic happiness is denied to them. So far as the question of money is concerned, very often they do not inherit any paternal property, but still make a place in life by themselves, of course depending upon so many other conditions.

The 3rd house has Mars as its lord who is an indicator for brothers. This house has the aspect of Saturn, Jupiter, Mars and Venus. This house is between Jupiter and Venus. These people have a good number of brothers and sisters. They are bold and have the capacity to bear troubles in their lives. They do not have much travel and they are rather revengeful in spirit, but somehow or the other they are not able to put these thoughts into action as much as they may desire to do so.

The 4th house has Jupiter as its lord. The house itself is between Mars and Saturn. This house has the aspect of Mercury and to that extent one can say, especially since Jupiter and the Moon, the indicator for mother, are friends, the native has a good mother, but still since this house is between two malefic planets, there will be some trouble in so far as the question of her health is concerned. They get a decent education but very rarely do they have good conveyances. They have a large circle of friends. Very often they own land of their own which they lose somehow or other later in life specially when they pass through the major periods of inauspicious planets.

The 5th house has Saturn in it with the aspect of the Moon. This house is between Jupiter and Saturn. These people are really intelligent but since Saturn happens to be the lord of this house, there are very strong indications for a perversity of thought and nature in them, and owing to the aspect of the Moon, they are generally easily misled. Owing to the absence of any malefic aspect on this house, one can say that there is some *poorva-punya* behind them, i.e., they must have done some good deeds in their previous birth, whose beneficial reward they may expect particularly with regard to achievements, devotion of children and the creative thinking.

The 6th house has Saturn in it with the aspect of Mars and the Sun, and this house is between Saturn and Jupiter. They generally try to steer clear of debts and the aspect of two malefic planets, the Sun and Mars on this house, assures them of freedom from disease, ill-health etc.

The 7th house has Jupiter as its lord, and this house is between two malefic planets and is aspected by Mercury. Jupiter and Venus are enemies, but Jupiter and Mercury are friendly. Hence they may marry well, but still a lot of domestic unhappiness and want of understanding between the husband and wife are always present and the wife's health may also suffer. They are highly sexed.

The 8th house has the aspect of Venus, Jupiter and Saturn. This house is between Jupiter and Venus. This house gives them a very long life and the aspect of these two benefic planets generally must be considered to be responsible for the troubles and tribulations they often pass through in their lives.

The 9th house has Venus in it with the aspect of Mars. This house is between Mars and Mercury. The aspect of a malefic Mars cannot be considered to be much good. Venus and the Sun, the indicator for the father, are enemies. Hence they generally do not inherit any paternal property or even if they do, the chances are that they lose it. In all these cases, a certain comparison has to be made; the conjunction of the Sun and Venus for Virgo Ascendant may be considered to be good so far as the question of the father is concerned because it is a conjunction between the lord of the 9th house Venus and the Sun, the indicator for father. But then the Venus becomes eclipsed, besides being an enemy of the Sun. Supposing Jupiter happens to be the lord of the 9th house and is in conjunction with the Sun, as in the case of Cancer Ascendant, Jupiter and the Sun are friendly. Therefore, the conjunction of Jupiter and the Sun is considered to be much better than the conjunction of the Sun and Venus. Take the case of Taurus Ascendant. The lord of the 9th house happens to be Saturn and we can say that the conjunction of the Saturn and the Sun is good, as in this case also they are enemies. Therefore, when one examines a horoscope, he must not be guided by the conjunction·of *Karaka* and *Bhavadhipati* alone, but he must consider whether they are friendly or inimical planets. For Taurus Ascendant or Virgo Ascendant, the conjunction of Mercury and *Sukra* will be that of the conjunction of the lords of 1st and 2nd houses. Again for Cancer Ascendant , the conjunction of the Sun and the Moon will yet be the conjunction of the lord of 1 and 2 houses. Can we say this conjunction is as good as the former? Of course not. For the Moon becomes eclipsed and becomes a malefic by virtue of its waning. Hence this conjunction of the Sun and the Moon is considered bad.

Therefore this distinction has always to be clearly made. The 10th house has Mercury in it with the aspect of Jupiter and Mars. This house is between Venus and the Moon. These people hold some high position and responsibility in their lives and they often try to be independent. There is not much religious fervour seen about them. They generally are not capable of harming others. They always think well of others.

The 11th house has the aspect of Saturn, Jupiter and Mars. This house is between Mercury and the Sun. These people earn well in their lives and often have a windfall or lottery or gains through inheritance.

The 12th house has the Sun in it with the aspect of Saturn and Jupiter. Somehow they are not able to enjoy their lives though they may have ample money. This house is between the Moon and Mercury.

Libra

This house is between Mercury and Mars. The lord of this Ascendant is Venus, and this house has the aspect of a friendly Mars and Saturn but still they are natural malefics. Therefore, during childhood, owing to the aspect of two natural malefics, there is a likelihood of their bringing ill-health to the native; but, later on, there is no such trouble. Here this Venus happens to be not merely the lord of the Ascendant, but also of the 8th house. Hence, it has to be considered that this Ascendant is slightly weaker than Taurus for which Venus will be the lord of the 1st and 6th houses. It is very curious to observe that there is an absence of the aspect of a benefic Jupiter either on Taurus Ascendant or Libra Ascendant, whereas the Taurus Ascendant has not the malefic aspect of Saturn, the aspect of Mars being common in both the cases; but the Libra Ascendant has the disadvantage of having the aspect of a malefic Saturn, which the Taurus Ascendant has not. This can be also counted as one of the factors for saying that the Taurus Ascendant is better than Libra.

Still these people generally rise in life. They dress well, can magnetise others with their charming personality and are generally peace-loving. But it has always been observed that their lives seem to be divided into three portions, in which the first is very good, the second indicates downward fluctuation and in the third portion they rise again. They are easily upset but quickly regain their mental balance and equilibrium. They enjoy good food, good music and are favoured in numerous attachments, love and life.

The 2nd house has as its lord Mars and this house is between Venus and Jupiter. This house has the aspect of Saturn, Jupiter, Mars and Venus and this shows that these people are bound to enjoy domestic happiness. But the aspect of Saturn on this house generally indicates frequent bickerings. They are able to save money but generally they become spendthrifts. They are generally polite and are polished in speech though at times can be rough and blunt. In fact, they do not make good speakers. One thing has to be remembered that Jupiter and Mars are friends. For, one is an indicator of wealth and the other is the lord of the house which indicates wealth.

The 3rd house has Jupiter as its lord and it lies between two malefic planets, Mars and Saturn, with the aspect of Mercury. Jupiter and Mars being friendly planets, these people generally have brothers and sisters but owing to the house being placed between two malefic planets, it is seen that there is not much give and take between them. These people are very thoughtful but not at all bold or courageous. The lord of the Ascendant and the lord of the 3rd house are enemies.

The 4th house has Saturn as its lord and it lies between Jupiter and Saturn. This house has the aspect of a benefic, the Moon. Hence they have a very good lady as a mother but somehow or other they lose their mother rather early in life or there is lack of understanding between the mother and son. They generally get a fairly good education and since Mars happens to be the lord of the 2nd house, and Saturn the lord of the 4th house, they are excitable or irritable but the aspect of a benefic Moon gives them the capacity to overcome these feelings. They are not generally revengeful by nature.

The 5th house has Saturn as its lord with the aspect of Mars and the Sun. They are fairly intelligent but somehow or the other, ill-luck generally dogs them. They have children but somehow or the other they are not happy with them. They are very fond of power and authority but in most of the cases they fail to use these to their optimum advantage.

The 6th house has as its lord Jupiter between Saturn and Mars. This house has the aspect of Saturn and Mercury. They are free from disease etc. and they try to steer clear of debts. Very often they make foreign trips. If Jupiter is strong, they have powerful adversaries to contend with.

The 7th house has Mars as its lord and this house has the aspect of Venus, Jupiter and Saturn. They, no doubt, marry well, but very often they marry twice owing to the aspect of Saturn on this house. Again these natives will do better by a late marriage than by an early matrimonial alliance. Also arranged marriage will not be conducive to their progress and happiness.

The 8th house has as its lord Venus and lies between Mars and Mercury. This house has the aspect of Mars. These people do not live upto a very old age however much Saturn and Venus may be friends. The aspect of Mars on the 8th house is indeed good; for it wards off much of the unhappiness connected with that house.

The 9th house has Mercury as its lord situated between Venus and the Moon, with the aspect of a very benefic Jupiter as well as Mars. These people generally hail from a very respectable family, but somehow, or the other, they lose their father early in life. They also tend to spoil the gains of their paternal inheritance.

The 10th house has the Moon as its lord with the aspect of Mars, Jupiter and Saturn and is between Mercury and the Sun.

Many doctors are born in this sign or at least such people who are interested in the art of healing. This is also suitable to favour legal professions and business particularly imports and exports. Of course, this does not preclude other lines of profession or avocation. These people are not very religious by nature.

The 11th house has the Sun in it and is situated between the Moon and Mercury having the aspect of Jupiter and Saturn. These people earn well in their lives, but still one thing should not be forgotten that Venus and the Sun are inimical planets and there is the aspect of an inimical Saturn on this 11th house. Therefore one will have to say that their income and financial gains will not be commensurate with the labour involved.

The 12th house has Mercury as its lord with the aspect of Jupiter. These people are generally good sponsors. Very often they try to live beyond their means and they know how to enjoy their lives.

Scorpio

This is the 8th sign of the Zodiac and is situated between Venus and Jupiter. Its lord is Mars, who also happens to be the lord of the 6th house. To this extent it must be considered to be better than Aries. For, the lord of the Ascendant in this case happens to be the lord of the 6th house, which is not as bad a house as the 8th, comparatively speaking, for Mars becomes the lord of the 8th house of Saturn, Jupiter, Mars and Venus.

This is considered to be one of the spiritual signs. The 2nd cycle of the nine *Nakshatras* ends here, as the first cycle ends with Cancer, and the third cycle ends with Pisces. Great spiritual people are born in this sign also, but somehow Cancer and Pisces seem to have been more patronised by them, than this Ascendant. Perhaps, it is due to the fact that Pisces and Cancer are owned by natural benefics while this house is owned by a natural malefic, Mars. Besides, the 12th house which is indicative of *moksha*, in the case of Pisces, belongs to Saturn, the planet of misery and sorrow, with the aspect of the Sun and Mars indicating that without real suffering no man would attain salvation. In the case of Cancer, the 12th house belongs to

Mercury, the planet for knowledge, aspected by Jupiter and Mars, indicating perhaps that without knowledge or *gyana*, no man can' attain salvation or *Mukti*. In the case of Scorpio, the 12th house belongs to Venus, the planet of pleasure and happiness, of refinement, love and beauty. There are chances in this case of a man devoting more of his time to pleasure.

One thing is very curious that there is the aspect of Mars on Aquarius and Gemini, perhaps meaning thereby that the native will fight a mental battle while trying to discard the material pleasures of life and turning his mind towards the spiritual side of life. These people are generally active, given to luxury and try to rise in life.

The 2nd house has Jupiter as its lord, and this house is situated between Mars and Saturn and has the aspect of Mercury. This Mercury happens to be the lord of not only the 8th house but also of the 11th house. Besides the lords of the 9th and 10th houses, the Moon and the Sun are friends of Mars. Hence these people generally have domestic happiness and never suffer from want. They are fairly truthful and if Mars is not well-placed, they become too subservient and difficult and even inclined to hit people below the belt.

The 3rd house has Saturn as its lord, and this house is situated between Jupiter and Saturn, with the aspect of a benefic Moon. They have brothers and sisters, but since Mars and Saturn are inimical, it can generally be seen that there is not much love lost between them. They are obstinate and *mulish* by nature.

The 4th house has Saturn as its lord and it is situated between Saturn and Jupiter, and has the aspect of the Sun and Mars. The Moon and Saturn are not inimical, so also the Moon and Mars. They generally have a long-lived mother, but yet a certain want of understanding between the mother and the native is often found. They are very excitable and irritable but they don't exhibit themselves. Unless Saturn and Mercury are well-placed, in their radical horoscopes, they do not get any great education. They are not able to have any landed property. They have a number of friends, but they are never useful to them;

often they are more selfish. They will generally try to use their friends.

The 5th house has Jupiter as its lord and it is between two malefic planets, Saturn and Mars. This house has the aspect of Saturn and Mercury. Hence a certain amount of meanness is seen about them and they lay claim to a great deal of intelligence. Unless Jupiter is well-placed they have no children, but a well placed Jupiter means a good number of children. They are fairly lucky in their lives.

The 6th house has Mars as its lord, and it is situated between Jupiter and Venus, with the aspect of Saturn and Venus. They generally don't run into debts and are free from disease. Their troubles are likely to occur in their old age. They might suffer from some disease connected with genital organs, a stone in the bladder, piles or diabetes.

The 7th house has Venus as its lord and it is between Mars and Mercury. This house has the aspect of Mars only. These people marry well, very often making their own choice.

The 8th house has Mercury as its lord and is situated between Venus and the Moon, two benefic planets, with the aspect of Jupiter and Mars. Saturn and Mercury are not adversaries and these people generally live long. They are usually able to tide over any misfortune that comes in their way.

The 9th house has the Moon as its lord, with the aspect of Jupiter, Mars and Saturn. This house is situated between Mercury and the Sun. The Moon and the Sun are not enemies. They inherit some paternal property and yet they are not able to derive full benefit therefrom. And very often they have to face litigation.

The 10th house has the Sun as its lord with the aspect of Saturn and Jupiter. This house is situated between the Moon and Mercury. They generally do well as servants. Very often they get into government service and rise slowly but steadily. Though they think they are very orthodox and religious, but very often it is more of a sham. But still, one thing has to be said that they work hard to achieve their ends. They don't allow obstacles to impede their progress.

The 11th house has Mercury as its lord and is situated between the Sun and Venus. This house has the aspect of Jupiter who happens to be the lord of the 2nd house. The absence of any malefic aspect on this house is interesting. They earn well. And are particularly favoured in business ventures.

The 12th house has the aspect of Saturn and Mars. No doubt they spend money, but it is more often for the benefit of others than for themselves. This does not mean that they are highly charitable because whatever expenditure there is, it is more for their own selfish ends. They are very highly utilitarian in their views. The conjunction of the Sun and Mercury as the lords of 10th and 11th houses is a great possibility and this, if it should occur without any other influence, will be a major drawback.

Sagittarius

This Ascendant has as its lord Jupiter with the aspect of Mercury. This Ascendant is between two malefic planets, Mars and Saturn, who however happen to be more or less friends of Jupiter. Yet the fact remains that the Ascendant is definitely between two natural malefics. It is generally said that people born in this Ascendant are lucky because there is generally a conjunction between the lords of the 9th and 10th houses, Sun and Mercury. But that conjunction may take place in a good house as well as a bad house. Beside this conjunction, one has to think of so many other conditions, which are the pre-requisites for the results of any malefic aspect on this Ascendant. Generally, these people are likely to rise in life but somehow or the other it is beyond any doubt, a great change comes in their lives somewhere between 35 and 42. In fact, that is a period of great importance in the native's life, ethier for the better or worse but generally good things happen.

The 2nd house has as its lord Saturn and it is between Jupiter and Saturn having the aspect of the Moon. Placed between these two planets, it's really very good. The aspect of the Moon is again better and these people are generally truthful but owing to the lord being Saturn, they sometimes are inclined to having rough speech. They are fairly well placed in life, though they do not have much domestic happiness.

The 3rd house has Saturn as its lord and it is between Saturn and Jupiter. This house has the aspect of the Sun as well as Mars. This shows that these people are generally bold and adventurous. But Mars and Saturn being enemies, the native creates some sort of misunderstanding, or at least want of understanding between himself and this brothers or sisters. They generally travel much on land.

The 4th house with its lord Jupiter, is between Saturn and the Mars, both of them malefic planets, with the aspect of Saturn and Mercury. Jupiter and the Moon, the indicator for the mother, are no doubt friendly planets. Still there is some suffering about the mother of the native. They have a fairly good and liberal education. They own land though it is not very remunerative in any way. They have a large circle of friends who generally will have some influence on their lives.

The 5th house with Mars as its lord is between Jupiter and Venus with the aspect of Saturn, Venus and Jupiter. They generally have an alert mind and because Jupiter and Mars are friends, they have children, but owing to the aspect of Saturn, may lose some of them. The aspect of two very benefic planets on this house shows that they are generally lucky, but the aspect of Saturn shows some break of luck now and then. They are generally independent in their views.

The 6th house with its lord Venus is between Mars and Mercury with the aspect of Mars. They steer clear of enemies and the aspect of Mars on the 6th house is good, in that it removes ill-health etc. But one thing they should take care of is not to incur debts, for if they do, somehow they would keep increasing.

The 7th house with its lord Mercury is between Venus and the Moon, two benefic planets with the aspect of Jupiter and Mars. Venus and Mercury are friends, so are Saturn and Venus. Jupiter and Mercury are not enemies. They generally marry well. Owing to the aspect of Mars, the wife's health many not be quite up to the mark.

The 8th house with the Moon as its lord is between Mercury and the Sun, with the aspect of Jupiter, Mars and Saturn. These people have a fairly long life and the aspect of Saturn and Mars must be considered to be good, in that, it removes the misfortunes indicated by that house. The aspect of Mars on that house shows some sort of accidental death or death probably due to an operation or with a weapon or explosion.

The 9th house with its lord the Sun is between the Moon and Mercury with the aspect of Saturn and Jupiter. However much Jupiter and the Sun may be friends, Saturn and the Sun are enemies. Somehow or the other they do not inherit any paternal property or by chance if they do, they generally lose it.

The 10th house has Mercury as its lord with the aspect of Jupiter and is between the Sun and Venus. They are afraid of doing any evil deeds, being fairly religious, though not orthodox. If other conditions in the horoscope are favourable, they attain fame and dignity in life.

The 11th house has Venus as its lord and is between Mercury and Mars, with the aspect of Mars and Saturn. This is a very strong case where one can positively say that the native does not at all get what he deserves in life by way of income, and one should not forget that Jupiter and Venus are also enemies. One is the indicator for fame, wealth etc., and the other being the lord of the 11th house indicates income.

The 12th house is that of Mars between Venus and Jupiter with the aspect of Saturn, Jupiter, Mars and Venus. They spend a lot of money. They like comforts; often times they try to lead a luxurious life. Owing to the aspect of both Jupiter and Venus, one thing has to be positively said that they are not selfish; they are very liberal and often liberal beyond their means owing to the aspect of Saturn.

Capricorn

The lord of this sign is Saturn, who also happens to be the lord of the 2nd house. Hence Saturn becomes a perfect benefic for people born in this Ascendant because this planet owns two benefic houses, and Saturn does not suffer from the disability of being the Lord of the Ascendant for that odium is only meant for Jupiter and Venus. The Ascendant itself is between Jupiter and Saturn with the aspect of a very benefic Moon. Therefore since the lord of the Ascendant is naturally strong, it is generally considered that people born in this Ascendant are lucky and likely to rise in life. This does not mean at all that every person born in Capricorn Ascendant will reach heights of fame and name, but all that can be said is that from the status in which he was born, he may certainly attain a much higher position and status in his life time.

The 2nd house again has Saturn as its lord and this house is between Saturn and Jupiter, with the aspect of a powerful malefic Sun as well as Mars. Therefore to expect, especially in view of the fact that Saturn happens to be the lord of the 2nd house, that these people are very truthful, is rather difficult. They may be courteous but since Saturn is the lord, perhaps there is more of not necessarily dishonesty, but, at least what is commonly called 'diplomacy'. One thing has also to be said, somehow or the other, owing to the aspect of Saturn and a powerful Sun, there is some amount of domestic unhappiness in their lives. Saturn and Jupiter are friends, therefore, they may earn money well, but, since the Sun and Mars aspect, the trouble will be whether they will at any time be able to save much.

The 3rd house has as its lord Jupiter and the house itself lies between two malefic planets, Saturn and Mars with the aspect of Mercury. Mercury and Jupiter being friends, generally these people are born with brothers and sisters and there is a likelihood of their doing well in life, but owing to the aspect of Saturn, no matter how much do they help them, it will be a matter of dispute, Jupiter being the lord of the 3rd house, especially with the aspect of Mercury and Saturn, these are not at all bold or adventurous people but more thoughtful, and to a certain extent speaking well. Because Jupiter happens to be the lord of the 3rd house and also happens to be a watery sign, these people generally travel overseas.

The 4th house has Mars as its lord, and this house is between Jupiter and Venus. This house has the aspect of Saturn, Jupiter and Venus. Hence these people get a fairly liberal education, but since Saturn is aspecting there will be some delay or a positive chance for a break. Again, one thing has to be observed here that Mars and Mercury are inimical planets and as such, their education may not be much useful to them in their lives. Mars and the Moon are friends. Hence a very respectable woman as a mother is seen. Again, one thing may be observed that the 3rd and the 4th houses have the aspect of Saturn and the lord being Mars, quite often they are intellectually dishonest. A certain amount of excitability of temper is definitely seen owing to the aspect of a malefic Saturn and the lord of the house himself being a fiery Mars. The very benefic aspect of Jupiter and Venus gives them the capacity to control their feelings to a very large extent but they can be vindictive if they feel like it.

The 5th house has Venus as its lord and is between Mars and Mercury. Both of these planets happen to be friends of Venus. This house has the aspect of Mars alone. Therefore, they have an agile mind and since the 5th house also speaks of *poorvapunya,* they are generally considered to be lucky in life. They have children. But again since Jupiter and Venus are inimical planets, it is just possible that their first born may not survive them.

The 6th house has Mars as its lord, and is situated between Jupiter and Venus, with the aspect of Saturn and Venus. They generally don't run into debt and are free from disease. Their troubles are likely to occur in their old age. They might suffer from some disease connected with genital organs, a stone in the bladder, piles or diabetes.

The 7th house has Venus as its lord and it is between Mars and Mercury. This house has the aspect of Mars only. These people marry well, very often making their own choice.

The 8th house has Mercury as its lord and is situated between Venus and the Moon, two benefic planets, with the aspect of Jupiter and Mars. Saturn and Mercury are not enemies and these people generally live long. They are usually able to tide over any misfortune that comes in their way.

The 9th house has the Moon as its lord, with the aspect of Jupiter, Mars and Satrun. This house is situated between Mercury and the Sun. The Moon and the Sun are not enemies. They inherit some paternal property and yet they are not able to derive benefit from it and very often they have to face litigation.

The 10th house has the Sun as its lord with the aspect of Saturn and Jupiter. This house is situated between the Moon and Mercury. They generally do well as servants. Very often they get into Government service and rise slowly but steadily. Though they think they are very orthodox and religious, very often it is more of a sham. But still, one thing has to be said that they work hard to achieve their ends. They don't allow obstacles to impede their progress.

The 11th house has the aspect of Jupiter, Saturn, Mars and Venus. The aspect of 4 planets on the 11th house is indeed good and they rise well in their lives. This house is between two very benefic planets, Venus and Jupiter.

The 12th house has as its lord Jupiter and is between Mars and Saturn, two malefic planets, and this house has the aspect of Mercury alone. However much they may be earning, they cannot enjoy life. Enjoyment in life as such seems to be denied to them. They may have much, but still not be able to enjoy it.

Aquarius

This is the 11th sign of the Zodiac. Its lord is Saturn. This house is situated between Saturn and Jupiter. This house has the aspect of two planets, the Sun and Mars, both of them are natural malefics though by virtue of the Sun being the lord of the 7th house, and Mars, the lord of the 10th house, they become temporarily benefics. The lord of the Ascendant besides being a natural malefic, also happens to be the lord of the 12th house, and hence it is said that the Aquarius Ascendant is not a fortunate one, since the Ascendant Lord becomes weak, and the Ascendant also is aspected by two malefics who are the enemies of Saturn. However lucky they might have been in their lives, it is generally seen that there is some suffering during the last period of their lives. It may be loss of money, or the loss of someone dear or any other factor causing unhappiness. In childhood, especially if the Moon is not well placed, they suffer from ill-health during their infancy but afterwards they won't have much to complain about. They may have a meteoricrise but they may also have a bitter fall in the end. So they must be very careful about this, because they are too ambitious, and hence probably the fall.

The 2nd house is that of Jupiter with the aspect of Saturn and Mercury. The house itself is between Saturn and Mars, two malefic planets. Since Jupiter and Saturn are more or less friendly planets, and Jupiter also being the lord of the 11the house, they generally always manage to get money. They are very prone to tell lies, and very plausible too. Their motto generally seems to be: "The end justifies the means".

The 3rd house has Mars as its lord, and the house is situated between Jupiter and Venus two benefic planets, and with the aspect of Saturn, Venus and Jupiter. They generally have many brothers and sisters, but there does not seem to be much love lost between them. These people are bold and adventurous, though always timid at heart. They are really thoughtful.

The 4th house has Venus as its lord, and is between Mars and Mercury. It has the aspect of Mars alone. The Moon the indicator for mother and Venus are not friendly though both of them are often there in a separation between the native and his mother or an early death. Somehow, there is a serious misunderstanding very often between the mother and the native. Venus and Mercury being friends they have a decent education and very often they are excitable by nature. They generally have landed property of their own and have conveyances.

The 5th house has Mercury as its lord with the aspect of Mars and Jupiter. They are really very intelligent and very quick in understanding, but if there is a malefic, they generally get perverted and become unhappy snobs. Of course when there is a malefic influence they are really very unhappy about them. They generally use their power more to do harm to others than good. Moreover, a benefic aspect on the house will certainly prevent all the things. Somehow they are able to escape from lot of hassles.

The 6th house with the Moon as its lord is situated between Mercury and the Sun. It has the aspect of Jupiter, Mars and Saturn. They generally try to steer clear of debt and disease and they travel a lot. Whenever they have a benefic aspect or a benefic in this house they become miserly.

The 7th house has the Sun as its lord and this house is situated between the Moon and Mercury, both of them benefics, with the aspect of Saturn and Jupiter. Saturn and Venus are friends. Saturn and the Sun are enemies, so also the Sun and Venus. They marry well, but somehow domestic happiness is denied to them. Very often they have a plurality of marriage. The later they marry the better it is. An early marriage is not at all good.

The 8th house has Mercury as its lord and is situated between the Sun and Venus. This house is aspected by Jupiter. Saturn and Mercury are not enemies and thus they generally have a fairly long life. Perhaps because of the aspect of Jupiter on this house they have some sort of misery or unhappiness in their lives.

The 9th house has its lord Venus and is between Mercury and Mars with the aspect of Saturn and Mars. The Sun and Venus are enemies, so also the Sun and Saturn. No doubt, they inherit some paternal property but they are generally unable to build up on it. Very often, they may lose their father early in life or they do not derive much help from him.

The 10th house has Mars as its lord and this house is between Venus and Jupiter, and is aspected by Jupiter, Mars, Venus and Saturn. They are really very versatile and are able to handle any sort of work given to them. Especially with the Sun as the lord of the 7th house, and Mars as the lord of the 10th house, they rise to public fame, but very often they do not understand their limitations. They are fairly religious, though they may not be orthodox.

The 11th house has Jupiter as its lord with the aspect of Mercury on this house. This house is between two malefic planets, Mars and Saturn. They earn very well in their lives but they are not able to save. They must always try to make it a point to be very careful about their money.

The 12th house has Saturn as its lord and the house is situated between Jupiter and Saturn. This house has the aspect of a very benefic Moon. They generally lead a life of luxury. They spend a lot of money more on their own self; a sort of eccentricity is seen in the matter of their expenditure. They generally travel much.

Pisces

This Ascendant is usually associated with Sun-the-*Atmakarak*, for this is the last of all Ascendants; this, according to *Kalapurusha*, is said to be the feet. This Ascendant is between Saturn and Mars and contains *nakshatras Poorva Bhadrapada* (last portion), *Uttara Bhadrapada* and *Revati* which means the influence of Jupiter, Saturn and Mercury. One may even say from this position that, while the first portion or the youth of the native may be happy, during the middle portion there will be troubles in life because the influence of Saturn is to be felt and then peace and happiness because of Mercury. Mercury especially for these people happens to be the lord of the 4th and 7th houses and hence a benefic. This Ascendant has as its lord Jupiter, a very benefic planet, and the *nakshatras* end here. It may be considered to be the end of all things. And the very first *nakshatra* of the next house is *Aswini*, of which the lord is Ketu, who happens to be the *Mokshakaraka*, perhaps, meaning thereby that if the native has not had the complete *gnana* he will have to go into Pisces and then come back in Aries.

This Ascendant has the aspect of Mercury as well as Saturn. Because Jupiter happens to be the lord of this house, generally these people are a bit obese. The aspect of Saturn on the Ascendant may indicate, especially if the native is born in *Shani-dasha*, some sort of ill-health during the first few years of this or her life until *Shani-dasha* is over, but generally these people are not very sick. They rise in the course of life.

The lord of the 2nd house is Mars and this house is between Jupiter and Venus and has the aspect of Saturn and Venus. Mars happens to be a friend of both Jupiter and Venus. Hence these people generally never suffer from want as such in their lives and there is a lot of domestic happiness about them. They also marry well or at least they make their own choice. They are generally truthful, perhaps, sometimes blunt or outspoken.

The 3rd house has Venus as its lord and has the aspect of Mars and the house itself is between Mars and Mercury. These people are generally bold and enterprising and because Mars and Venus are friendly planets, these people have generally a number of brothers and sisters. They have frequent small journeys on land. They are not bold or courageous. They generally have the capacity to bear the troubles of life with equanimity.

The 4th house has Mercury as its lord and is between Venus and the Moon. This house has the aspect of Mars and Jupiter. They have a fairly good education. The Moon the indicator for mother and Mercury being friends, they generally have a very good and long-live mother. They have a large circle of friends. They are generally able to own modern conveyances of their own and have all comforts and luxuries.

The 5th house has the Moon as its lord and is between Mercury and the Sun. Jupiter, Saturn and Mars aspect this house and therefore they have a clear/keen intellect. They have a quick understanding but owing to the aspect of Saturn, they can also be a bit perverse. The Moon and Jupiter are friendly planets. They have children but owing to the aspect of Saturn, there may be some loss, probably of the eldest child. They exercise power and authority well.

This house speaks of *Poorva-punya*. Because the Moon is a benefic with the aspect of two friendly planets Jupiter and Mars, they are generally considered to be lucky, though owing to the aspect of Saturn, some fluctuations of fortune here and there can be indicated.

The 6th house has the Sun as its lord and this house is between the Moon and Mercury. This house has the aspect of Jupiter and Satrun. The aspect of Jupiter should not be considered to be good while that of Saturn must be considered as such.

These people generally have a fairly good health, especially after their youth; and one thing they must try to remember is not to run into debts. They generally travel much.

The 7th house has Mercury as its lord and this house is between the Sun and Venus, both of whom happen to be friends of Mercury. This house has the aspect of Jupiter. Mercury and Venus are friends. Therefore they often marry well and wisely.

The 8th house has as its lord Venus and is between Mercury and Mars with the aspect of Saturn and Mars. The aspect of Saturn on the 8th house must be considered to be very good. Besides, Saturn and Venus are very friendly. Hence they have a long life. The aspect of two malefic planets is indeed very good in that, it moves much of the malefic tendencies of this house. That really is a negative advantage.

The 9th house has as its lord Mars and this house is between Venus and Jupiter, both of whom happen to be friends of Mars. Here it can be seen that the 2nd house, the house that indicates domestic happiness, wealth etc., is between Jupiter and Venus, so also the 9th house which is called the *dharma-sthana, Pithru-sthana, Guru-sthana* etc., is between the same two very benefic planets Jupiter and Venus. This house also has the aspect of Saturn, Jupiter and another benefic Venus, though Venus may happen to be a temporary malefic for people born in the sign, Pisces. Mars and the Sun are friends, so also Jupiter and Mars. Hence generally these people inherit some paternal property. The word 'some' is used because of the aspect of Saturn, otherwise, one will have to say that these people inherit a large amount of paternal property. In later life, they become very religious and begin to read sacred books and texts.

The 10th house has Jupiter as its lord and this house is between Mars and Saturn. This house has the aspect of Mercury alone. Therefore, these people generally become religious and they often want to enter greatly into public life. They generally do good social work which somehow or other, does not bring credit or a good name. By no means, are these people inclined to do evil to others.

The 11th house has Saturn in it and is situated between Saturn and Jupiter and this house has the aspect of the Moon. Mars and Saturn are inimical planets. Somehow their expected income is not realised unless there are other conditions in the horoscope to expect it. But since Jupiter and Saturn have to be considered more friends than enemies and since Jupiter and Mars are friends, they are able to earn fairly well though they may not be able to accumulate wealth.

Saturn happens to be the lord of the 12th house and this house is between Saturn and Jupiter. This house has the aspect of Mars and the Sun. To that extent it is a very good thing in that it removes much of the troubles that have to be indicated by this house; expenses, losses, etc. But still, owing to the aspect of two malefic planets, they are not able to enjoy themselves much in their lives or at least in the way in which their status in life would warrant.

11

SOME PECULIARITIES OF ASCENDANTS

Aries

Mercury and Saturn are *Marakas* (death inflicting), being the lords of the 3rd and 11th houses. Venus, though the lord of the 2nd and 7th houses, will not kill unless Venus occupies the 2nd house and is aspected by Saturn.

Jupiter, being the lord of the 9th and 12th houses may become a *Maraka* if it occupies the 10th house.

Raja-yoga : A combination conferring high public honour, name and fame is formed in the following cases :

Jupiter in Pisces and the Moon in the 4th house. Jupiter in Sagittarius and Saturn in Libra, the Mars in Capricorn, the Sun in Aries and Jupiter in Sagittarius.

Jupiter, Saturn and the Sun or the Moon, Jupiter and the Sun occupying the same house. ·

Jupiter and the Moon in Aries or Saturn and Mars in Capricorn or Venus in Libra. Jupiter and Saturn in Aquarius.

Jupiter, Mercury and Mars are associated in the 6th, 8th or 12th house or any two of them in the 6th or 12th house or in mutual reception in those houses. If Mars, Jupiter, Saturn and Venus, all occupy the 4th, 9th or 10th houses. The Sun in Aries and the Moon in Cancer.

Persons born in Aries, the Ascendant may be prone to small-pox, danger from weapons, fever, wounds and skin diseases.

If Mars associates with the lord of the 6th house, there will be troubles in the head during their Sub-Periods.

If Mercury and Mars occupy the 6th house, there may be accidental injuries, small-pox and leprosy, during their major-period.

If Mars and Venus occupy the 7th house, his earnings will be insignificant. If Mars should occupy the 8th house along with the Sun and Venus, he will be moderately prosperous.

If the Sun and Mars, or Jupiter and Venus, occupy the 9th house or if Saturn occupies the 7th house, during Mars major-period, there will be prosperity.

If the Moon be placed in the 4th house, the Sun in the Ascendant Mars in the 10th and Jupiter in the 7th house, there will be considerable prosperity during periods (*Dashas*) of each of them.

Mercury gives unsatisfactory results for a Aries Ascendant especially when it is strong in the Natal Chart.

A combination conferring high public honour.

Ordinary Yoga giving planets :

The Sun is a full benefic.

Jupiter and Saturn are half benefics.

The Sun in Aries, Leo, Scorpio or Sagittarius.

The Moon in Taurus, Cancer, Leo or Sagittarius.

Mars in Aries, Gemini, Cancer, Virgo or Capricorn.

Jupiter in Cancer, Leo, Virgo, Scorpio, Sagittarius or Capricorn.

Saturn in Aries, Capricorn or Aquarius.

Mercury in Scorpio or Pisces.

Ketu in Gemini, Virgo or Pisces.

Venus in Taurus, Cancer or Sagittarius.

Saturn and Jupiter associated in Sagittarius, Cancer or Aries.

Jupiter and Mars associated in Cancer.

The Sun and Mercury together in Aries, Leo or Sagittarius.

Note: In all the combinations mentioned above, there should not be the aspect or conjunction of any other planet.

Taurus

Jupiter, the Moon, and Venus are death inflicting planets, or fatal planets or planets with fatalistic tendencies.

The Sun and Saturn are benefics.

Mercury is a half benefic.

Raja-yogas

Saturn, the Sun and Mercury together occupying the 1st, 5th, 10th or 11th house.

Jupiter and Mercury associate or aspect each other.

Mercury in Taurus, Gemini, Leo, Virgo, Capricorn or Aquarius.

The association of Mars and Venus or Jupiter and Venus or Jupiter and Mars.

Exceptional Raja-yoga

Jupiter, Mars and Venus, associating in the 6th, 8th or 12th house.

Yogas

The Sun in Gemini, Virgo, Leo, Acquarius, Pisces. The Moon in Taurus, Libra, Sagittarius or Pisces. Mars in Cancer, Libra, Sagittarius, Aries.

Rahu in (Dragon's head) Sagittarius or Pisces.

Jupiter in Aries, Cancer, Libra, Sagittarius or Pisces. But Jupiter in Aries will give this *Yoga* in the beginning and then harm in the end.

Saturn in Leo, Scorpio or Aquarius. Ketu in Cancer, Libra, Pisces or Aries. Venus in Libra, Sagittarius, Capricorn, Aquarius or Aries.

The Sun and Mercury together in Leo, Virgo, Capricorn or Aquarius.

Venus and the Moon, in Libra. Jupiter in *Kendra* or a *Kona* will not give much good results.

If Jupiter, Mercury and Mars together occupy a house, there will be trouble, from debts, during the major-period of Mercury as well as loss of honour, change of residence, hatred of friends and relations and depression in spirit and possible death or parting with of near and near ones deaths.

Note: In all the above combinations there should not be the aspect or conjunction of any other planet.

Gemini

The Sun, the Moon, Mars and Saturn are *Marakas*, Ketu occupying 2nd, 7th or the 12th house with Moon and *Kuja* becomes a *Maraka*.

Yogas

Venus alone gives prosperity. Venus and Mercury together give *Rajayoga*. If Rahu and Jupiter occupy the 2nd house, death occurs during Rahu's major-period, Jupiter's sub-period or vice versa, or in their *dasha* major-periods in the sub-period of other malefic planets.

When the Sun and Mercury are occupying the 3rd house, Mercury gives good *Yoga*.

If Venus, Mars and the Moon occupy the 2nd house, there will be much wealth during Venus's major-period. With Mars in the 2nd house, Saturn and the Moon in the 8th house, there will be mixed results during Saturn's major-periods and much wealth during Mars's sub-period.

With Saturn and Mars in the 2nd house, the Moon in the 8th house, there will be loss of previously acquired fortune during Saturn's and Mars' major periods.

With Mars and the Moon occupying the 11th house and Saturn, the 9th house, there will be much wealth during their periods.

Jupiter and Saturn in the 9th house give pilgrimages to sacred rivers and shrines during their periods.

Saturn and the Sun occupying ascendant give long life.

If Venus occupies the 12th house, acquisition of much wealth and happiness during Venus's major-period is assured to the native. Saturn and Venus are half benefics.

Raja-yogas

Jupiter in Cancer or Gemini gives *rajayoga* in the beginning and harm in end. In Sagittarius, it generally does harm.

Jupiter and the Moon in Pisces, there will be *yoga* during Jupiter's major-period and during the the Moon major-period there will be *yoga* only if the Moon is waxing.

Mars, Saturn and Venus together in the 6th, 8th or 12th house.

Ordinary Yogas

The Sun in Scorpio or Capricorn. The Moon in Cancer, Virgo, Libra, Aquarius or Pisces.

Mars in Aries, Leo, Taurus or Capricorn. Rahu in Leo, Scorpio, Capricorn or Aries. Jupiter in Virgo, Libra or Aquarius. Saturn in Aries, Vrishabha, Scorpio or Pisces. Saturn in Aquarius gives *yoga* in the beginning and harm in the end. Mercury in Aries. Libra or Aquarius. In Cancer, *Yoga* in the beginning and harm in the end. Ketu in Leo, Scorpio, Aries or Taurus. Venus in Taurus, Libra, Scorpio or Capricorn. Jupiter and Mercury together in Virgo or Pisces. *Yoga* in the beginning and harm in the end during their major-periods. Sun and Mercury in Virgo or Aries together. Saturn and Mars together. Venus and Mars together. Saturn and Venus together.

Note: There should not be the aspect or conjunction of any other planets in any of the above mentioned conditions.

Cancer

Saturn, Mercury, Venus and Sun are *Marakas*. These planets cannot give good results. The Sun will not kill of its own accord but will do so when under a malefic influence. Mars gives good benefits and is a full benefic. The Moon is a good planet.

Raja-yogas

Mercury and Venus in the 12th house. There will be *Raja-yoga* during Venus major-period.

Jupiter and the Moon in ascendant, in their sub-period. The Moon in the ascendant and Mars in the 7th house. Mars and Jupiter in Pisces, Aries or Scorpio. Saturn and Jupiter in Sagittarius, Aquarius or Gemini. The Sun and Mercury in Aquarius, Gemini, Virgo or Sagittarius. Venus and the Moon in Taurus, Cancer or Libra. Jupiter and the Moon in Cancer or Aries. Jupiter, Mercury and Saturn in 6th, 8th or 12th house.

Ordinary Yogas

Mars in the 5th or 10th house confers much wealth and riches. Venus in 2nd or 12th house gives good results. Also Jupiter, Mars and Moon in the 2nd house.

The Sun and Venus in the 5th house give wealth, fame and prosperity and creative talents. If Mercury and Venus are in the 5th house, good results during the major-period of Mercury are promised. Mercury, Venus and the Moon in the 11th house, Jupiter in ascendant and the Sun in the 10th house give wealth, fame, courage and good qualities.

The Sun and Mars in the 10th house give wealth. The Sun and Mercury in ascendant and Venus, the Moon, Mars and Jupiter in the 11th house give poverty during the Sun's major-period and good results during the major-period of the other planets.

If Saturn and Rahu occupy the 5th house and Jupiter and Mercury the 11th house, there will be pilgrimages to sacred places during Rahu's major-period.

Yoga

The Sun in Leo, Scorpio, Aries or Taurus
The Moon in Libra, Pisces or Taurus.
The Moon in Cancer; *yoga* in the beginning and harm in the end.

Mars in Aries, Taurus, Scorpio or Pisces.
Mars in Capricorn; yoga in the beginning and harm in the end.

Jupiter in Cancer, Libra, Scorpio, Pisces or Aries. Saturn in Aries, Gemini or Sagittarius. Mercury in Gemini, Sagittarius, Aquarius or Taurus. Ketu in Sagittarius, Taurus or Gemini. Venus in Libra. The Sun and Mars together or the Sun and Mercury together in Aries or Leo.

Note: There should not be the aspect or conjunction of any other planets in any of the above-mentioned conditions.

Leo

Saturn, Venus and Mercury are *Marakas*. Mercury cannot of himself cause death. He becomes a *Maraka* only if he associates with Saturn and occupies a death-inflicting house. Rahu and Ketu are *Marakas* only when they occupy death-inflicting houses.

Good Planets

Mars always gives good results. Jupiter and the Moon generally do not give much good results. Venus in the 3rd house gives good results. Venus in the 10th house gives no *yoga* but only difficulties. Jupiter in the Ascendant, Mars in the 9th house, Saturn in the 3rd house and Mercury and the Sun together in the 2nd house give *raja-yoga*.

If Mars associates with the Moon, there will be obstacles in education and dullness of intellect, but during major-period of Mars there will be *yoga*.

Mars and Venus, Saturn and the Moon, Saturn and Jupiter, Jupiter and the Moon together give *Raja-yoga*.

Venus and the Moon in Capricorn or Cancer; Saturn, Jupiter and the Moon together in 6th, 8th or 12th houses or Saturn, Jupiter and the Moon exchanging their houses in 6th, 8th or 12th houses cause very powerful *Raja-yoga*.

Ordinary Yogas

The Sun in Leo, Sagittarius, Aries or Gemini.
The Moon in Libra, Capricorn, Pisces, Taurus or Gemini.
Mars in Scorpio, Sagittarius, Aries, Taurus or

Gemini. Rahu in Capricorn, Pisces, Gemini or Cancer.
Jupiter in Cancer, Sagittarius, Capricorn or Pisces.
Saturn in Libra gives *Yoga* in the beginning and harm in the end.

Saturn in Capricorn, Pisces, Aries or Cancer.
Mercury in Leo, Virgo, Sagittarius, Aries, or Gemini.
Ketu in Libra, Capricorn or Gemini.
Venus in Taurus, Libra, Scorpio or Sagittarius.
Venus and the Moon together.

The Sun, Mars and Mercury in conjunction with or with the aspect of Jupiter. Mars and Venus when they are together if aspected or associated with Jupiter, spoil *yoga*.

Other Results

Jupiter and Venus, if in association yield no *yoga*.
Jupiter and Mars in association give good results generally during their major-periods.

If the Sun, Mercury and Mars associate with or aspect each other there will be much wealth, so also with the Sun, Mercury and Jupiter if they are associated with or aspect each other.

If the Sun and Mercury associate, there will be some wealth.

If the Sun, Mars and Mercury occupy Ascendant, Mercury's major-period causes benifits and accrual of much prosperity.

If Mars and Saturn occupy the 12th house, Saturn gives good results during his major-period.

Note: In all the above combinations, there should not be the aspect or conjunction of any other planets.

Virgo

Jupiter, the Moon, and.Venus are *Marakas*.
The Sun will not kill.
Mercury and Venus are full benefics.
Saturn is half benefic and generally gives bad results.

Good Planets

Mercury in association with Venus gives good results. The Moon in the Ascendant with Ketu gives good results even though he is a *Maraka* planet. Jupiter and Venus in the 4th house give good result during their major-periods.

If Saturn occupies the 11th house, Saturn will give very good results during his major-period.

Mars cannot give a *yoga*; generally gives bad results. Saturn and Jupiter in Cancer; Venus, the Moon and Rahu in Taurus; Mercury and Mars in Gemini give good results during the sub-period of benefic planets. Saturn, though a lord of the 5th house, generally causes adverse results and tensions.

Raja-yoga

Mercury in Virgo; Venus and Mercury together; Jupiter and Venus together; the Sun, Mars and Saturn together in the 6th, 8th or 12th house give *Raja-yoga*.

Venus in pisces, gives *Raja-yoga* during her major-period in the beginning and much harm in the end of the period.

Ordinary Yogas

Occur under: The Sun in Scorpio, Aquarius, Aries, Cancer or Leo. The Moon in Libra, Sagittarius, Capricorn, Taurus, Gemini or Cancer. Mars in Scorpio, Aquarius, Aries, Cancer or Leo.

Rahu or Ketu in Scorpio, Aquarius, Cancer or Leo. Ketu in Aries will not give *Raja-yoga*.

Saturn in Scorpio, Aquarius, Aries or Leo. Mercury in Virgo, Libra, Sagittarius, Capricorn, Taurus, Gemini or Cancer. The Sun and Saturn, Saturn and Mars or the Sun and Mars associating.

Other Results

If Venus and the Moon are together during the Sun's major-period, there will be much wealth. During Venus' the major-period, no wealth and during the Moon's major-period, there will be mixed results, good and not so good.

Venus and the Moon in the 7th house; Jupiter in the 11th house and Sun in the 8th house, give during major-period Jupiter and Venus *yogas*, but these periods may not be good with regard to marital happiness as the spouse's health may be afflicted.

If Jupiter and Mercury are in the 4th house and if Saturn and Venus occupy the 6th house, there will be much wealth during their major-periods.

Jupiter in Sagittarius, Scorpio, Gemini and Cancer give good result, but in Pisces gives bad results.

Venus and Mercury if aspected by or in conjunction with Mars, the *yoga* is spoiled.

Venus and the Moon in Libra give much wealth but in Scorpio ordinary results.

Note: In all the above combinations or positions there should not be the aspect or conjunction of any other planets.

Libra

The Sun, Mercury and Mars are *Marakas*.
Sun is more powerful in killing. Mars will not kill.

Good Planets

Saturn and Mars are full benefics. Mercury is half benefic. Saturn gives better results than Mercury.

Venus gives good results.
The Moon and Mercury together give good results.

Raja-yogas

Jupiter in the 6th house, Saturn in the 9th house and Mars and Mercury in the 11th house.

Saturn in the Ascendant and the Moon in Cancer.

Mercury and the Moon together in Gemini, Cancer, Capricorn or Aquarius.

Jupiter, Venus and Mercury together in the 6th 8th or 12th house. The Moon, the Sun, Mercury, Saturn and Mars all together. Mercury and Venus in Pisces, Scorpio or Virgo. Jupiter in Cancer gives very bad results.

Ordinary Yogas

The Sun in Scorpio, Sagittarius, Aquarius or Leo. The Moon in Capricorn, Aquarius or Libra. In Cancer she causes both auspicious results as also some adverse results/setbacks.

Rahu or Ketu (Dragon's head or tail) in Sagittarius, Pisces, Scorpio, Leo or Virgo, but Ketu in Taurus will not give *yoga*. Mars in Leo.

Venus in Taurus or Pisces, gives *yoga* during his major-period in the beginning but some adversity and struggle towards the end of the periods. Jupiter in Scorpio, Capricorn or Virgo. Mercury in Libra, Pisces, Scorpio, Cancer, Leo or Vigro.

Saturn in Capricorn, Cancer, but Saturn in Aquarius, Gemini or Libra gives *yoga* and does harm afterwards. Mercury and the Moon, Saturn and the Moon and Mercury and Venus *yoga*.

Other Results

If Jupiter and Venus occupy the same house, or aspect each other, or are aspected by Mars and Saturn, there will be small-pox and wounds during the blackties of Jupiter and Venus if these two occupy the houses of Mars and Saturn or during Jupiter's sub-period Venus' major-period or vice versa.

If Mars associates with Saturn and Mercury, there will be accrual of much wealth, and prosperity.

If Venus, the Sun and Mercury occupy the Ascendant, it would lead to prosperity, and the acquisition of motor vehicles, immovable property, and wealth.

If Mercury, Venus and Saturn occupy the Ascendant and if the Moon and the Sun occupy the 7th house, there will be prosperity and happiness during the major-period of Mercury.

If Saturn occupies Aquarius with Jupiter, Mercury and Mars and if Rahu (Dragon's head) occupies the 10th house, there will be prosperity during Mercury's major-period. The native's spiritual interests will get kindled and the native will undertake pilgrimages to holy place.

The Sun, Mars, Saturn and Mercury associating with or aspecting each other will cause immense happiness, accrual of wealth and prosperity.

Note: In all the above combinations or positions, there should not be the aspect or conjunction of any other planets.

Scorpio

Mercury, Venus, Saturn are *Marakas*. Jupiter, though lord of the 2nd house is generally not a *Maraka*.

The Sun, the Moon and Jupiter are full benefics.
The Sun and the Moon confer good results.
Jupiter causes beneficial results.

Mars causes similar beneficial results as those caused by Jupiter.

The Sun alone is the *yoga*-giving planet, though, even this is not much.

The Sun is auspicious during its sub-periods during the major periods of benefic planets.

Jupiter in 3rd house generally produces generosity and charitableness.

Raja-yogas

The *Raja-yogas* occur with the Sun, Mercury and Venus in the 7th house during Mercury's major-period.

Mars, Mercury and Venus associating or exchanging their places in 6th, 8th, 12th houses.

The association or exchange of any two of these ordinary conjunctions.

Ordinary Yogas

Jupiter, the Moon and Ketu (Dragon's tail) occupying Cancer give very good results during Jupiter period; only during Ketu period no good results are noticed.

The Sun in Sagittarius, Aquarius, Pisces or Cancer. The Moon in Pisces, Cancer, Leo or Virgo. Mars in Aries, Gemini, Libra or Capricorn. Rahu or Ketu in Capricorn, Aries, Gemini, Virgo Libra.

Ketu (Dragon's tail) in Gemini will not cause *yoga*.

Jupiter in Sagittarius, Pisces, Leo or Virgo.
Saturn in Capricorn, Aquarius, Aries and Leo.
But in Libra, it causes *yoga* and then adverse results.

Mercury in Aries, Gemini, Libra and Capricorn.

Venus in Libra, Aries or Gemini, in Pisces and Cancer rather adverse results.

The Sun and Saturn in conjunction in Aquarius, Pisces, Cancer, or Leo.

The Sun and Jupiter in Sagittarius, Aquarius, Pisces, Cancer, or Leo.

Jupiter and the Moon associating with or aspecting each other or occupying each other's house. Saturn and the Moon; Mars and Venus; Mercury and Mars or Mercury and Venus associating.

Other Results

Jupiter and Mercury associating or aspecting each other, there will be accrual of much wealth.

Jupiter and Mercury in the 5th house and the Moon in the 11th house will lead to much wealth and prosperity.

With the Sun in Cancer and the Moon in Leo, there will be good result in the major-period of both the planets.

The Sun and the Moon associating is not quite auspicious but their aspecting each other causes *yoga*.

Note: There should not be aspect or conjunction of any other planet in the combinations mentioned above.

Sagittarius

The Moon, Venus and Satrun are *Maraka* planets. Saturn kills only when he is associated with Mercury or the Sun; otherwise it does not kill. Jupiter gives ordinary result and occasionally causes adverse result without killing. The Sun is a full benefic. Mars is half benefic.

Good Planets

The Sun and Mars cause beneficial results. Saturn in the 5th house causes auspicious results. Saturn in Libra, the 11th house, causes very good results and *yoga*, but Saturn does not cause *yoga* if he occupies the 5th or the 11th house for any other ascendant.

The Sun and Venus in the 9th house when Saturn is in 3rd house. During Saturn's major-period, there will be beneficial results.

The Sun, Mars and Rahu together in Aquarius or Leo; there will be bathing in holy rivers during their major-periods. Mercury in the 11th house with the aspect or association of Jupiter, will result in prosperity and happiness.

Raja-yoga

The Sun and Mercury in association, or occupying each other's house, cause *Raja-yoga* but the association or aspect of the Moon spoils the *yoga* completely. Venus and the Moon together in Aquarius, Taurus, Cancer or Scorpio will cause *yoga* in the the ascending order.

Mars and the Moon or Venus and the Moon or Mars and Venus, or Venus, Mars and the Moon in Taurus, Cancer or Scorpio, or exchanging their places in these signs, cause *Raja-yoga*.

Ordinary Yogas

The Sun in Pisces or Leo.
The Moon in Aquarius, Scorpio or Taurus.
Mars in Aquarius, Taurus, Cancer, or Scorpio.
Rahu in Aquarius, Taurus, Cancer, Libra or Scorpio.
Ketu in Aquarius, Taurus, Libra or Scorpio.
Jupiter in Sagittarius, Pisces, Aries, Leo or Virgo.
Saturn in Aquarius, Taurus or Libra.
Merucry in Leo, Libra or Sagittarius.
Venus in Taurus, Cancer or Scorpio.
Jupiter or Mercury together, or the Sun and Jupiter together.

Note: There should not be the aspect or conjunction or any other planets in the combinations mentioned above.

Capricorn

Jupiter, Mars and the Moon are *Maraka* planets. Saturn, though a killer, cannot kill of his own accord. The Sun though the lord of the 8th house, will not generally kill but gives very ordinary result. Mars Jupiter and Saturn are half benefics.

Good Planets

Mercury in the 8th house. Jupiter in Ascendant with the aspect of Venus; there will be good health but it will not be conducive to financial benefits. Venus as the lord of the 5th house gives good result, but as the lord of the 10th house confers ordinary resluts.

Venus and Mercury in the Ascendant, the Moon in the 5th house and aspected by Jupiter, makes one very affluent and prosperous.

If Jupiter be in the the Ascendant, Mars and Venus be in the 4th house and be strong, there will be monetary gain through brothers during major-periods of Jupiter.

The Sun, the Moon and Mercury in Ascendant, and Venus and Mars in the 12th house, there will be accrual of wealth through brothers and if Saturn and Mercury occupy the 9th house, there will be prosperity. Rahu in the 12th house, and aspected by Jupiter, or associated with him, confers good results.

Raja-yogas

Venus gives *yoga* of his own accord. The Moon in Cancer and Mars in Capricorn. Mercury and Venus in Taurus and the Sun in the 4th house; there will be *yoga* during the Sun's major-period.

Jupiter in Pisces, Gemini, Leo or Sagittarius. Mercury and Venus; Venus and Mars, the Sun and Jupiter; the Sun and Mercury or the Sun, Mercury and Jupiter in association or exchanging their positions in Gemini, Leo and Sagittarius.

Ordinary Yogas

The Sun in Pisces, Gemini or Sagittarius.
The Moon in Taurus, Virgo or Libra.
Mars in Taurus, Aries, Virgo or Scorpio.

Mars in Pisces is not inauspicious.
Rahu (Dragon's head) or Ketu (Dragon's tail) in Pisces, Gemini, Leo, Scorpio or Sagittarius.

Saturn in Aries, Libra or Capricorn.
Saturn in Libra causes yoga in the beginning and harm in the end.

Mercury in Scorpio, Virgo or Libra.
Venus in Aries, Scorpio, Virgo or Libra.
The association of Jupiter and Mercury or Venus and Saturn.

Other Results

Saturn and Mercury in association in Aquarius or Vigro give wealth.

Mercury and Mars in Aries, Virgo, Libra or Scorpio give good results.
Mercury in Sagittarius causes *yoga*.

Note: There should not be conjunction or aspect of any other planets in the combinations mentioned above.

Aquarius

Jupiter Mars, and the Moon are *Marakas*.
Jupiter does not kill of his own accord.

Good Planets

Venus is a full benefic.
Mars is half benefic.
Venus invariably causes benefic results.
Mercury and Saturn cause ordinary results.
The Sun and Mercury in the 5th house cause benefic results.

If Jupiter occupies the Ascendant and Venus occupies the 4th house there will be mixed result during Venus' major-period; Jupiter will not cause good result but during Sun's major-period there are good results.

If Jupiter occupies any angle and Mars or the Moon occupies the 5th house, there will be wealth during Mars' or the Moon's major-period.

Jupiter and Ketu (Dragon's tail) in the Ascendant with the aspect of Mars make a person immoral.

Raja -yoga

Mars and Venus in association. If Mercury and the Sun occupy Gemini and if Venus occupies Leo and Jupiter be in Cancer, there will be *Raja-yoga* during the Sun's major period.

Mercury the Moon and Saturn or any two of them in association in Cancer, Virgo, or Capricorn, confer *Raja-yoga* but with all the three it is very powerful.

Ordinary Yogas

If the Sun is with Venus in Ascendant and Rahu is in the 10th house, there will be a conjunction during Rahu's and Jupiter's major-period.

If Jupiter is in the Ascendant and Saturn is in the 2nd house, there will be mixed results during Jupiter's major-period and obstacles to conjunction during Saturn's major-period.

If the Sun, Jupiter and Mercury are in the 3rd house, there will be very good *yoga* during the Sun's major-period only.

The Sun in Aries or Sagittarius.
The Moon in Aries or Virgo or Capricorn.
Mars in Aries, Taurus, Gemini, Cancer, Libra, Scorpio, or Sagittarius.

Rahu and Ketu (Dragon's head or tail) in Aries, Cancer, Virgo, Sagittarius or Capricorn. Ketu (Dragon's tial) in Virgo will not give *yoga*.

Jupiter in Taurus, Gemini, Libra, Scorpio, Sagittarius or Pisces.
Saturn in Aries, Cancer, Virgo, Sagittarius, or Capricorn.
Venus in Taurus, Gemini, Libra, Scorpio.

Jupiter and Mercury, Merucry and the Moon; Saturn and Mercury or Saturn and the Moon in association.

Note: There should not be aspect or association of any other planet in the above-mentioned combinations.

Pisces

Mercury, Venus, Saturn and the Sun Marakas.
Venus is more powerful in killing.
Saturn is more powerful than Venus in killing.
Mars and the Moon are benefics.

Good Planets

Mars and the Moon cause benefic results.
Jupiter causes ordinary results.
Saturn in the 12th house causes good results.
The Moon in the 12th house causes poverty and disturbs the
yoga during Jupiter's major-period and the Moon's sub-period.

If Jupiter occupies 5th house, the native will be blessed with
many daughters but he will have one male issue.

Vensu does not give good results.
If the Moon occupies the 2nd house and Mars the 5th house,
there will be accrual of wealth during the Moon's major-period.

If Jupiter occupies the 5th house, Venus occupies the 8th house,
Saturn occupies the 9th house, and the Moon and Mars 11th
house, there will be very good results.

If Mercury, the Moon and Mars occupy.
Capricorn, there will be accrual of wealth and motor vehicles
during their major-period.

If Saturn, the Moon and Mars occupy the 11th house and Venus
occupies the 6th house, there will be wealth and carriages during
Venus' major-period.

If Mercury, Jupiter, the Moon and Mars occupy Gemini without
the aspect or association of other planets, there will be fame,
wealth etc. during their major-periods and sub-period.

If Jupier occupies the 10th house, there will be good results.

If the Moon occupies the 3rd house, the Sun occupies the 6th
house, Mercury occupies the 7th house, Venus occupies the 12th
house, Jupiter occupies the 10th house, Saturn occupies the 12th
house, and Mars the 11th house, there will be prosperity.

If Jupiter, Mars and Venus occupy Capricorn, there will be no trouble, in Venus' sub-period and during Jupiter and Mars' major periods.

Raja-yoga

The Sun, Venus and Saturn associating without the aspect or association of other planets in Simba Aquarius or Libra, but preferably in the first two in Libra, the aspect of these planets on the 2nd house affects domestic happiness.

Other-Yoga

Mars and Jupiter in association.
The Sun, the Taurus, Libra Capricorn or Aquarius.
Mars in Aries, Cancer, Scorpio, Sagittarius or Capricorn.
Rahu or Ketu in Taurus, Leo, Capricorn or Aquarius.

Ketu in Libra cannot cause *yoga*.
Jupiter in Gemini, Cancer, Scorpio, Sagittarius or Capricorn.

Saturn in Taurus, Leo, Libra, Capricorn or Aquarius.

Saturn in Cancer and Libra causes *yoga* in his major period but in the end cause adverse results.

Mercury in Gemini, Cancer, Scorpio, or Capricorn. Mercury in Virgo cause *yoga* during his major-period, in the earlier part but causes adverse results towards the end.

Venus in Leo or Libra.
Jupiter and Mars aspecting or associating with each other.
The Moon and Mercury associating. The Moon and Mercury do not cause *yoga* in Libra.

Jupiter and the Moon associating, or Mars and the Moon associating, or the Sun and Venus associating or the Sun and Saturn associating or Saturn and Venus being together, causes auspicious results.

Note: There should not be the aspect or association of any other planets in above combinations.

12

PLANETS AS LORDS OF HOUSES

Sun

Leo Ascendant

The Sun-Mercury : The Sun is the king of all planets, and owns only one house — Leo. Suppose a native is born in the Leo Ascendant. The Sun is its lord. We will have to consider whether the Sun - Mercury conjunction is good or bad. Because this conjunction will be the lord of the 1st and 2nd houses besides of the 1st and 11th it must be considered to be very good, in that the native will get wealth, provided this conjunction does not occur in an unfavourable place from Jupiter, the indicator for wealth, and from the Ascendant.

The Sun-Venus : Venus is the lord of the 10th house as well as the 3rd house. No doubt Venus gets eclipsed when she is in conjunction with the Sun but that is a different matter. Still, Venus is the lord of the 10th house indicating profession and when she is in conjunction with the lord of the Ascendant, the person is likely to rise in his professional career.

The Sun-Mars : It is the conjunction of the lords of 1st and 4th houses as well as of 1st and 9th. This conjunction as of the lords of 1st and 9th houses is very good mother, in that the native is likely to have a respectable father. Besides, the chances of inheriting some paternal property are there. Again, Mars is the lord of the 4th house which speaks of a very good mother, but again here also, one will have to take into consideration the position of the Moon as the indicator for mother with reference to the Sun and Mars. When we take the question of education, we have to take the Sun-Mars with reference to Mercury, the indicator for *vidya*, i.e., education.

The Sun-Jupiter : Jupiter is the lord of the 5th and 8th houses, and the conjunction of 1st and 5th houses is indeed very good; the conjunction of 1st and 8th also must be considered to be good for longetivity, for whenever the lord of the Ascendant is in conjunction with any *bhavadhipati*; that *bhavadhipati* becomes strong. The 5th house indicates not only children but *poorva-punya* and *Adhikar* (authority) also. The Sun-Jupiter conjunction therefore must be considered to be good in both the cases; provided, it is not in an unfavourable position from the 10th house or its lord. This conjunction insofar as it relates to the 8th house must not be in an unfavourable position from Saturn, the indicator for longevity.

The Sun-Saturn : Saturn is the lord of the 6th and 7th houses, the 6th house indicating ill-health etc. and the 7th house, partner and conjugal happiness. Whether the person will be sickly or not, he will have to be considered by the respective strengths of the Sun and Saturn. If the Sun be weak and Saturn be very strong, the native will have some ill-health or the other. The Sun and Saturn are adversaries. But the Sun as the lord of the Ascendant being in conjunction with the lord of the 7th house, must be considered to be good; the native may get a good wife but there may not be much understanding between them. The Sun and Saturn are enemies, so also the Sun and Venus: but Saturn and Venus being bosom friends, will be responsible for getting the native a devout wife. With this conjunction in a female's horoscope, we will have to bring Jupiter into play with the Sun and Saturn, instead of Venus as in a man's case.

The Sun-Moon : This conjunction must necessarily be considered to be bad because, it wll be round about *Amavasya*. Generally, it is said that during the waning Moon all benefics are weak and all malefics are strong. That itself imparts a certain amount of weakness to the horoscope.

Mars

This is a strong fiery planet, but of course less strong than the Sun. This is a warrior. This planet owns two houses Aries and Scorpio.

Aries Ascendant

Mars-Venus : This conjunction must necessarily be considered to be very good, for it is the conjunction of the lords of 1st and 2nd and 1st and 7th houses. In the first place, there is a positive indication that the native may marry bliss because Mars and Venus are friends, at least not enemies. So, as far as the question of wealth is concerned, that will have to be considered from the position of Jupiter vis-a-vis Mars and Venus.

Mars-Mercury : This conjunction must necessarily be considered to be bad, because Mercury is the lord of the 3rd and 6th houses and therefore a malefic planet. However, this conjunction must be considered to be good, if it takes place in the 6th, 8th or 12th house from the Ascendant. But if it takes place in any other house, it is likely to produce ill-health as well as enemies. If Mars is exalted, he may eventually overcome both. The conjunction will bless the native with good brothers and courage as well.

Mars-Moon : This conjunction is indeed very good showing a very noble mother. Here, the Moon is not only the indicator for mother but also the lord of the 4th house. The native will have a number of friends placed high as well as low in life. For education this conjunction must be examined with reference to the position of Mercury vis-a-vis Mars and the Moon.

Mars-Sun : This conjunction gives children though one or two miscarriages may happen. More or less will depend on the position of this conjunction with reference to Jupiter, the indicator for children.

Mars-Jupiter : This conjunction is of the 1st and 9th houses as well as of 8th, 9th and 12th; as of 1st and 9th it is good so also of 8th and 12th. The conjunction of 1st and 9th must take place in a favourable house, and of 8th and 12th must necessarily take place in an unfavourable but more of it, if well placed from Sun—the *Pitrukarak* (indicator for father). This Conjunction in a favourable position from Ketu the *Mokshkaraka* (the indicatior for salvation) may turn the native's thoughts towards God at the end of his life. This conjunction, as of 1st and 12th houses, makes the native a bit extravagant but also charitable.

Mars-Saturn : This conjunction must be considered to be good. This conjunction of 1st and 10th houses shows a good position in life with power and authority; as of the 1st and 11th a good income of course, even here one will have to take into consideration both Jupiter and Venus, because Jupiter is the indicator for wealth and Venus is the lord of the house indicating finance.

Scorpio Ascendant

Mars-Jupiter : This conjunction, as of 1st, 2nd and 5th houses is better compared to the same conjunction in Aries Ascendant, for this Jupiter is a perfect benefic, being the lord of 2nd and 5th houses, while for Aries Ascendant, Jupiter owns the 12th house also. It may be that Jupiter is *Maraka*, (death inflicting) but that is not the point. In fact this is the finest conjunction, only second to the Mars-Jupiter conjunction for the Pisces Ascendant. With this conjunction in the Ascendant, 2nd, 5th, 10th, or 11th house must be considered to be very good; the native will have wealth and will definitely be above want; the native will have a fair share of domestic happiness.

This conjunction as of 1st and 5th houses makes the native very intelligent, quick-witted and fond of authority which he knows well how to wield. The native will have children.

Mars-Saturn : This conjunction as of 1st, 3rd, 4th and 6th houses is a double-edged weapon. They are mutual enemies, but the Moon, the indicator for mother, is a friend of both. It has often been seen that there is some want of understanding between mother and son, however good and respectable the mother may be. So far as the question of education is concerned, it has to be seen whether they are passing through any malefic major-period during their youth, in which case there is every chance of their education being broken or delayed. The extent of the progress of education will depend on the position of these two planets vis-a-vis Mercury, the indicator for education. This conjunction of 1st and 3rd houses makes the native a bit arrogant and self-opinionated. This conjunction of 3rd and 6th must take place in an unfavourable house, *viz.*, 6th, 8th or 12th.

Mars-Venus: This conjunction as of the 1st and 7th houses is always good. Here one thing has to be checked out whether it takes place in a benefic house or a malefic house. In the opinion of the writer, the conjunction of Mars and Venus as the lords of 6th and 12th houses either in the 6th house or in the 12th house has been a better position than elsewhere. So they get a good wife.

Mars-Mercury: This conjunction will be that of 1st and 8th houses, 1st and 11th, and 6th and 8th. As of 1st and 11th, it is very good if in a good house and in a favourable position from Jupiter, but in an unfavourable position, it is not pleasant. As of 1st and 8th or 6th and 8th houses it is better to have it in an unfavourable position, for the lord of the ascendant becomes strong. For longevity this conjunction will have to be examined from Saturn the indicator for longevity.

Mars-Moon: The conjunction, as of the 1st and 9th is good, provided it is in a favourable position both from the Ascendant and the 9th house. Whether the native will inherit paternal property will depend on its position with reference to the Sun, the indicator for father.

Mars-Sun: This conjunction is excellent. The native will rise to power, but how long he is going to maintain that power will depend on other factors.

Mercury

This planet is the lord of Gemini and Virgo. Generally speaking, it is not such a strong planet, because it is impotent. This planet always speaks of education etc., and many lawyers, humane judges, and some doctors also are born under this sign.

Gemini Ascendant

Mercury-Moon: This conjunction is indeed very good, being of one and two, but if the Moon be waning and very near *amavasya*, it does not produce very good results, even though it is favourably placed from Jupiter, the ·indicator for wealth. Domestic happiness is also fairly good and there is not much to complain about.

Mercury-Sun : This conjunction is not very pleasant because the Sun is the lord of the third house, and not because Mercury gets eclipsed. The Sun and Mercury are always almost together and Mercury does not suffer from the disability of being eclipsed. The Sun and Mars are friends, but Mercury and Mars are enemies. The native may have brothers but there may not be much agreement between them though very often the native will be very helpful to his brothers or brothers' children. The lord of the 4th house also is Mercury and very many cases have been seen where the native has lost his mother early in life whenever the Moon was not well-placed though as between Mercury and the Moon, they might have been very well positioned. The native generally has a liberal and good education, provided, in his young age, no malefic planetary period as that of Rahu or Mars, or even Saturn, intervenes. It Mercury is not well placed, it is often observed that the native does not have adequate tranquillity of mind.

Mercury-Venus : This conjunction is necessarily very pleasant and favourable. Venus owns the house of intelligence and Mercury, knowledge; the Moon also is favourable, the native rises very well in life and becomes a good speaker or orator. He will have children; even here, this conjunction will have to be considered with reference to Jupiter. Because Venus is also the lord of the 12th house, the native will be very spendthrift by nature but that will be for a good and not for an evil purpose. If it is favourably placed from Ketu, the native may develop interest in religion and philosophy.

Mercury-Mars: Mars owns the 11th house. The conjunction of one and eleven is good, but it must take place in a good house, preferably with the aspect of Jupiter. This conjunction in a bad house will be good insofar as it removes the disability of Mercury being in a bad house. Mercury-Moon-Mars conjunction will be very good, because they are lords of 1st, 2nd and 11th houses. So far as the question of ill-health is concerned, generally Venus being the lord of the 12th house, many instances have been seen where the natives suffer from diabetes as well as from piles and fistula, when other conditions for them are favourable, *viz.,* Saturn is in or aspecting the 12th house or Venus etc.

Mercury-Jupiter : This conjunction as the lords of 1st and 7th is good, as Mercury and Jupiter are not enemies, Mercury and Venus and the Moon are enemies. In a woman's horoscope, Mercury-Jupiter conjunction is very good, but it is not so good in a man's horoscope. Anyway, they marry fairly well. This conjunction with Jupiter as the lord of the 10th house is indeed good. The native is likely to rise in life and attain some position in his particular vocation.

Mercury-Saturn : This conjunction of the lords of the 1st, 8th and 9th houses is nescessarily very good and gives the native a long life, Saturn himself being the indicator for longevity.

Virgo Ascendant

Mercury-Venus : This conjunction is excellent, for it is the conjunction of lords of the 1st and 2nd houses as well as of the 9th, 10th, provided there is no aspect of conjunction of any malefic planet and is favourably placed from Ascendant. The native will have fairly good health and will have good domestic happiness. So far as the question of wealth is concerned, this conjunction has to be considered with reference to Jupiter.

Mercury-Mars: This conjunction is necessarily bad, because Mars is the lord of the 3rd and 8th houses, it may be that so far as longevity is concerned, it is good, but then it spoils the lord of the ascendant, for the lord of the ascendant must not be in conjunction with any malefic planet when placed in a good house. If it is placed in an evil house, it will be really good. The longevity depends upon its position from Saturn, its indicator. For brothers, it is a very bad position, for Mercury and Mars are natural enemies. Very often it is seen that these people have no brothers or sisters and whenever they have, there is a definite lack of understanding between them; generally it makes them a bit obstinate and mulish, for Mercury becomes a malefic in association with Mars.

Mercury-Jupiter : This conjunction will be more or less the same as for Gemini ascendant. Here again Mercury and Venus are friends. Mercury and Jupiter are not enemies. But Jupiter and Venus are enemies. Therefore, there's bound to be some sort of want in his domestic happiness. Though Jupiter and Venus are enemies, after all both are benefics.

Mercury-Saturn : This conjunction is of the 1st and 5th houses and of 1st and 6th. The native will have children, because Jupiter is friendly to both. Of course how many or how few will depend upon the position of these two planets with reference to Jupiter. The health of the native is likely to be more delicate than strong, because Saturn is the weakest of all planets and Mercury himself is a weak planet gaining strength from the planet with whom it is in conjunction.

Mercury-Moon : This conjunction of the 1st and 11th houses is very good. Here, it must not be taken as the conjunction of the 10th and 11th houses. In a favourable position of course it is very good, again depending upon its position from Venus and Jupiter.

Moon

This is indeed a natural benefic, but is considered a malefic when waning. She owns Cancer. This is the fourth sign in the Zodiac and in the *Kalapurusha* body it is the breast. The Moon being the lord of that house and she being the indicator for mother, this sign of Cancer will always be at an advantage when the Moon is waxing and not waning, because it is the lord of the ascendant to be strong. It is a feminine planet and represents the mind in human beings.

Cancer Ascendant

The Moon-Sun : This conjunction of the lords of the 1st and 2nd houses may be considered to be good, but that will be round about *Amavasya* when all the benefic planets are weak and the malefic planets strong. Hence, it will not be a happy conjunction though it may be treated as a good one.

Moon-Mercury : This conjunction need not be described as of great enemies. Mercury for this Moon, is as enemy but both of them are benefics. It will be the conjunction of 1st and 3rd houses and 1st and 12th, which indeed is bad, especially when the native is likely to lose a lot of money in his life. This conjunction especially well placed from Ketu inclines the native for spiritual development. This sign Cancer by itself is a sign that is inclined for spiritual development.

Moon-Venus : This conjunction is indeed good. They are enemies, though natural benefics; the Moon, as the indicator for mother, and Venus, as the lord of the fourth house indicating the mother, shows a very good and excellent lady as his mother, especially when this conjunction takes place in a favourable house, both from the ascendant and the 4th house. This house speaks of education as well. Mercury and Venus being friends, the native is likely to have a good and liberal education, provided the conjunction is favourably placed from Mercury. The native is likely to have conveyances. As that of the 1st and 11th houses, this conjunction indicates a good income, but the accumulation depends upon its position from Jupiter, the lord of the 9th house and the Sun, the lord of the 2nd house.

Moon-Mars : This conjunction of friends and as of lords of 1st, 5th and 10th houses is necessarily good; the native will have children. That will depend upon its position from Jupiter. The native is certainly intelligent and there is a quickness of intellect. The power of understanding will really be great. He will rise to some position of power and authority.

Moon-Jupiter : This conjunction will be of the 1st and 6th houses and 1st and 9th. As of the 1st and 6th houses, it is not pleasant, as the 6th house represents ill-health, disease etc. Whether the native is going to be always sickly or otherwise, will have to be examined from their comparative strength. If Jupiter is stronger, it will indicate frequent minor ailments; if the Moon is waning, the health may not be very robust. These people should be very careful not to contract debts, for though their intention and desire to repay will be very strong, they may not be able to do so, owing to their liberal and expensive nature. As of 1st and 9th houses, it is indeed very good, especially as Jupiter is a friend of the Sun, indicator for father and the Moon is not an enemy of either. The native is likely to inherit some paternal property, provided this conjunction takes place in a favourable house, not only from the Ascendant but also from the 9th house and from the Sun.

Moon-Saturn : This conjunction is of 1st, 7th and 8th houses. As of 1st and 7th, it is indeed very good. Here a point may be stressed that Saturn and Venus are friends. Therefore, they are likely to get a good wife, but again Saturn and the Sun representing domestic happiness are enemies; so also Venus and the Sun. Very often Cancer-born people either do not have much domestic happiness or have a plurality of wives.

Saturn as the lord of the 8th house, with the Moon, the lord of the Ascendant must be considered to be good, for whenever the lord of the Ascendant is in conjunction with any *bhavadhipati,* that particular *bhava* becomes strong. Therefore, Saturn himself being the indicator for longevity, a long life is to be predicted. So far as the question of *yoga* is concerned, this conjunction in any unfavourable house is preferable.

Venus

This is a natural benefic, in fact very nearly as good as Jupiter, with only this difference that Venus is a luxury-minded planet whereas Jupiter is more spiritually inclined. This planet owns two houses — Taurus and Libra.

Taurus Ascendant

Venus as the lord of Taurus becomes the lord of the 6th house also and is therefore less harmful. The Taurus Ascendant has the advantage of having benefic planets as lord of evil houses and of having lords of benefic houses (except the Sun) as friends of Venus.

Venus-Mercury : This conjunction will be of the lords of 1st and 2nd houses besides of 1st and 5th, and therefore very pleasant, in that the native will have wealth as well as children, of course, that depening upon its position from Jupiter. People born in this Ascendant are considered to be generally lucky in life. They are fair and honest of speech, and have fairly good domestic happiness.

Venus-Moon : This conjunction is of the 1st and 3rd as well as 6th and 3rd. As has been remarked earlier, the Moon, though a malefic, by virtue of its being the lord of the 3rd house is a natural benefic and more so when she is waxing. Mars is a friend of both Venus and the Moon. The natives have brothers and sisters, but because Venus and the Moon are natural enemies, it is possible that there may not be much agreement between them. They are not very adventurous people.

Venus-Sun : This conjunction of the 1st and 3rd houses is good, but Venus suffers from the disability of being eclipsed which is a weak point. A good mother is promised, yet Venus and Moon being enemies, somewhat of misunderstanding between them or some unhappiness to her is thus likely. Mercury as a friend of both the Sun and Venus, will give good education, especially when favourably placed from the 4th house. They have many friends to whom they are generally useful. They are intelligent, with quickness of perception. The question of health will depend upon the position of Venus herself and also upon the aspects which the 6th house from the Ascendant has.

Venus-Mars : This conjunction is of 1st, 6th, and 12th. The conjunction is of the lord of the 7th house and of Venus, the indicator for wife, is definitely good; a very good and excellent lady as the wife is seen, but still Mars and Mercury, the lord of the two houses being inimical, sometimes a nagging wife is seen. This conjunction in any favourable place is indeed good. This conjunction in 6th, 8th or 12th house is much better, for it will be the conjunction of the lords of 6th and 12th houses. The conjunction of the lord of the 12th house is conducive to a very great *raja-yoga*, provided there is not the aspect or conjunction of any other planet. This conjunction anywhere else is good.

Venus-Jupiter : This conjunction is of 1st, 6th, 8th and 11th houses. The conjunction of 1st and 11th houses in a favourable position is indeed good, and especially if Mercury also is favourbly placed from it. If Mercury joins it in a favourable position, the native will have great wealth. It must be remembered that this conjunction in the 11th house does not produce good results.

Venus-Saturn : This conjunction of 1st, 9th and 10th is excellent, more so because they are friends. In a benefic house, it is good, but in the 9th or 10th house, it is better. The question of inheriting paternal property will depend upon its position from the Sun. The native is likely to rise to some position of eminence.

Libra Ascendant

Venus, as the lord of Libra, becomes the lord of 1st and 8th houses, showing that Venus is weaker. Perhaps to prove this fact, there is the aspect of Saturn on this house.

Venus-Mars : This conjunction is of 1st, 2nd, 7th and 8th houses. This conjunction for a Libra Ascendant is a better proposition than for the *Vrishabha* Ascendant, where it will mean the conjunction of 1st, 6th, 7th and 12th houses. The native has good domestic happiness, a good wife, but the question of wealth will depend upon its position from Jupiter. The native is fairly honest and truthful.

Venus-Jupiter : This conjunction is of 1st, 3rd, 6th and 8th houses. Venus and Jupiter are enemies though benefics. Here again, it may be pointed out that malefic planets own benefic houses. Jupiter owns 3rd and 6th, two bad houses. Mercury owns 9th and 12th. 12th is a bad house. Therefore, a benefic planet becomes a temporary malefic. But a malefic planet becomes a temporary benefic and a line of distinction must necessarily be drawn between a natural benefic as in the case of Mars for Virgo Ascendant. The native has brothers but generally it has been seen that there is not much love lost between them. The conjunction is better in the 6th, 8th or 12th houses.

Venus-Saturn : This conjunction is of the 1st, 4th, 5th and 8th houses. These two are friends. So also Mercury, the indicator for knowledge. The natives have very good education, provided they do not have a bad *dasha* like that of Rahu during the education period. The native has many friends, but friendship is not continued. A good lady for mother is seen but if the Moon is unfavourably placed an early demise is likely. He is intelligent but often a bit mulish and obstinate. The conjunction of the lords of the 8th house and the indicator of longevity gives a long life.

Venus-Mercury : This conjunction of 1st and 9th houses is excellent; but paternal inheritance will depend upon its position from the Sun. Its unfavourable position may mean both an early death of the father as well as loss of inheritance. This conjunction in the 12th house without any aspect or conjunction of any other benific planet is excellent.

Venus-Moon : This conjunction is of the 1st and 10th houses. It may be that these are not friends, but still the native is honest. He has some position or power of authority and he is fairly honest. He generally is not inclined to do evil for evil's sake. One thing cannot be denied that he is selfish.

Venus-Sun : This conjunction is of 1st and 11th houses. No doubt it is good especially when favourably placed from Jupiter and Mars. But Venus, the lord of the Ascendant, will have the disability of being eclipsed. The question of wealth will depend upon the position of Mars. The native has children. This conjunction of the 1st, 6th and 10th houses is bad. However, the question of ill-health will depend upon the comparative strength of Jupiter and the Sun, and also upon the kind of aspects on the six houses.

Pisces Ascendant

Jupiter as the lord of the Pisces Ascendant is at a better advantage because he owns the 10th house — a stronger angle than the 4th house. Therefore, this must be considered to be a better Ascendant than Sagittarius.

Jupiter-Mars : This conjunction of the 1st, 2nd, 3rd and 10th is indeed beautiful and is better than that for Sagittarius, where Mars is the lord of the 12th house. It is as good a conjunction as of Mercury and Venus for Virgo Ascendant. The native gets wealth and paternal property, the latter depending on its position from the Sun. He is truthful and has fairly good domestic happiness. He rises in life as well, if the conjunction is in a benefic house.

Jupiter-Venus : This conjunction of 1st, 3rd, 8th and 10th houses is definitely bad for *yoga*, but it gives longevity. In an unfavourable house it is better for causing *yoga*. The native has brothers and there is also agreement between them. He has a certain amount of pride about himself, as well as aloofness. He is not very bold or courageous.

Jupiter-Mercury : This is the conjunction of 1st, 4th, 7th and 10th houses. A liberal education is seen if it is well-placed from the Moon. Slow in making friends but steadfast and helpful to them, the native is slightly selfish, but can keep an open mind. A good wife is seen; but a tendency for plurality of marriage is also indicated, if the 7th and 2nd houses are afflicted, because Jupiter and Venus are enemies.

Jupiter-Saturn : This is the conjunction of the 1st, 10th, 11th and 12th houses, as of 1st and 11th it is good; as of 10th and 11th which is bad, it should be ignored. It is productive of very good income if favourably placed both from the Ascendant and Mars. The native is a good servant but not a good master. As of 1st and 12th, in an unfavourable position, is better. The native is fairly religious and if well-placed from Ketu, he is spiritually-minded because the Pisces Ascendant has the inherent capacity to produce spiritually-minded people.

Jupiter-Moon : This conjunction of the 1st, 5th and 10th houses is good. The native has fame, a good name and dignity. The question of wealth will depend upon the position of Mars. The native has children. This conjunction in 1st, 9th or 10th house is indeed very good.

Jupiter-Sun : This conjunction of the 1st, 6th and 10th houses is bad. However, the question of ill-health will depend upon the comparative strength of Jupiter and the Sun, and also upon the kind of aspects on the 6th house.

Saturn

This planet is a natural malefic and is considered to be a planet of woe and misery, trial and tribulation and of perseverence and hard work.

Capricorn Ascendant

This planet is the lord of the 1st and 2nd houses and therefore a perfect benefic, and it is preferable if it is well-placed from Ascendant.

Saturn-Jupiter : This is the conjunction of the 1st, 2nd, 3rd and 12th houses. Jupiter is a benefic as well as the indicator for wealth. This conjunction in 1st, 5th, or 11th house is preferable. Saturn being placed from a favourable position from Jupiter is a better proposition. In the conjunction, the lord of the Ascendant has the disability of being with the lord of the 3rd and 12th houses; which makes native very expensive.

Saturn-Mars : Though these two are enemies, it is the conjunction of the 1st, 2nd, 4th and 11th. The conjunction of the 1st, 2nd and 11th is necessarily good, provided it is in a favourable position from the Ascendant and Jupiter. Mars and the Moon are friends, Saturn and the Moon are not adversaries. But Saturn and Mars are enemies. A very good mother is seen. Still, some want of undertanding between the mother and son has very often been observed, especially when the conjunction is unfavourably placed from the Moon. The native receives a fairly good education, the extent depending upon its position from Mercury, the indicator for education and learning. It gives conveyances, but more so, if favourably placed from Venus. The native gets landed property but he may not be able to derive the full benefit from ancestral property.

Saturn-Venus : This conjunction of 1st, 2nd and 10th houses is good. Saturn and Venus are friends. The native has quickness of intellect. He gets children also, but the position with reference to Jupiter will have to be considered seriously. In many cases, unhappiness through children has been observed. The native is very ambitious, fond of authority much and very often rises to position of honour. The native speaks of philosophy, but very rarely practises it, and he is not very religious

Saturn-Mercury : This is the conjunction the 1st, 2nd, 6th, and 9th houses. The native inherits good paternal property if well-placed from the Ascendant and the Sun. It creates many enemies and the native generally tries to ride rough-shod over weaker ones. The native manages generally to maintain fairly good health. This conjunction in a good house is in indeed preferable.

Saturn-Moon : This conjunction of the 1st, 2nd, 7th houses is good. The native gets a good wife who generally comes from a good family, often times better than his own and has a fair amount of domestic happiness.

Saturn-Sun : This conjunction of the 1st, 2nd and 8th houses is very good for longevity, because Saturn is also an indicator for longevity. But this conjunction has also the effect of reducing the strength of the lord of the Ascendant by eclipsing it, and the closer the conjunction, the worse it is.

Aquarius Ascendant

Saturn is a natural malefic and the lord of the 1st and 12th houses. As of the 1st, it is a benefic; as of the 12th, it is a malefic. Hence, this Ascendant as well as Saturn must be considered weak. Unlike other Ascendant this requires to be fortified very well before any *yoga* can be predicted.

Saturn-Jupiter : This conjunction of the 1st, 2nd, 11th and 12th houses is good. In a favourable place both from the Ascendant as well as the 2nd house, it produces very good results. The native is generally truthful and enjoys a fair amount of domestic happiness.

Saturn-Mars : This is the conjunction of the 1st, 3rd, 10th and 12th houses. The native generally does not have many brothers and if he has, there is not much agreement. He is outwardly very bold but timid at heart. He rises to a position of power and eminence with dogged labour. He is very exacting by nature. A sense of false dignity is seen in him. He is helpful to his friends.

Saturn-Venus : This conjunction of the 1st, 4th and 9th and 12th houses is good. The native has a very good lady as mother, who is either unhappy or dies early in life. When well-placed from Mercury, it gives good education. The native gets conveyances. By inclination he is fond of sycophants. The native is generally able to save some property. Inheritence of paternal property depends on its position from the Sun. This conjunction is good in any house, but in the 12th house it is the best. This by itself is a great *Raja-yoga* and additionally, if the lords of 6th, 8th and 12th houses are also weak, it becomes exceptionally good.

Saturn-Mercury : This is the conjunction of the 1st, 5th, 8th and 12th houses. As the conjunction is of the 1st and 5th houses in a favourable position from the Ascendant and Jupiter, and without any malefic aspect on the 5th house, it is bound to give good children and make the native happy about them. The same conjunction as of 8th and 12th houses in the 6th, 8th or 12th houses must be considered to be a better proposition in as much as the evil in the horoscope is eliminated. This will be productive in the 12th, Saturn-Mercury conjunction will also give a long life though there is this odium that after all the native may have some sort of perversity in his character and it sometimes also makes the native a snob.

Saturn-Moon : This is the conjunction of the 1st, 6th and 12th houses. It must be mentioned here that the Moon in the 2nd house for this Ascendant has always given very bad results at the end of life. This conjunction, if it takes place in the 3rd, 6th, 8th or 12th house is good, because it is of 12th and 6th houses. In any favourable house from the Ascendant, it is very bad, but in an unfavourable position, it is slightly better, as the evil is reduced; this does not produce a very great *raja-yoga*. It is very favourable for long travels.

Saturn-Sun : This is the conjunction of the 1st, 7th, and 12th houses. It leads to plurality of marriage. Saturn and the Sun are enemies. So also Venus and the Sun; but Saturn and Venus are friends. The native gets a good wife, but still, if the Sun is stronger than Saturn, the wife is dominating. The wife comes from a fairly good family, and if the Moon in the two horoscopes of the husband and wife is unfavourably placed from each other, it leads to great domestic unhappiness, despite Jupiter, a peaceloving planet, owning the 2nd house.

13

HOW TO EXAMINE A HOROSCOPE

Any pain or pleasure experienced by a person perhaps only affects his body and mind. And in some cases not even the mind. They never affect the soul. Therefore, if we have to examine the material prospects in a man's life in this world, we have to consider the strength of the Ascendant and its lord, and the lord of the birth sign. As this represents the body of a man, if we do not correctly understand the strength of the Ascendant and its lord, our prediction will most likely go awry. If the Ascendant or its lord are weak, it may affect his material prospects or his capacity to lead a fruitful and enjoyable life.

An Ascendant Lord may be considered to be strong in the following cases:

(1) When he is in his own house,
(2) When he is with friends,
(3) When he is in an angle or trine,
(4) When he has the conjunction of benefics,
(5) When he has the aspect of benefics,
(6) When he is in a friendly *navamsa*,
(7) When he is in a friendly *drekkana*,
(8) When he is in exaltation,
(9) When he is between benefics,
(10) When he is in a friendly sign,
(11) When he is in the 11th house from Ascendant.

The Ascendant Lord may be considered to be weak in the following cases:

(1) When he is in an inimical sign,

(2) When he is in conjunction with malefics,

(3) When he is in the 3rd, 6th, 8th or 12th house from Ascendant,

(4) When he is between malefics,

(5) When he has the aspect of malefics,

(6) When he is in depression or is eclipsed,

(7) When he is in an inimical *navamsa*.

(8) When he is in an inimical decanate.

The Ascendant is considered to be strong when:

(1) There are benefics in it,

(2) There are the aspects, of benefics,

(3) The Ascendant is between benefics.

Note: Here the benefics and malefics mean the natural benefics and malefics, not the planets which have become temporary benefics or malefics by virtue of ownership, e.g., Jupiter as the lord of the 3rd and 6th houses is a malefic, Saturn becomes a perfect benefic when he is the lord of 4th and 5th houses as in the case of a Libra Ascendant. But when "between benefics" occur, it means only natural benefics and when "between malefics" occur, it means between natural malefics.

The Ascendant is considered to be weak when:

(1) Ascendant is hemmed in between malefics,

(2) There are malefics in the Ascendant,

(3) There are malefics aspecting it, or

(4) When the birth is in a malefic *navamsa* or *drekkana*.

Then we have to find out if 1st, 2nd, 4th, 5th, 7th, 9th and 10th houses are benefic and if their lords are strong or weak, for these houses and their lords together are usually expected to give good results. These must therefore be strong.

We have also to find out if the lords of 3rd, 6th, 8th and 12th houses are strong or weak. These houses and their lords generally bring misery, tensions, trouble and unhappiness to a native. These must be weak. For, the minus or negative quality will be reduced and as this decreases, the strength increases.

We should also see whether individual planets are in an adverse position to each other, i.e., planets which are situated in the 6th and 8th house to each other generally give a very bad result, in their major periods and sub periods, whatever may be their respective lordship. These points must be very carefully noted before one begins to predict.

As a matter of guidance a few points are given below:

Even though the lord of the Ascendant is in exaltation or a friendly sign, if that house of exaltation happens to be 3rd, 6th, 8th or 12th house from the Ascendant, then, the Ascendant Lord should not be considered to be powerful, i.e., an exalted Mars for a Scorpio Ascendant, an exalted Jupiter for a Sagittarius Ascendant and exalted Venus for a Libra Ascendant are comparatively weak and may mar the native's fortune.

If the Ascendant Lord happens to be in an angle, or trine and even if that house happens to be a house of debilitation, or an inimical sign, the Ascendant Lord should not be considered to be weak.

Though the Ascendant Lord be a malefic by nature, if he should happen to be in 3rd, 6th, 8th or 12th house, he should not be considered to be in a good position and expected to give good results. The ascendant lord or the lord of Ascendant, though a malefic by nature, becomes a benefic by virtue of his being the *lagnadhipathi* and his position in the 3rd, 6th, 8th or 12th houses is not conducive to any good.

Benefics (natural) always increase the effects of the houses which they occupy or aspect. Malefics (natural) destroy the result of the houses which they occupy or aspect. Therefore, it is very good to find benefics occupying good houses and malefics occupying evil houses. For, the natural benefics would improve the results of the houses they occupy and the natural malefics would destroy the evil of those houses, they occupy. Malefics in 3rd, 6th, 8th and 12th houses remove the evil effects of those houses. If a native does not have quarrels or misunderstanding it is good and these effects will result if the malefics occupy or aspect the houses which indicate these things. If a native does not contract debts or suffer imprisonment or major illness, it is good. If a native does not waste or lose money, it is good.

If the Ascendant Lord be in an angle or a trine he must have the aspect and/or conjunction of benefics alone. He must not have in any case the aspect of malefics or the conjunction of malefics or the conjunction or the aspect of the lords of 3rd, 6th, 8th and 12 houses.

If the Ascendant Lord is situated in 3rd, 6th, 8th and 12th houses, he must have the aspect and/or conjunction of the natural malefics alone and there should not be, in any case, the aspect or conjunction of any natural benefics. This position is conducive to *yoga*.

When a planet is situated in a certain house, if the lord of that house be situated in the house of exaltation of the occupying planet, the occupying planet gets exalted, the strength or extent of the exaltation will depend on the actual degree or position of the lord of the house in the house of exaltation.

Example: If the Sun should be in Cancer and if the lord of that house, the Moon occupies Aries, the Sun gets exalted but this exaltation will depend on the degree and position which the Moon occupies in Aries; as in Aries, the Sun gets different strengths according to its position.

If the same Moon should occupy Libra, the Sun is debilitated and the degree of debilitation depends on the position or degree which the Moon occupies in Libra.

But if the Moon should occupy Taurus when the Sun is in Cancer, the Sun also becomes powerful.

Some astrologers hold the opinion that if a certain planet should be debilitated in a sign, and if the lord of that sign occupies his own house or his house of exaltation, the occupying planet loses its debilitation and causes *Raja-yoga*, e.g., if Jupiter is in Capricorn, he is debilitated but if Saturn is in Capricorn or Aquarius or Libra, Jupiter loses his debilitation and causes *Raja-yoga*.

Some others say, that if Jupiter be in Capricorn and if Saturn should occupy Capricorn or Aquarius, he will be *neecha* or debilitated and if Saturn should occupy Libra, Jupiter gets *Neechabhangam*, or loses its debilitation and if Saturn be in an angle from the Moon, Jupiter bestows *Neechabhanga Raja-yoga*. This view is more acceptable. Yet others hold that when a planet is in debilitation, if the planet which has that house as its sign of exaltation or the lord of the house be situated in an angle from the Moon, the planet loses its debilitation, e.g., Saturn is in debilitation in Aries and if the Sun, the planet which has Aries as its sign of exaltation, or if Mars, the lord of Aries, be in an angle from the Moon, Saturn is said to lose his debilitation.

When an exalted and a debilitated planet together occupy a sign, the debilitated planet is said to lose its debilitation, e.g., with the Sun and Saturn in conjunction in Aries, the Sun will not lose its strength and Saturn will lose his debilitation.

The following combinations will generally result in *yoga* if the planets are situated in benefic houses from Ascendant without the aspect or conjunction of malefics and preferably without the conjunction or aspect of even benefics. The conjunctions of lords of the 1st and 2nd, 1st and 5th, 2nd and 11th, 1st and 11th, 4th and 5th, 9th and 10th, 4th and 9th, 5th and 7th, 5th and 10th, 7th and 9th, 1st and 9th, 1st and 4th, 1st and 10th, 2nd and 9th, 2nd and 5th houses. In short, the conjunction of the lord of a quadrant or angle with the lord of trine or trikona is good. The lord of the angles if they happen to be benefics do not give a good result. The Moon, because it owns only one house is not a malefic even if it owns an angle.

Benefics should be lords of trines, when they will cause good results. Malefics should be the lords of angles when they will give good results. Benefics as lords of trines occupying angles and malefics as lords of angles occupying trines give very good results.

With the lords of the 6th, 8th and 12th houses, the conjunction of any two of these planets in the 6th, 8th or 12th house without any other aspect or conjunction gives *yoga*. The conjunction of all the three planets in 6th, 8th or 12th house without any aspect or conjunction, gives *Raja-yoga*. The exchange of houses or the mutual reception by or of any two or the lords of 6th, 8th and 12th houses without any aspect or conjunction is good and gives *yoga*.

The lord of 1st in 5th, of 5th in 9th, and of 9th in 1st house gives yoga.

Planets must be in advance of their houses and never behind, e.g., if the lord of the Ascendant goes to the 12th house, if the lord of the 12th goes to the 11th house; and the lord of the 11th to the 10th and so on, this particular position causes poverty, misery and trouble and tensions.

If several planets are in an advance by one house of their own, they give good results.

The *parivarthanam* or exchange of places by the lords of the benefic house is always good, i.e., two lords of 1st in 9th and the lord of 9th in 1st is good but the exchange of houses by the lords of 6th, 8th or 12th is not good, though the lords of these houses may be benefics. The conjunction of benefactor with the *bhavadhipathi* is always productive of much good for the house; e.g., the conjunction of Jupiter, the *puthrakarka* with the lord of the 5th house, the *puthrasthandhipathi* is very good, for the house. Ordinary or very good results will depend on the position these two planets occupy in a chart. Their conjunction in angles or their mutual aspect from angles or trines will be beneficial. But their occupying malefic houses or having the conjunction or aspect of the malefic planets will reduce the good effects which these combinations may generally cause.

If Jupiter, Mercury and Venus, all three are situated in the 6th, 7th and 8th houses from the Moon (all the three houses being thus occupied) and are not aspected by or in conjunction with malefics, the native will have *Raja-yoga*, which will give him immense and good fortune, wealth with peace of mind and happiness, Similarly, if Saturn, Mars, the Sun, Rahu or Ketu, or any three of them are situated in 6th, 7th and 8th houses from the Moon (all the three houses being thus occupied) and are not aspected by other planets, the native will also have *Raja-yoga*, but this will bestow him only with wealth and riches, peace of mind and family happiness being somewhat impaired.

If the three benefics Mercury, Venus and Jupiter are all together in 6th, 7th, or 8th house from the Ascendant and are not aspected by malefics, the native is blessed with *yoga*.

Benefic planets in any two of the 6th, 7th, or 8th houses from the Moon also bless the natives with *Raja-yoga*. Also any planets in these houses bestow *Raja-yoga*.

The conjunction or mutual aspect or mutual reception of any two lords of the 2nd, 5th, 9th and 11th houses gives Yoga, provided there is not aspect or conjunction of any of the lords of 3rd, 6th, 8th or 12th houses. But if this conjunction takes place in 6th, 8th or 12th houses, it may cause only adverse happenings.

Weak or debilitated malefic planets or strong and powerful benefic planets in angles or trines give good results.

The conjunction of the lords of the 1st, 9th and 10th in the 10th house from Ascendant without any malefic aspect or conjunction gives exceptional *Raja-yoga*. This fails to cause the conjunction of the lords of 9th and 10th houses in Ascendant desired results.

If Jupiter, Mercury, Venus and the full Moon are without any malefic aspect or conjunction in a Chart, the native will have *yoga* irrespective of any other conjunction or adverse factors. Cancer occupying the *Bhava* is not good, the exception being *Saturn-ayush karak* in the 8th house. Some hold that even the aspect of a *karak* on its *Bhava* is not good.

In the event of a man being born in the major period of a benefic, the person will at least towards the end of his life see better days and die, though he may undergo very many difficulties during the beginning or middle portion of his life.

In the event of the native being born in the major period of a malefic planet, the person may suffer during the last period of his life, even though he may have had very great *yoga* during the other period.

If the lord of any house occupies the angle or trine from the Ascendant, he will give results of the *Bhava* which he owns.

If the lord of any house occupies the angle or trine from his own house and if the latter is powerful, he gives good results of that house.

If the lord of any house be the Sun, Mars, or Saturn and if it occupies 3rd house from the Ascendant, he gives good results.

If the lord of any house occupies its own house that house becomes auspicious.

If the lord of any house be in association with benefics or aspected by benefics, the results of that house will not be so good.

If the lord of any house or any house is between benefic planets, the results of that house will be good but if they are hemmed in between malefics, the results will be inauspicious.

If the lord of any house or any house is associated with or aspected by both benefics and malefics, the result will be of mixed nature.

If the lord of any house occupies a friend's house or his house of exaltation, it gives beneficial results, but if he occupies his house of depression or the inimical house, it causes inauspicious results. Rahu and Ketu give very good results during their major periods under the following conditions. These two planets must be in an angle or a trine or the 11th house from the Ascendant; the lord of the house occupied by Ketu or Rahu must be in an angle or trine from the Ascendant and preferably from the Moon ascendant also. This is a very good position for an excellent period during Rahu or Ketu's major periods. If one of these planets Rahu and Ketu fulfils the conditions given above and his major period occurs, the native will have very good *yoga* in proportion to the strength of the lord of the Ascendant and subject to the conditions mentioned below.

If Mars should aspect Rahu or Ketu, these two planets Rahu and Ketu become more or less ineffective, that is to say, they lose all their power, and are incapable of producing either good or bad results. During the periods of these planets, the effects of lords of sub-periods only will prevail. If Rahu is in the 6th, 8th or 12th house, from the Ascendant and if the conditions mentioned above are satisfied, Rahu will give the full effects of the house occupied by it, which is evil but when such conditions pervail, the aspect of Mars will be very beneficial, for the malefic effects of Rahu are nullified by the aspect of Mars.

If in a horoscope, all the planets are hemmed in between Rahu and Ketu, the native will not have *yoga,* having ordinary results or bad results depending on the strength of the lord of the Ascendant and other positions which have already been discussed. This is called *Kalasarpa Yoga*. This *yoga* entails considerable effort and struggle but has been found in the natal charts of many world leaders, who have distinguished themselves in various walks of life.

If the lord of any house occupies exaltation in a sign and depression in the *Navamsa*, the results will be inauspicious.

If the lord of any house occupies depression in a sign and exaltation in the *Navamsa*, the results of that house will be beneficial.

All planets and all lords of houses occupying the 11th house from the Ascendant give good results. Venus in the 11th house either from the Ascendant or from the Moon or from Lord of the major period has always produced very bad results. Even if it is in the 11th house it will not produce good results. This position is always a weakening factor in a horoscope. Conversely, Venus occupying the 12th house, either from the Ascendant, or the Moon Ascendant, or from the Lord of the major period is always good whereas any other planet in such a position must be considered to be bad. If the lords of the 6th, 8th and 12th houses occupy *Kendras* or *Konas* that they cannot give good results.

The lord of the major period gives not only the results of the house of which he is the lord but will also give the results of those planets with whom the lord of the major period associates and which aspect the lord of the major period and the results of the house which he occupies.

When the results of the lord of a period are to be taken or predicted, it should be noted whether the lord of the major period occupies friend's house, an enemy's house, exaltation or depression. If it is a friend's house, he gives good results; if in an enemy's house, bad results; exaltation, very good results and depression, very bad. When results are to be predicted, the position the lord of the major period, the houses of which he is the lord, the planets in conjunction and the planets which are aspecting should all be carefully noted.

The mutual aspect or conjunctions of the Sun and Saturn; Mars and Mercury; and Jupiter and Venus always tend to decrease the general strength of a natal chart, the more so when these do not have the conjunction or aspect of any other planet.

The sub-periods of Jupiter, the Sun and Mars are productive of extremely bad results, whatever may be their ownerships, during the major period of Venus, Saturn and Mercury respectively or vice versa.

But during these periods, there will be very good *yoga* if one of these two planets of the pair, Jupiter and Venus, Saturn and the Sun, or Mars and Mercury, is in exaltation and the other is in debilitation, e.g., Jupiter's major period and Venus' sub-period or vice versa will be very bad. But if one of these, Jupiter or Venus, is in exaltation and the other is in debilitation, the results will be very agreeable and good and the period would be conducive to the native's rise and prosperity.

If the lord of a sub-period occupies the 7th house from the lord of the major period, there could be ill health to the person or his wife or tensions to the native.

If the lord of a sub-period occupies the 6th or 8th house from lord of the major period, there will be quarrels, blames and/or losses.

If the lord of a sub-period occupies the 12th house from the lord of the major period, there will be no peace of mind. There would usually be some disputes, litigation and fluctuations of financial fortunes, useless expenditure during his sub-period.

At the beginning of its period if a planet be situated in a favourable sign from Ascendant or the Moon, or the Ascendant preferably from both according to the transits, the results of his major period will be good.

The major period of a planet which comes between two good major periods (meaning *yoga karak dashas*) will generally be good whatever be the *adhipatya*. The major period of a *yoga-giving* planet, if it happens to be between two bad periods (*avayogakarak dashas*), the results will not be good.

The points explained above may be used for examining the strength of any house of a birth chart. But it should be remembered that though a particular house may be very strong, the results of that house will not be effective if the lord of the Ascendant is not strong.

The cumulative effect of the results from the ascendant, the Moon Ascendant and the house in which the Ascendant Lord is situated as ascendant must be considered. In arriving at this result, the following order may be adopted with advantage :

The Ascendant,

The Moon Ascendant,

The house occupied by the Lord of the Ascendant.

14

ANALYSING A HOROSCOPE AND MAKING PREDICTIONS

This is the most interesting part of Astrology. The basic prerequisites for a man who ventures into the predictive field are :

1. Patience,
2. A certain amount of intuition,
3. An open mind without any sort of prejudice,
4. Desire to speak the truth,
5. Application of previous experience and, above all,
6. Faith and Trust in God.

Without these, the astrologer is not likely to make a mark in this highly specialized field.

It must be remembered that astrology is not a science as accepted in its ordinary sense but a divine science that attempts to reveal the FUTURE, which is engulfed in mystery. It is for your well-being and hence not mandatory, or obligatory or dictatorial. This forms one of the parts (limbs) of the *Vedas* and even the *Vedas* themselves are not complete without it.

We have now learnt what the Zodiac is, what the planets are, their characteristics, the good and bad conjunctions, their aspects etc. We have now to put all these together and analyse the final result.

The Ascendant or the ruling sign of birth is the quintessence of all the other houses. So the effects and qualities of all the lords of other houses as well are inherent in the lord of Ascendant and it is therefore sino genesis. By the effects and qualities of the lords of other houses is meant the effects and qualities displayed by those planets as owners of the different houses and not their individual effects or qualities. Therefore, these two things must be remembered well and the first priority should be given to these two aspects.

Generally, if we want to examine the 5th house regarding children, we will have to look into all its allied aspects — wife, family and *karma*, that is to say, the 7th, the 2nd and the 10th house as well. With regard to the 2nd house, you will have to look into 7th, 9th, 10th and the 11th houses — disease, misery and ailments and so on for all other houses.

Then with regard to enjoyment of pleasures, you will have to look into the 4th, 7th and the 12th houses, i.e., mental peace and happiness, wife and conjugal happiness, and enjoyment in general.

For health, you will have to examine the 6th, 8th and 11th houses — disease, misery and ailments and so on for all other houses. Ask for yourself what are the basics which make up the particular point which you are examining and look into all of them and also remember the particular aspect being judged in the natal chart.

The following guidelines should be borne in mind while trying to predict the effects of different houses :

1st House

Remember the house, its lord, its benefactors, the Sun and the Moon. (Vigour and Body).

2nd House

Remember the house, its lord : Jupiter, Mercury and Venus are indicators of wealth, speech and spouse respectively.

3rd House

Remember the house, its lord, Mars and Saturn, indicators of brothers and courage and suffering respectively.

4th House

Remember the house, its lord, Moon, Mercury, Venus and Mars benefactors of mother, learning, conveyance and land/property respectively.

5th House

Remember the house, its lord, Jupiter, Mercury and the Sun, benefactors of children, intelligence and father respectively.

6th House

Remember the house, its lord, Mars and Saturn, indicators of adversaries and untoward and unpleasant happenings and ill-health.

7th House

Remember the house, its lord, Venus and Mars, indicators for the spouse and sexual appetite respectively.

8th House

Remember the house, its lord, Saturn, indicator of longevity and all sorts of mental and physical sufferings and afflictions.

9th House

Remember the house, its lord, Jupiter and the Sun, indicators of the preceptor and father respectively.

10th House

Remember the house, its lords the Sun, Saturn, Jupiter and Mercury, indicators of fortune, employment or livelihood, wealth and learning of a vocation respectively.

11th House

Remember the house, its lord, Jupiter, indicator of wealth, financial gains, business and elder brothers.

12th House

Remember the house, its lord, Saturn and Mars indicators of sorrow and imprisonment; Venus, indicator of material desires and pleasures; Jupiter, indicator of spiritual attainment, and Dragon's tail (Ketu) indicator of *moksha* or liberation of soul.

Of course the aspects, conjunction etc. must also be taken into account. When these houses are examined, we must also probe into the houses to that *bhava*, that is to say, if you have to examine the 10th house, you must examine the 7th house also, because it is the 10th house from the 10th. But when you look at the 7th house here, you must not mistake it for *kalatra* or the wife's *bhava*. View it also in the same way as you would examine the 10th house. In doing this, the strength of the Ascendant and its lord should not be lost sight of. The results and the effects of all the houses, their lords and indicators will only be in proportion to the strength of the lord of the Ascendant.

Supposing the sum total of all the pleasures in the world is 100, see how much the native is destined to be blessed with. You have a general idea of a natal chart by observing if there are malefics in angles and trines, if the lords of benefic houses are in malefic places, if the lords of benefic houses are strong or weak and the lords of malefic houses are strong or weak. Then proceed thus: Give the lord of the Ascendant, say 50 points. Examine all the *bhavas*, each separately as regards their aspects, associations etc. and put all these together giving them 25 points to the relative position of all the planets towards each other — 25 points. As in illustration :

Good	Adverse
Lord of the Ascendant therefore benefic	1
" " " natural benefic	1
" " " owns another benefic house	1
" " " is in an angle *(kendra)*	1
" " " has a beneficial aspect	1
" " " is between malefics	1
" " " has a malefic conjunction	1
" " " is in an inimical sign	1

Out of the total 8 points which we were able to assign to the lord of the Ascendant, the native secures 5 good points and 3 adverse points. The resultant 2 points are thus good ones. Therefore in the final analysis, the native gets only 20 good points.

Good	Adverse
Then, in the ascendant, there are two benefics	2
A malefic is aspecting	1

Then for the 2nd house and so on. Suppose all these 12 houses are assigned 100 points in all, out of which there are 80 good points, meaning 4/5th of the total, for these you will have to give 20 points, since we have a maximum of 25 points.

Then the relative position of planets to one another; *shasta-asthakas*, inimical, *sama-sapthakas* etc. must be taken into consideration. Suppose you give 10 points here, the whole horoscope now gets 50 points. This is certainly an average horoscope. In a horoscope like this, in *yoga dasha* the results will be just about half of what these planets ought to give. In horoscopes which get a larger number of points, the results of these *dashas* will be more beneficial. In adverse periods, the results will be comparatively less severe in intensity.

It may be difficult for a beginner to calculate all this, but as a few illustrations are worked out, it will not be necessary to work on paper and there will be a clear mental picture. Some experience will convince you about the utility of this method and it works well for all ordinary purposes.

In cases where in the Ascendant, the Moon and the lord of the Ascendant are situated, examine for confirmation from the houses occupied by the Sun, Jupiter and Venus as Ascendants. For, Jupiter is the benefactor of wealth etc. Venus is the benefactor of all material pleasures, comforts and enjoyments and the Sun is *Atma* and vigour.

In cases where all the four, i.e., lord of the Ascendant, the Moon, Jupiter and Venus are present in the Ascendant, it is always very good to examine the horoscope in the same way from the *navamsa* chart. Take the *navamsa* Ascendant as the birth sign and then proceed to find the average strength.

In cases where the lord of Ascendant gets a good number of benefic points and if in the other two divisions the adverse points are more, drop these out of consideration, for, a strong and well placed Ascendant lord will overcome much of the other weaknesses or deficiencies in the chart.

See in what birth star a planet is placed and who is the lord of this star according to *Vimshotri dasha* system, e.g., for *Aswini*, Ketu and if this planet be in an enemy's birth star or if the planet is situated in a star whose lord owns malefic houses from the Ascendant, reduce the *yoga* of the planet concerned.

Example: A man is born in the Libra Ascendant. If Mars is in the 9th sign Gemini and in *Punarvasu* star whose lord is Jupiter, Mars will not give good results, but will give more or less the effects of Jupiter which is bad, since Jupiter is the lord of the 3rd and 6th sign from the Ascendant.

The above points are by no means exhaustive. These are only a few illustrations to guide the reader. It will be found that all the information given in this and the previous chapters, must be freely used. These are generalised here. The results mentioned may vary, if there are other very strong reasons, such as powerful aspects, combinations etc.

Never exaggerate the results, especially the good ones. For, then one will be dishonest not only to himself, but also to the native who consults him to interpret his horoscope.

15

FEMALE HOROSCOPES

These is not much difference between male and female horoscopes except in the case of the 8th house which is the *mangalya* house. From this house, you predict the motherhood, or the period of the married state of a woman, tne death of her husband, her marital happiness etc. About her husband, we shall have to examine the 7th house, just as the 7th house in a man's horoscope has to be examined with regard to his wife.

The complexion of the body must be considered from the Ascendant and, the Moon Ascendant, as also in examining those most inexplicable traits, i.e., grace, beauty, sex appeal, tenderness, gait, peculiar physical and mental charm etc., the things which are woman's personal qualities. Besides the Ascendant, the 4th house, denoting family comforts should also be examined in detail.

In these days when the fusion of the West and the East is going on and no definite stage has yet been reached, it is very difficult to predict about conditions which essentially belonged to man, but which are now being explored and encroached upon by women. Widow remarriage is one of the most significant points which requires broad elucidation. In examining the *bhagya* of a woman, the method adopted hitherto was, that the good or evil in a woman's horoscope affects her father before she is married and her husband after she is married. Times are changing fast, so are men and a host of other things such as the mode of life, social norms and life style. Food habits are becoming more complex and intricate. So, the astrologer has to be a bit wary when he has to examine a woman's horoscope. In this chapter, a few hints will be given to guide the esteemed reader while analysing the horoscope of a woman.

A woman, born in an odd sign with the Moon also in an odd sign, is devoid of modesty, grace, etc. She has masculine traits and specially if this happens in a strong malefic ascendant, say, Leo, without benefic aspects, it is advisable for her to take up some profession, rather than running the risk of an early marriage. In such cases, the strength of the lords of the ascendants of the natives about to marry must be examined carefully.

If in one of them, the Ascendant and the Moon Ascendant, be an odd sign and the other an even sign, the effects mentioned above will be less marked.

If both the Ascendant and the Moon Ascendant be in even signs, the woman is really a woman in the true sense and more so when the Ascendant and the Moon Ascendant have beneficial aspects.

If the Ascendant or the Moon Ascendant should be strong, and there are malefics in it, and if the Moon, Mercury and Venus are not strong and if the Sun also is not strong, the woman is unsteady and would face hassles in her family/marital life. The aspect of Saturn and/or Mars on the 7th house from the Ascendant or on their lords or on the 2nd house and 1st lord is not desirable.

If Aries, Scorpio, Capricorn, and Aquarius be the ascendants and if the Moon and Venus be situated in such an ascendant and if strong malefics aspect it, such an ascendant and benefics do not aspect it, both the woman and her mother may be suspect about their character or reputation particularly in the Indian conditions, though it may not be so in the western social conditions.

If the Moon and Mercury both are situated in the ascendants, the woman is generally selfish and jealous.

If the Moon and Mercury be situated in the Ascendant, without the aspect of malefics, the woman will be of a good character, able, kind; sympathetic and charitable; more so, if the Sun is also strong in the natal chart.

If the Moon and Mercury, Venus and Jupiter or Mercury and Venus be situated in Ascendant, she will be gentle and exceptionally bright.

If three malefics be situated in Ascendant, the woman will be the reverse of that mentioned above and may have to struggle in life.

If the ascendant be an odd house and the Sun, Mars and Jupiter be strong and Mercury, the Moon and Venus be weak, she will be of masculine nature and may have humorous flirtations/attachments.

If the 7th house from Ascendant or the Moon be weak and not aspected by any benefic, the husband will be wicked. If Mercury or Saturn be in the 7th house and unaspected, the husband is likely to be impotent. If the Sun be in it, the husband rejects her. If Mars be in it and aspected by malefics, she may become a widow early in life.

If Saturn be in the 7th house and be aspected by malefics or even if Saturn be in conjunction with or aspects the lord of the 7th house, the woman marries late. Several malefics in the 7th house make the woman a widow. If a malefic be in the 7th house and aspected by another malefic, her husband rejects her. If there are benefics in the 7th house and the *navamsha lagna* be that of a benefic, the woman will be healthy and loved by her husband.

If Saturn and Venus be in each other's *navamsa* and aspect each other or if Taurus or Libra be the Ascendant and the *navamsa* be Aquarius, the woman may commit unnatural acts. She will assume a masculine nature and have sexual relations with other women.

If a malefic be in the 8th house, she could become a widow and this may happen during the period or sub-period of the planet whose *navamsa* is occupied by the lord of the 8th house.

If in the 8th house there be a malefic but a benefic from the 2nd house aspects the 8th house strongly, she predeceases her husband.

If a number of benefics be in the 8th house, she predeceases her husband.

A benefic planet in the 9th house with a malefic in the 7th house would make the female native a *sanyasini* or a religious philosopher or *yogi*.

If the lord of the 9th house and Jupiter be in the 6th, 8th or the 12th house, she may marry an old man, but if these two associate with Rahu or Ketu, the husband will be a villain or of unsavoury reputation.

A number of illustrations like those mentioned above can be enumerated such as :

The Sun in the 7th house gives a husband with fiery lustful eyes;

The Moon makes him voluptuous but sickly; Mars, cruel and indolent;

Mercury wealthy, good and learned;

Jupiter wealthy, long lived, powerful and lustful;

Saturn old, infirm, obstinate and wicked;

Venus lively, playful, wealthy and learned in the art of sexual enjoyment;

Rahu and Ketu low, evil-minded and selfish and so on.

However, these planets in the 7th house in their *navamsa* give a playful, gentle, good, happy, devoted and a learned husband, who has control over the senses, very old husband, handsome, loving and lustful husband respectively.

The conjunction or mutual aspect of the lord of the ascendant and the lord of the 7th house, or the lord of the 7th house and the lord of the 8th house, in a female horoscope is good. The former bestows conjugal happiness and the latter bestows a long life to the husband.

In a man's horoscope, the latter condition is positively bad, but the former is good. Further, though the respective planets may be natural or even temporary enemies, the results of the 7th house will be good, though this combination may not be so good for other matters.

It will be found that in all the above cases, the general characteristics of the planets have been taken into consideration; though these will be the main features, they are subject to varied modifications, changes etc. by aspect and/or conjunctions. In some cases, the results mentioned will be very pronounced and in others they will not be so apparent.

A number of other details can be given with reference to the *trimsamsa* etc. but they are not included herein. It will be thus seen that to make a woman a noble and true, these benefics, i.e., Jupiter, Venus, the Moon and Mercury should be as strong as possible. When the Sun is strong in a female horoscope, preferably in exaltation, many other drawbacks can be countered most conveniently and effectively.

The concept of marriage is undergoing vast changes on Indian scene and more and more girls are choosing to have love marriages instead of the arranged ones. The married women want to assert their own rights and their professional independence. More and more of them are taking up jobs and after marriage they neither want to give up their jobs nor their hard earned status, professional and financial and other assets. They can do so while their marriage remains intact. The love affairs from a female chart have to be ascertained from the 5th house. The 7th house stands for marital status and 12th house denotes conjugal affairs and the pleasures of the bed. To know whether a female native will go in for an arranged marriage or a love marriage, the 1st, 5th, 7th, 9th and 12th houses of the birth chart have to be carefully analysed alongwith Mars. If Mars is joined by Rahu and aspected by Saturn, the type may go in for a love marriage after carefully considering the compatibility angle with the husband to be.

As mentioned elsewhere in the book, the 1st, 5th and 9th houses in a native chart, particularly of female nativity are the most important ones and must be analysed properly as these throw light on the various important traits of a female native, including her love life.

16

MARITAL BLISS

Time for Marriage

It is very important to choose an auspicious date and time for one's marriage. Almost all Indian *panchangs* (Ephemeris) indicate important and auspicious dates and times for celebrating marriages. While certain sections of Hindus will have no objection to solemnizing the marriage in the month of *Ashadha* (provided the Sun has not moved into Cancer), others take objection to this. There is perfect agreement among the believers in the occult lovers that the time, the date, the day of the week, constellation and planetary position obtaining at the time of marriage should be auspicious from all the relevant angles. And this question comes up after the marriage proposal has been accepted by the two parties, and the compatibility seen to.

The lunar months of *Magha*, *Phalguna*, *Vaisakha* and *Jyestha* are considered to be most auspicious. *Kartika* and *Margasira* are only satisfactory. The other lunar months are not considered to be good and are thus not recommended. Some learned scholars feel that the marriages can be solemnized in the months of *Pushya* and *Chaitra* provided the Sun is in Capricorn and Aries respectively.

The following lunar days *viz.*, from the 11th day (the dark half or *Krishan Paksh*) to the New Moon, *Riktha Thithi*, 8th, 12th and 6th are unsuitable and should be thus not considered. The auspicious lunar days are the 2nd, 3rd, 5th, 7th, 10th, 11th and 13th of the *Shukal Paksh* (brighter half).

Among the weekdays : Mondays, Wednesdays, Thursdays and Fridays are more auspicious, Sundays and Saturdays medium, and Tuesdays are usually unsuitable.

The best and most auspicious asterisms (*Nakshatras*) are *Rohini, Margasira, Magha, Uttara-Phalguna, Hasta, Svati, Anuradha, Mula, Uttarashadha, Uttarabhadrapada* and *Revati*.

The first quarter of *Magha* and *Mula* and the last quarter of *Revati* are not auspicious. The other constellations not indicated are not suitable and should be avoided.

The following *yogas* should be rejected :

Vyatipata, Dhruva, Mrityu, Ganda, Vajra, Souta, Vishkambha, Atiganda, Vyaghata and *Parigha.Vishtikarana* must invariably be discarded.

Among the Zodiac signs, Gemini, Virgo and Libra are the best. Taurus, Cancer, Leo, Sagittarius and Aquarius are medium. The rest are considered to be good from the marital angle.

In deciding the *Mahurta* (auspicious time) for marriage, the 21 evil *doshas* which are normally avoided for auspicious works should first be considered. Sometimes, it becomes impossible to avoid them, in which case, it may become necessary to resort to other benefic neutralising influences after considering the totality of the circumstances of the natal charts of the bride and bridegroom to be.

An important aspect to be considered is that the Moon should not be in the 6th, 8th or 12th house from the girl's birth sign (*Janam Rashi*). And the constellation chosen should be such as is suitable for the girl's birth star (constellation). It should be an even star *viz.*, 2, 4, 6, 8, 11, 13, 15, 17, 18, 20, 22, 24, 26, 27. Although the ninth star is not even, yet it is also suitable. Similarly, the star numbers 18 and 27 whose addition number also comes to 9 are also suitable. In the case of a bride, the 1st, 10th and 19th stars are acceptable but not in the case of the groom.

Other important considerations are :

(1) The 7th house must be unoccupied by any planet.
(2) Mars should not be in the 8th house.
(3) Venus or Jupiter should not be in the 6th house.
(4) The Ascendant should not be hemmed in between malefics.
(5) The malefics should not occupy the Ascendant.
(6) The Moon in the election chart should not be associated with any other planet.

Apart from the above, the usual *Tarabala, Panchaka,* etc. aspects should be looked into. There are some special combinations which can neutralize adverse planetary influences. An attempt should be made to find out a really propitious moment. Jupiter, Mercury or Venus placed in the Ascendant, malefics in the 3rd house could constitute a powerful factor in making the Ascendant strong and powerful. The following are some of the good combinations which are favourable for the matrimonial election chart *(Muhurta).*

Mahendra Yoga, an auspicious combination requires Jupiter to occupy the Ascendant, Venus in the 8th house and the Sun in the house of gains or the 11th house.

Next to it in prominence is *Vishnupriya Yoga* which requires Venus to stay in the Ascendant with Jupiter in Mid Heaven (the 10th house) and the Sun and Mercury in the house of gains.

Sreenatha Yoga and *Samundra Yoga* are not so auspicious but give benefic results, when Venus occupies the house of income in the 2nd house, Jupiter and the Sun in twelfth and eighth signs respectively and Saturn in the sixth house. Similarly, Venus in the ascendant, Mercury occupying the 2nd house, Jupiter in the 4th house and Saturn in the 11th house could usher auspicious results for marriage ceremony.

Combination of Mercury, Jupiter and Venus in the ascendant signifies *Vijaya yoga.* Venus and Jupiter in the ascendant signifies *Vijaya yoga.* Venus and Jupiter in the Ascendant forms *Jaya yoga,* when either of them is elevated.

The following *Yogas* are also acceptable for matrimonial alliances :

(i) Saturn in 3rd house, Jupiter in 6th, the Sun in 10th and Mars in 11th — *Pushya Yoga.*

(ii) Mars in 3rd house, Saturn in the 6th, Venus in the 9th, Jupiter in 12th — *Maharshi Yoga.*

(iii) Venus in the ascendant, Jupiter in 11th house — *Ardhama Yoga.*

17

EFFECT OF INAUSPICIOUS
GANDANTHA CONSTELLATIONS
AT BIRTH

Let us nrst define what a *gandantha* constellation is. The junction
of the following pairs of stars, viz :

(1) *Jyeshta* and *Mula.*
(2) *Aslesha* and *Makha.*
(3) *Revati* and *Aswini* for a period of 7-1/2 *ghatikas* (three
    hours) is called *gandantha* and such junction produces much
    evil to persons born at such a junction.

These asterisms are called Gandantaras [Vulnerable Points]
and are considered to be highly inauspicious for the child and in
some cases for the parents and relatives. If there is a solar eclipse
or if the moon is on the horizon, the situation becomes more
critical. But if the child born under these inauspicious asterisms
survives he is expected to attain a very high position or status in
life and in some cases may attain the position of a minister.
Governor or an industrial magnate.

(A) The three hours must be taken to include the 1-1/2 hours
    at the end of the 1st star and 1-1/2 hours at the beginning
    of the 2nd star.
(B) The junction of *Jyeshta* and *Mula* for a period of 7-1/2
    ghatikas is technically called *Abhaukta Mula.* Any girl or
    boy born at such a junction brings about the ruin of the
    family into which he or she is born.

(C) If a person be born in *Jyeshta,* different effects are predicted for the ten divisions in which the *adyantam* (total) *ghatikas* of *Jyeshta* are divided.

If birth takes place during the :

(1) 1st division, the danger is to the grand mother.
(2) 2nd division, the danger is to the grand father.
(3) 3rd division, the danger is to the maternal uncle.
(4) 4th division, the danger is to the mother.
(5) 5th division, the danger is to the child.
(6) 6th division, the danger is to domestic animals, cattle and loss of wealth.
(7) 7th division, the danger is in both parents' families.
(8) 8th division, there is a danger of severe affliction to the whole race.
(9) 9th division, the danger is to the father-in-law if the child is a girl.
(10) 10th division, there is a danger of loss of almost everything.

Jyeshta

(A) If a girl is born during *Jyeshta* on a Tuesday, her eldest brother may face the danger of death.
(B) If a girl is born during *Mula* on a Sunday, her father-in-law may face the danger of death.
(C) If a person is born in the first *pada of Jyeshta,* his or her eldest brother may face serious danger.
(D) If a person is in born in the second *pada of Jyeshta,* the youngest of his elder brothers may face danger.
(E) If a person is born in the third *pada of Jyeshta,* his or her father may face danger of death.
(F) If a person is born in the fourth *pada of Jyeshta,* the born person himself may face danger of death.

Mula

(1) If a person be born in the first *pada of Mula,* his father may die.
(2) If a person be born in the second *pada of Mula,* his mother may die.
(3) If a person be born in the third *pada of Mula,* there will be loss of wealth.

(4) If a person be born in the fourth *pada of Mula*, there will be happiness.

The 15 divisions of Mula :

(1) If a person be born in the 1st division, his father may die.
(2) If a person be born in the 2nd division, the death of his father's brother may occur.
(3) If a person be born in the 3rd division, the death of a sister's husband may occur.
(4) If a person be born in the 4th division, the death of the paternal grandfather may occur.
(5) If a person be born in the 5th division, the death of the mother may take place.
(6) If a person be born in the 6th division, the death of the mother's sister may be caused.
(7) If a person be born in the 7th division, the death of mother's brother is likely.
(8) If a person be born in the 8th division, the death of a paternal uncle's wife may occur.
(9) If a person be born in the 9th division, the death of every thing is indicated.
(10) If a person be born in the 10th division, the death of all cattle is indicated.
(11) If a person be born in the 11th division, the death of servants is indicated.
(12) If a person be born in the 12th division, the death of the born child is possible.
(13) If a person be born in the 13th division, the death of his eldest brother may occur.
(14) If a person be born in the 14th division, the death of his sister may take place.
(15) If a person be born in the 15th division, the death of mother's father is indicated.

A slesha

(1) If a person be born in the first *pada*, there is no danger to any person.
(2) If a person be born in the second *pada*, there is the risk of losing money.
(3) If a person be born in the third *pada*, risk of losing mother.

(4) If a person be born in the fourth *pada,* the risk of losing his father is there.

Other Inauspicious Nakshatras

(1) If a person be born in the first *pada* of *Mula, Makha* or *Aswini,* there is the risk of death of the father.

(2) If a person be born in the fourth *pada* of *Revati, Jyeshta* or *Aslesha,* there is risk of death of both the parents and the child.

If a person be born during the above mentioned *ganda* stars :

(1) He loses his father if the birth takes place during the day.

(2) He loses his mother if the birth is during the night.

(3) He himself dies if the birth be in the junctions of day and night. The *ganda* period is 3-1/4 *ghatikas* at the end of *Revati, Aslesha* and *Jyeshta* at night, at the beginning of *Aswini, Makha* and mentioned stars in the junction between day and night.

The Moon

(A) Child born in the day in the Sagittarius Ascendant when the Moon is in *Purvashada,* may lose his father.

(B) Child born in the Cancer Ascendant, when the Moon is in *Pushya,* may lose his father.

(C) The child born when the Moon is in *Purvashada* or *Pushya* in the Ascendant, may lose his father if the birth be in the first *pada* of the star; may lose his mother if the birth be in the second *pada;* may lose the offspring till then born if the birth be in the third *pada;* may lose the mother's brothers if the birth be in the fourth *pada.*

(D) If, when the Moon is in the first *pada* of *Uttara-phalguni* or in the second and third *padas* of *Pushya,* or in the third *pada* of *Chitra,* or the first half *pada* of *Bharani* or in the third *pada* of *Hasta* or in the fourth *pada* of *Revati,* a boy is born the father may die, and if a girl is born the mother may die.

Duration of Danger

(A) The (risk or danger) period when the birth is in 1st *pada* of *Aswini* is 16 years.

(B) The *ganda* (risk of danger) period when the birth is in 1st *pada* of *Makha* is 8 years.

(C) The ganda (risk of danger) period when the birth is in *Jyeshta* is 1 year.

(D) The *ganda* (risk of danger) period when the birth is in *Chitra* is 4 years.

(E) The *ganda* (risk of danger) period when the birth is in *Aslesha* is 2 years.

(F) The *ganda* (risk of danger) period when the brith is in *Revati* is 1 year.

(G) The *ganda* (risk of danger) period when the birth is in *Uttraphalguni* is 2 months.

(H) The *ganda* (risk of danger) period when the birth is in *Pushya* is 3 months.

Other *Gandanthas*

(1) If a child is born in *Purvashada*, father may run the risk of death in the 9th month.

(2) If a child is born in *Hasta*, the father may die within 12 years.

(3) If a child is born in *Abhukta Mula*, (that is to say, at the junction of *Jyeshta* and *Mula*), the father may die soon after birth.

(4) If somehow the child born in *Abhukta Mula* lives long, he may bring his family into prominence and be prosperous. He may even command an army.

(5) The number of *ghatikas* of the 14th of *Krishna Paksha* should be ascertained and this be divided into six equal divisions.

   (a) If a child be born in the first portion of *Bahula* 14, it is auspicious.

   (b) If the birth be in the second portion of *Bahula* 14, father may face danger of death.

   (c) If the birth be in the third portion of *Bahula* 14, mother may face risk of death.

   (d) If the birth be in the fourth portion of *Bahula* 14, mother's brother may face risk of death.

   (e) If the birth be in the fifth portion of *Bahula* 14, brothers may face severe affliction and risk of death.

   (f) If the birth be in the sixth portion of *Bahula* 14, the child itself may die.

(g) If any child be born on the new Moon day or in any portion of new Moon in the early morning, that child unless it be a girl, may bring adversity to the family.

Further Probabilities

(1) If a child be born under the same star as father's or under the 10th star from the father's, the father may die.

(2) If a child be born in the same birth Ascendant or the same *nakshatra navamsa* as the father, the father may die soon after birth.

(3) If a child be born in *Musala* or *Mudgara yoga*, there may be adversity and losses to the family.

(4) If a child be born in *Vishti karana*, he may be poor and may have to struggle for survival.

(5) If a child be born in *Gulika yoga*, he may have a defective limb.

(6) If a person be born in *Rikta tithi* he may become barren.

(7) If a person be born in *Yamakantaka yoga*, he may be a cripple.

(8) If a person be born in a star assailed by a planet, he may suffer from a disease.

(9) If a person be born in *Vyatipata yoga*, he may have a defective limb.

(10) If a person be born in *Parigha yoga*, the child born may die.

(11) If a person be born in *Vaidhruti yoga*, the father may face risk to life.

(12) If a person be born in *Vishkumba yoga*, there may be loss of wealth.

(13) If a person be born in *Sula yoga*, he may suffer from colic pain.

(14) If a person be born in *Ganda yoga*, he may have disease in throat or enlargement of thyroid gland.

Other Predictions

(1) If a child be born with teeth, there may be damage to the family from the 2nd to the end of 4th month.

(2) If at the birth of a child, the teeth begin to grow, the father may die in the 6th month.

(3) However, if nothing happens during the six months, then all may go on well.

Calculation of *Nakshatras*

(1) (A)   The star in which the Moon is placed at the time of birth, is called the birth star (*janma nakshatram*)

   (B)   The 10th star from the birth *nakshatra* is called the *Karma nakshatra*.

   (C)   The 16th star from the *Janma nakshatra* is called the *Sanghatika nakshatra*.

   (D)   The 18th star from the *Janma nakshatra* is called *Samadurga nakshatra*.

   (E)   The 19th star from the *Janma nakshatra* is called *Adhana nakshatra*.

   (F)   The 23rd star from the *Janma nakshatra* is called the *Vainashika nakshatra*.

   (G)   The 25th star from the *Janma nakshatra* is called the *Jathi nakshatra*.

   (H)   The 26th star from the *Janma nakshatra* is called the *Abhishika nakshatra*.

   (I)   The 27th star from the *Janma nakshatra* is called the *Abhishika nakshatra*.

(2) (A)   If the above stars, *janma*, *karma* and others are hidden or concealed by the intervention of malefic planets at the time of birth, the child born may face risk of death.

   (B)   If the above stars are concealed by benefic planets, they may produce beneficial results.

(3) (A)   The *ganda* in the months of *Ashada*, *Pushya*, *Margasira* and *Jyeshta* affects human beings.

   (B)   In the month of *Makha*, the *ganda* is death.

Thee Effects *Vela* (Time)

(1) If born in the *Satva* portion, the child is eloquent and aware of the duties of the wise, persevering, pure, lustrous, learned, beautiful, with no enemies.

(2) If born in the *Rajas* portion, the child is happy, wealthy, famous handsome, strong, a conqueror of foes, love sick, unkind to relations.

(3) If born in the *Tamas* portion he would be getting others' wealth and women, be unhappy, steal and quarrel with relations and elders, and be fickle-minded.

(4) A day of 24 hours consists of 16 *artha jamas;* each *artha jama* is 3-$3/4$ *ghatikas* or one hour and half. *Tamas, Satwa* and *Rajas* govern the *artha jamas* in the order given below :

On Sunday the first and last *artha jama* is *Tamas.*
On Monday the first and last *artha jama* is *Satwa.*
On Tuesday the first and last *artha jama* is *Rajas.*
On Wednesday the first and last *artha jama* is *Tamas.*
On Thursday the first and last *artha jama* is *Satwa.*
On Friday the first and last *artha jama* is *Rajas.*
On Saturday the first and last *artha jama* is *Tamas.*

The Effects of *Kala Hora*

(1) Each day is divided into 24 *kala horas* or hours, Jupiter, Mars, the Sun, Venus, Mercury, the Moon and Saturn are the lords of these *hora* for all the hours in succession.

The *hora* in any day of the week begins with the planet by which the day is named. The *hora* in the night of any day begins with the fifth planet from that by which the day is named.

The 1st *hora* on Monday is of the Moon.
The 2nd *hora* on Monday is of Saturn.
The 3rd *hora* on Monday is of Jupiter.
The 4th *hora* on Monday is of Mars.
The 5th *hora* on Monday is of the Sun.
The 6th *hora* on Monday is of Venus.
The 7th *hora* on Monday is of Mercury.
The 8th *hora* on Monday is of the Moon.
The 9th *hora* on Monday is of Saturn.
The 10th *hora* on Monday is of Jupiter.
The 11th *hora* on Monday is of Mars.
The 12th *hora* on Monday is of the Sun.
The 13th *hora* on Monday is of Venus and this is the beginning of the night on Monday, and so on.

(2) (A) The effect of a birth in a *hora* of the Sun is pain and fatigue.

(B) The effect of birth in a *hora* of the Moon is prosperity.

(C) The effect of birth in *hora* of Mars is sorrow and sickness.

(D) The effect of birth in *hora* of Mercury is learning and wealth.

(E) The effect of birth in *hora* of Jupiter is every blessing.

(F) The effect of birth in *hora* of Venus is conjugal bliss.

(G) The effect of birth in *hora* of Saturn is loss of property.

Children born in these *padas* are prone to *gandas* in *Balarishta*, for they are powerful in causing death. But these are subject to other conditions mentioned elsewhere. If the counteracting influences are greater, these will have no effect. The junctions of Leo, Scorpio or Sagittarius have no effect. The junction of *Revati* and *Aswini*, *Aslesha* and *Makha* and *Jyeshta* and *Mula* are very dangerous.

These are *Bala-Arishta Nakshatras Padas* (Quarters):

Aswini	2	4		
Rohini	1	2	3	4
Makha	2			
Chitra	2			
Jyeshta	3			
Dhanishta	2			
Bharani	2			
Mrigasira	1			
Uttara	2			
Visakha	4			
Mula	2	3		
Satabhisha	1			
Krittika	3			
Pushya	1			
Hasta	3	4		
Anuradha	3			
Uttara-ushada	1			
Uttara-bhadrapada	4			

18

AYURDAYA OR LONGEVITY

Perhaps the most difficult part in the study of astrology is the fixing of a person's span of life. It is said that a man's life is shortened or lengthened by his deeds, conduct and manner of living.

Those are long-lived who are virtuous in thought and deed, who are pious and devoted to God, who eat wholesome and simple food, who keep their senses under control, who preserve their character, who observe good conduct and who do *Pranyama*.

Premature or untimely death is the lot of people who commit sins, covet other's property, possess stealing tendencies, abuse God and pious people and are gluttons.

Sudden and unexpected death is said to occur to people who do not believe in the moral forces, who are wicked, who are enemies of God and men, who unlawfully take property of the others, who are a source of terror to all, who are torchbearers, who abandon their duties, who live by sinful deeds and do not obey holy or sacred laws.

However carefully and correctly one may try to fix the longevity of a native's life, the native himself may overcome death. Generally speaking, astrology helps one to probe into this question and the following points must be noted carefully.

There are four stages in life :

(1) *Balarishta* (or death in early life),
(2) Short life (death within 30 years),
(3) Middle life (death within about 60 years),
(4) Long life (death between 60-75 years).

The first is *Balarishta*. This means death in early life, in childhood. There is some difference of opinion on this aspect among occultists. Some people think death at 5 years, 8 years or 12 years is to be considered as *Balarishta*.

There is another school of thought whose belief is that the death in the first *dasa*, whatever be its duration, whether a few days or a long period of years as in the case of Venus major period, must be considered to be *Balarishta*.

Death in the 2nd major period from birth will be *Alpayu* or a short life.

For *Balarishta*, the following points have to be very carefully noted. There are Four *sandhis* or meetings :

(1) *Nakshatra sandhi,* ending of one *nakshatra* and beginning of the other *nakshatra* gh. 1 or 36 minutes either way. Some others hold a shorter period also.
(2) Ascendant *sandhi* : ending of one Ascendant and the beginning of the other, 12 minutes before and after. Some others hold 6 minutes.
(3) *Tithi Sandhi* : There are 15 *tithis* in *Shukal Pakshami* and 15 *tithis* in *Krishna Pakshami,* in a month. The end of a *tithi* and the beginning or the either way. Some others hold a shorter period.
(4) *Dina Sandhi,* the junction of day and night or night and day, 12 minutes either way are serious. Two *sandhis* may cause ill-health, three *sandhis,* serious ill-health. If all the four *sandhis* should operate simultaneously, the chances of death of the native may go up.

For a birth by day in the dark half or birth by night in the bright half, there will be an easy escape from *Balarishta*, even if the Moon occupies 6th or 8th house and is aspected both by malefics and benefics.

The Moon being in the 6th, 8th or 12th house from the Ascendant, especially with the aspect of malefic planets, is a strong case of *Balarishta*. Here also, if the house occupied by the Moon is that of a natural benefic, the *Balarishta* effect may vanish. For instance, with the Moon being in Taurus, the 6th house for Sagittarius Ascendant may be a case of *Balarishta* but because the Moon happens to be in the house of Venus, a natural benefic, the evil is comparatively reduced provided there is no aspect of any malefic planets even though the aspect of a benefic planet is denied. The Moon being in the 6th house, say, in Aries is again definitely not a *Balarishta* since that house happens to be that of Mars, a natural malefic, the *dosha* is great even though there may not be a malefic aspect and though there may be an aspect of a benefic. The ascendant between malefic planets, say, Saturn and Rahu on either side, and the ascendant itself having the aspect of malefic planets, is a strong point for *Balarishta*.

So also the Moon being heavily afflicted as being between malefics and having malefic aspects is again a factor for *Balarishta*. All these points have to be noted very carefully before deciding the short, medium or long life of the person whose chart is being analysed. Of course, there are so many other conditions but the few important ones have been spelled out here.

As is the case with every other house, the 8th house has to be judged from the strength of the house itself, the lord of the house, the 3rd house and its lord, the strength of Saturn, the relative positions of Saturn and the lord of the 8th house and the Lord of Ascendant.

There are three important houses which are death-inflicting; the strength of these and their lords is given here in their ascending order.

(1)   The lord of the 7th house,
(2)   the planets in the 7th house,
(3)   the lord of the 1st house,
(4)   the planets in Ascendant.
(5)   the planet in conjunction with the lord of the Ascendant,
(6)   the lord of the 2nd house,

(7)   the planets in the 2nd house,

(8)   the planets in conjunction with the lord of the 2nd house.

After deciding about the kind of horoscope with reference to a short, middle or long life, we can examine the *Maraka* planet. If in a short-lived horoscope, about the age of 30, the person is passing through the *dasha* period of a planet, it will kill in one of the malefic or strong *maraka bhuktis* as explained above and elsewhere under the chapter on the *dashas and bhuktis* (Chapter 19).

If after deciding that a horoscope is medium-lived even though the person may be passing through a strong *maraka dasha* at the age of about 30 years or thereabouts, the person may not die during this *dasha* but he may have other serious problems. These must be carefully remembered in predicting or finding out about the *maraka* (death inflicting) planet. Also consult the chapter on some peculiarities of ascendants (Chapter 11). In cases where the longevity and *maraka dasha* factors coincide, death may take place in the sub-period of a *maraka*, malefic enemy of the *dasha-natha*, whichever is stronger. The lord of the 11th house is always a potential *maraka*.

The maximum age of a native is said to be 120 years. Natives will have generally long life if 4 or more planets occupy 1st to 4th houses from Ascendant. Persons have medium life if 4 or more planets occupy 5th to 8th houses from Ascendant. Natives have a short life if 4 or more planets occupy 9th to 12th houses from the Ascendant.

There is a short life in the following conditions :

(1)   The Lord of Ascendant being weak, malefic planets occupy 6th and 8th houses from Ascendant, without the aspect or conjunction of any benefic planets,

(2)   The Lord of Ascendant being weak and malefics occupying angles,

(3)   The lord of the Ascendant and the Ascendant being without the aspect of benefics and malefic planets being in the 2nd and the 12th houses from Ascendant and its lord,

(4) the lord of the Ascendant and of the 8th house, exchanging their houses without any beneficial aspect but with malefic aspects or associations,

(5) the lord of the Ascendant being a malefic occuyping the 8th house, and the lord of the 8th house being with the aspect of malefics alone, and not the aspect of benefics,

(6) lord of Ascendant and the 6th house, together in the 6th house,

(7) the lord of the Ascendant being weak and the lord of the 8th house not occuyping an angle,

(8) the Moon being between the lords of 1st and 8th houses with Jupiter in the 12th house from Ascendant,

(9) waning Moon and Ascendant both being aspected by or being in conjunction with malefics without the association or aspect of any benefic planets,

(10) either Ascendant or its lord and the lord of the house occupied with malefics alone without any beneficial aspect or conjunction,

(11) the lord of the Ascendant and the 8th house occupy fixed signs or if one occupies a movable sign and the other a dual sign,

(12) the Ascendant being a dual house and the Moon occupying another dual sign,

(13) the lord of the 8th house and Saturn both being depressed and Ascendant having malefics in it,

(14) Saturn and the Moon occupying the 7th house,

(15) the aspect or association of malefics with the lord of the 8th house and Saturn without a benefic aspect or conjunction,

(16) the lord of the 8th house and Saturn occupying malefic *navamsas*,

(17) the association of the Moon and Saturn eleswhere when the Sun is in the 8th house from the Ascendant,

(18) the Sun and the Moon in the Ascendant and malefics in the 8th and 12th houses from Ascendant,

(19) the lord of the Ascendant in conjunction with Ketu,

(20) the Moon in the 6th, 8th or 12th house and malefics in the 8th and 12th houses.

There is a medium life span generally in the following circumstances :

(1) The lord of the Ascendant being strong, Jupiter occupying an angle or trine, and malefics in the 6th, 8th or 12th houses,

(2) the association of benefics with the lord of the Ascendant, benefics in the 4th house and the lord of the Ascendant being aspected by Jupiter,

(3) the lord of the Ascendant being strong and aspected by benefics and the Moon being in Aries,

(4) the lord of the Ascendant in the 9th house and the lord of the 5th house in Ascendant,

(5) the lord of the Ascendant being in conjunction with Jupiter or occupying an angle or trine,

(6) the lords of the Ascendant and the 8th house exchanging their houses and having no malefic aspect or conjunction,

(7) the lord of the Ascendant, Jupiter and/or Venus being in angle,

(8) the lord of the Ascendant and the lord of the 8th house in benefic houses with the benefic aspect,

(9) the lord of the Ascendant and the Moon being together and aspected by benefics,

(10) the lord of the Ascendant and the Sun being friends,

(11) the Ascendant being a movable sign, and the Moon occupying a movable sign,

(12) Saturn in Ascendant, Jupiter in the 4th house and the Sun and the Moon in the 10th house,

(13) Jupiter and Moon together in a house with the aspect or association of the lord of Ascendant,

(14) lord of the 8th house in the 8th house and benefics in quadrants or *kendras* from the 8th house,

(15) the lord of 1st and 9th houses being associated or aspecting each other or occupying each other's sign without any malefic aspect,

(16) Ketu in Ascendant, the Moon in the 5th house and Jupiter in the 9th house being strong, without any of these having a malefic aspect,

(17) Jupiter and Venus in the Ascendant or the 4th house and Saturn in the 10th house with the Moon in the 6th house,

(18) the lord of the 8th house and Saturn being in conjunction, preferably with a benefic aspect,

(19) when the benefics are in angles from the 8th house in an angle or a trine from the Ascendant and having the aspect of Jupiter and Venus.

There is long life in the following cases :

(1) The lord of Ascendant in an angle with the aspect or assoication of Jupiter and Venus,

(2) exaltation of any 3 planets, the lord of Ascendant being in association with any one of them and the 8th house being free from any malefic aspect and having beneficial aspect of association,

(3) Saturn or the lord of the 8th house being in conjunction with an exalted planet or having in its aspect the exalted planet not being an enemy of Saturn,

(4) malefics in the 3rd, 6th and 11th houses, benefics in an angle or trines and the lord of Ascendent being strong,

(5) the lord of Ascendant being strong and occupying an angle, malefics in 6th and 12th houses, and the lord of the 10th house in exaltation,

(6) the lord of Ascendant and the lord of the house occupied by the lord of the 8th house being in it or together,

(7) the lord of Ascendant occupying an angle, trine exaltation when Ascendant is a dual sign,

(8) Ascendant being a dual sign, two malefics occuyping an angle from lord of Ascendant,

(9) Jupiter and the Moon together in Cancer, Mercury and Venus together in an angle and other planets, in 3rd, 6th, 11th houses,

(10) all planets occuyping 7 to 12 houses,

(11) five or more planets occupying the 5th or the 9th house from Ascendant with the exception of the lord of the 8th house,

(12) all planets occuyping odd houses when Ascendant is an odd house,

(13) lords of the Ascendant 8th and 10th houses occupying angles or trines and Saturn being strorg,

(14) Jupiter, Mercury and Venus occuyping together anyone of the angles, without any malefic aspect,

(15) the Sun, Mars and Saturn together in 3rd, 6th or 11th houses without any association or aspect,

(16) Jupiter in the Ascendant, Venus in 4th house and Saturn and Moon in the 10th house without the aspect or association of malefics,

(17) Jupiter, Mercury and Venus in the 5th or the 9th houses, Saturn in exaltation without the aspect or association of malefics,

(18) the Sun, Mars, Saturn and Rahu in 3rd, 6th, 11th houses with aspects of benefics.

Death

Death may take place generally during the following major periods :

During the major period of a planet occupying the 30th degree of a house,

During the native's 4th major period if it is of Saturn; the 5th dasha if it is of Mars; 6th major period if it is of Rahu.

During the 3rd, 5th or 7th *dasha* of a planet, from that of a planet in depression, in the 6th house, or eclipsed by the Sun *(Astangata)*.

Death is likely to occur in the period of the strongest of the following planets, as they are *Chhidra grahas*.

(1) During the period of the lord of the 8th house,

(2) during the period of the planet in the 8th house,

(3) during the *dasha* of the planet aspecting the 8th house,

(4) during the period of the greatest enemy of the lord of the 8th house,

(5) during the period of the planet in association with the lord of the 8th house.

19

DASHAS AND BHUKTIS
(Major-Periods and Sub-Periods)

By this time, the reader must have learnt how to assess the horoscope regarding its general strength and the strength of the lord of *lagna*, for, the influence of *dasha* depends on this most important point.

Of course, the strength of the lord of *dasha* also may be examined in the same way as the lord of *lagna*. Please refer to the chapter on "How to Examine a Horoscope". Having decided its strength, find out what a planet is capable of producing—good or not so good results; good if he is the owner of benefic houses and bad if he owns bad houses.

Here also a subtle distinction can be made between the *dasha* of a natural benefic becoming a malefic as the lord of 3rd and 8th houses from *lagna* as in the case of *Kanya lagna*.

The idea contained here is that a natural malefic will not be so bad a owner of bad houses as a natural malefic owning bad houses. The natural trend or inclination of the planets is taken into consideration. Then again, the reverse case may be examined. Jupiter in the previous case, for, Mars owns a stronger *kona* or trine, the 9th while the lordship of the 2nd house is common to both. Given the same conditions, the *dashas* of Jupiter and Mars will go equally well so far as money and preferment in service etc., are concerned, but there will be more peace and mental happiness in the *dasha* of Jupiter, a natural benefic indicating plenty than in the *dasha* of Mars, a natural malefic, being forced to do good against its own inclination. A *dasha*-lord gives the effects which are his own as *karaka* or indicator, those of the houses which he owns, those of the houses which he occupies, and those of the planets which are in conjunction with it, or are aspecting it. Of course, common sense will prevent an astrologer from predicting that a young boy in his early teens passing through a favourable Guru *dasha* will have children, or if he is passing through a favourable *dasha* of the Sun as the lord of the 9th house in conjunction with *Budha*, in the case of *Dhanus lagna*, will have preferment in service or a vocation. Such obvious things will have to be ruled out.

Then what becomes of the effects of this *dasha*? During this period, the parent or guardian gets the benefit, incidentally improving. Instances are not wanting and show that where it has been observed that until a certain age, a boy's education progressed very satisfactorily and thereafter a number of failures before success and in some cases a complete breakdown, or success after certain initial setbacks, as a result of such periods.

People with an apparently very powerful horoscope with a number of *yogas* have not achieved much in life, compared to apparently mediocre horoscopes. The astrologer is then put into great difficulty in trying to solve this problem. Many things are then thought of, like *navamsa*, *dasamsa* and so on. They are all very true. They must be paid attention to. But very often we forget one important thing — the lord of *lagna*. The I is the pivot. I have friends, I have wealth, I have good parents, I have a good wife and family and so on. Therefore it is necessary that though the planetary positions have promised certain things, I should be capable of receiving and enjoying them.

How is this I or the lord of the Ascendant placed from these *yoga* giving planets? If badly and adversely placed, the effects will not be much evident, though at a particular period, the promise has been fulfilled, the next period will completely wipe out everything. If the lord of *lagna* is unfavourably placed from *yoga-karakas*, and very well-placed from *avayoga-karaka* planets giving good and evil results, respectively, the native will get the latter more than the former. An intelligent student of astrology should never lose sight of this fact.

The Lords of Sub-Periods

These also must be considered in the same way as the lords of the Major-Period. Having ascertained its capacity to do evil or good, the position of the sub-period lord from the *dasanatha* must be seen. Favourable positions such as 2nd, 4th, 5th, 9th, 10th or 11th houses from *dasha* lord will be productive of very good results; 1st and 7th houses mediocre results while positions in 3rd, 6th, 8th or 12th houses are positively indicative of bad results. Major-period lord and the sub-period lord being natural friends is much better than being temporary friends. Both the major-period lord and sub-period lord if they happen to own good houses, and if the sub-period lord is well placed from the major-period lord, of course, yield benefical results.

Experience shows that if the major-period lord and the sub-period lord be the owners of evil houses — 3rd, 6th, 8th or 12th and if they are placed unfavourably from each other, especially in 6th, 8th, or 12th houses from each other, very good results are seen during their *dashas* and sub-period. The extent of benefit depends on the strength of the Ascendants and its lord and the general strength in the make-up of the natal chart of the individual.

One can be fairly accurate in his predictions about a *dasha*, if the following points are kept in view :

1. Examine the *dasha* lord from the Ascendant.
2. Examine the *dasha* lord from natal Ascendant.
3. Examine the *dasha* lord from the position of the lord of Ascendant.

Examine also the sub-period lord in the same way as the lord of the major and having arrived at a conclusion, consider the sub-period lord with reference to major-period lord. Make the house where lord of the major-period is situated in the Ascendant for the time being, and then see what houses from this house, the sub-period lord owns. If he owns benefic houses, both from Ascendant and major-period lord and is favourably placed as explained above, the results will be very satisfactory. The sub-period lord being a malefic from the Ascendant and well-placed from major-period lord, will yield bad results but if the sub-period lord owns good houses from major-period lord and is well-placed from him, the bad results will be less pronounced.

Again, the sub-period lord being a benefic from Ascendant and well-placed from Ascendant lord, but if he happens to own bad house or houses from the major-period lord, the good results will be less pronounced.

It may be mentioned here, that Venus in the 11th house from Ascendant or the Ascendant Moon, or from the major-period lord has always produced very bad resutls, more so especially without the association or aspect of any other planet. Venus as the lord of the 11th house is much worse than any other planet. The 11th house is a good one only because it is the 12th house from the 12th house, meaning a loss of loss etc. But it is the 6th to the 6th house, *bhava* to *bhava* and therefore bad. The house itself is considered good but its lordship is bad.

If the major-period lord is good and the sub-period lord is bad, and if they are adversely placed from each other, the results will not be very bad. If the major-period lord is bad and the sub-period lord is good and adversely placed from each other, the results will not be good. If well-placed, the results will not be disagreeable.

Sthula Kala-Dashas

The following are the major-period for every person from his birth. The dashas of planets who give trouble during the said *kala* major-period are also given. If the currentm major-period of a person according to *Vimshotri* falls in such cruel planets major-period, the planet cannot give good results, as shown below.

				From	The cruel major-period according to the *Vimshorati*.
1st	*Sthula*	*Kala*	**Period**	Mars. Birth to 2 years.	Saturn.
2nd	"	"	"	Budha. 3 to 8 years.	Rahu.
3rd	"	"	"	Guru. 9 to 24 years.	Moon.
4th	"	"	"	Sun. 25 to 42 years.	Venus.
5th	"	"	"	Sani. 43 to 61 years.	Ketu. (Dragon's tail)
6th	"	"	"	Rahu. 62 to 93 years.	Mercury.

Example : A child getting a Rahu Major-Period according to *Vimshotari dasa* will not get good results between 3 to 8 years for, according to *sthula kala-dasa* will be that of Mars, for which the cruel planet is Rahu.

From 1st, 4th and 9th houses and from the Sun, happiness of and from the father should be predicted.

From the lords of 1st, 3rd, 8th and 10th *ayurdaya*.

From 2nd, 5th, 7th and 10th houses, pilgrimage matters.

From the 3rd, 9th and 11th houses, matters regarding brothers. From Jupiter and 5th house children.

From the 7th and 2nd houses and Venus the wife, and her accomplishments. In the case of a woman, consider Jupiter instead of Venus.

From the 12th, going to far and distant places, including foreign lands.

From the 10th house, the Sun, Mercury, Jupiter and Saturn, all the results of the 10th house.

The Lords of the 5th and 9th houses give good results, including foreign lands.

The Lords of the 3rd, 6th and 12th houses give good results.

The Moon, Jupiter, Venus and Mercury as lords of angles cannot give good results.

Malefics as lords of angles give good results.

The Lords of 5th and 9th houses, must be treated as benefics, whether natural benefics or not.

The Lords of angles though natural malefics must be treated as benefics in bestowing results.

The Lords of the angles if they are natural benefics must be considered as malefics in giving results, during their major-period.

The Lords of 3rd, 6th, 8th, 11th and 12th houses from the Ascendant or the Moon.

The Ascendants are malefics even though they may be natural benefics.

Generally speaking, if the 4th *dasha* from birth be that of Saturn, the 5th be that of Mars, the 6th be that of Jupiter and if the 7th be that of Rahu, the person passes through great difficulties and may also die during these major-periods. If any one of these planets owns bad houses from the *lagna* and is strong or exalted, the danger is very great; if debilitated or completely eclipsed, the trouble will be less.

The aspect of benefics though they may be lords of malefic houses, e.g., Jupiter, must always be considered good and beneficial. The aspect of malefics, though they may be lords of benefic houses, for instance Saturn, must always be considered to be bad.

20

GOCHARA — THE TRANSIT OF PLANETS

This is a method by which the present condition of a native is examined with the help of the transitory position of planets with reference to the position of the Moon in the radical horoscope. Some look into this with reference to the Ascendant also. It must be borne in mind that this only helps the major-period and sub-period results or, in a sense serves as a moderator. One cannot rely on the results of transits alone. The question will be why the Moon alone and not the Ascendant, is relevant for assessing results of day-to-day transits. In the Ascendant there is the *Atma* also—besides the general structure of the physical body and the *Atma* is beyond the influence of planets. But the Moon is the mind besides having to do with the body. The purpose is to find out how the body and the mind are being influenced by the transits of planets.

The following general rules may be observed in examining the results of *Gochara* [Transits]. Even when a planet is favourably placed, it will not give good results if it suffers from *vedha* and there are a number of these *vedhas*.

When the planet is moving in houses mentioned in the top line from the Moon, it is expected to give good results. But if there is a planet in any of the houses mentioned under, the planet gets *Vedha* and gives inauspicious results. For instance, the Sun in the 6th house from the Moon gives bad results but if any planet, excepting Saturn, is moving at that time in the 12th

house from the radical Moon, the Sun will give the bad results
of the 12th house and not the good results of the 6th house in
which he is moving. In the same way results for all other planets
should be considered. Conversely, if the Sun is passing though
9th, 12th, 4th or 5th houses and if any planet excepting Saturn is
in 3th, 6th, 10th or 11th house respectively, the Sun would give
good results of 3th, 6th, 10th or 11th houses as the case may be.
It must be remembered that there is no *vedha* between the Sun
and Saturn, as between the Moon and Mercury.

The following chart will give good indication of the result
of transits.

Chart

Planet	Houses	Good / *Vedha*
The Sun	3rd 6th 10th 11th 9th 12th 4th 5th	Give good results from the Radical *Vedha* Houses.
The Moon	1th 3rd 6th 7th 10th 11th 5th 6th 12th 2nd 4th 8th	Good Houses. *Vedha* Houses.
Mars	3rd 6th 11th 12th 9th 5th	*Good* Houses. *Vedha* Houses.
Saturn	3rd 6th 11th 12th 9th 5th	Good Houses. *Vedha* Houses.
Mercury	2nd 4th 6th 8th 10th 11th 5th 3rd 9th 1st 8th 12th	Good Houses. *Vedha* Houses.
Jupiter	2nd 5th 7th 9th 11th 12th 4th 3rd 10th 9th	Good Houses. *Vedha* Houses.
Venus	1th 2nd 3rd 4th 5th 8th 9th 11th 12th 8th 7th 1st 10th 9th 5th 11th 3rd 6th	Good Houses. *Vedha* Houses.

Besides the sign *vedha* mentioned above, there are many
others. Planets in a particular sign cause *vedha* to planets in
other sign. For instance, Mercury when passing through a sign,
if there are no planet or planets in the 3rd, 5th, 8th, 9th and 12th
houses, gives good results and so on for all other planets. The

anga-gochara, paksha-bala, sankranti result, birth constellation and week days and so on also have to be considered. For ordinary purposes, the reader is requested to note in what house from the Moon a planet is moving.

According to the rules given above the results will be good or bad. For instance, with the Sagittarius sign, the Jupiter in the 11th house, i.e., Libra is expected to give good results. In this sign there are 3 *nakshatras*: *Chittra*, *Swati* and *Visakha*. Their respective lords are Mars, Rahu and Jupiter. Jupiter will give better results when moving either in *Chittra* or *Visakha*, than in *Swati* whose lord is Rahu, and an enemy of Jupiter, and so on for all other planets.

Then the most important point which stands above all these, is the *ashtaka-varga*. If a planet is moving in an unfavourable sign from the Moon and if in its own *ashtaka-virga* the planet gets more than four points, the evil is considerably decreased. If there are less than four points bad results are even more pronounced, as the points decrease in number and if there are no points, there is real trouble and danger. Of course in favourable positions, more points mean better results. Less points mean comparatively less favourable results.

In some parts of India, the child's name is given as far as possible from the letter denoted by the Constellation or at least the name is given beginning with the letter indicated by the constellation *pada* and another name also is given for ordinary purposes. When a person without a horoscope consults an astrologer, he is able to find out the major-period through which the native is passing. Of planets which have a much less period, the difference in the major-period will be correct up to 2 years at the most if he was born in the major-period of Venus who has a span of 20 years. If he was born in the major-period of a planet which has a much less period, the difference in the balance of major-period will be much less. Generally from the Ascendant as well as from the Moon Ascendant, the major-periods are examined and in the absence of a regular horoscope, from the the Moon Ascendant astrologer can decide the exact major-period he is passing through and with the help of the present transitory movement of the planets, he can arrive at a definite and right conclusion fairly well. This method is not followed in some parts of India. It will be very advantageous. to astrologer they consult by naming their children after the letter of the *nakshatra pada* of their birth.

21

ASHTAKA - VARGA OR THE EIGHT GROUPS

(a) This chapter is called the *ashtaka-varga* or the group of eight, because calculations for this *varga* have to be made in respect of eight groups viz., the seven planets and the Ascendant. It is with reference to these eight group calculations that events in a man's life are predicted after determining the benefit and adverse influences that the various planets cause during their transit through the twelve signs of the Zodiac, or the twelve houses of a natal chart. The *ashtaka-vrga* signifies the eight sources of energy for each planet, including the Ascendant. Rahu and Ketu are omitted from this system because of their shadowy nature.

(b) In order to prepare the *ashtaka-varga*, one should have the *rashi* horoscope of the native. It is only with reference to the *rashi* chart that *ashtaka-varga* horoscope can be prepared and results predicted therefrom.

(c) The *ashtaka-varga* horoscope consists of 8 parts: the one for each planet and the eighth is the sum total of all the planets.

They are named below :

(1) The Sun's *ashtaka-varga*.
(2) The Moon's *ashtaka-varga*.
(3) Mars *ashtaka-varga*.
(4) Mercury's *ashtaka-varga*.

(5) Jupiter's *ashtaka-varga.*

(6) Venus *ashtaka-varga.*

(7) Saturn's *ashtaka-varga.*

(8) The *sarvashtaka-varga.*

The first seven are called the *bhinnashtaka-varga* in contrast to *sarvashtaka-varga.*

(d) The method of preparing the *ashtaka-varga* horoscope is this. Take the planets in order one by one from the *rashi* horoscope of the person and in a blank horoscope form place some mark or point in the respective houses as mentioned in the following rules and then total the number of marks of points and place the total number in that house for that planet's *ashtaka-varga* horoscope. That would be that planet's *ashtaka-varga* and so on for each planet.

These marks or points are called the benefit points in each house.

The benefic points in any house will not exceed eight. The number of benefic points deducted from 8 is the number of malefic points in that house.

1. Place Marks or Points for the Sun in the —

(a)	1st, 2nd, 4th, 7th, 8th, 9th, 10th, 11th	houses	from the Sun's house
(b)	3rd, 6th, 10th, 11th	"	the Moon's "
(c)	1st, 2nd, 4th, 7th, 8th, 9th, 10th, 11th	"	Mars' "
(d)	3rd, 5th, 6th, 9th, 10th, 11th, 12th	"	Mercury's "
(e)	5th, 6th, 9th, 11th	"	Jupiter's "
(f)	6th, 7th, 12th	"	Venus' "
(g)	1st, 2nd, 4th, 7th, 8th, 9th, 10th, 11th	"	Saturn's "
(h)	3rd, 4th, 6th, 10th, 11th, 12th	"	the Ascendant "

2. Place Marks or Points for the Moon in the —

(a)	3rd, 6th, 7th, 10th, 11th	houses	from the Sun's house
(b)	1st, 3rd, 6th, 7th, 10th, 11th	"	the Moon's "
(c)	2nd, 3rd, 5th, 6th, 9th, 10th, 11th	"	Mars' "
(d)	1st, 3rd, 4th, 5th, 7th, 8th, 10th, 11th	"	Mercury's "
(e)	1st, 4th, 7th, 8th, 10th, 11th, 12th or 2nd	"	from the Jupiter's house
(f)	3rd, 4th, 5th, 7th, 9th, 10th, 11th	" .	Venus' "
(g)	3rd, 5th, 6th, 11th	"	Saturn's "
(h)	3rd, 6th, 10th, 11th	"	the Ascendant "

3. Place Marks or Points for Mars in the —

(a)	3rd, 5th, 6th, 10th, 11th	houses	from the Sun's	house
(b)	3rd, 6th, 11th	"	the Moon's	"
(c)	1st, 2nd, 4th, 7th, 8th, 10th, 11th	"	Mars'	"
(d)	3rd, 5th, 6th, 11th	"	Mercury's	"
(e)	6th, 10th, 11th, 12th	"	Jupiter's	"
(f)	6th, 8th, 11th, 12th	"	Venus'	"
(g)	1st, 4th, 7th, 8th, 9th, 10th, 11th	"	Saturn's	"
(h)	1st, 3rd, 6th, 10th, 11th	"	the Ascendant	"

4. Place Marks or Points for Mercury in the —

(a)	5th, 6th, 9th, 11th, 12th	houses	from the Sun's	house
(b)	2nd, 4th, 6th, 8th, 10th, 11th	"	the Moon's	"
(c)	1st, 2nd, 4th, 7th, 8th, 9th, 10th, 11th	"	Mars'	"
(d)	1st, 3rd, 5th, 6th, 9th, 10th, 11th	"	Mercury's	"
(e)	6th, 8th, 11th, 12th	"	Jupiter's	"
(f)	1st, 2nd, 3th, 4th, 5th, 8th, 9th, 11th	"	Venus'	"
(g)	1st, 2nd, 4th, 7th, 8th, 9th, 10th, 11th	"	Saturn's	"
(h)	1st, 2nd, 4th, 6th, 8th, 10th, 11th	"	the Asacendant	"

5. Place Marks or Points for Jupiter in the —

(a)	1st, 2nd, 3rd, 4th, 7th, 8th, 9th, 10th, 11th	houses	from the Sun's	house
(b)	2nd, 5th, 7th, 9th, 11th	"	the Moon's	"
(c)	1st, 2nd, 4th, 7th, 8th, 10th, 11th	"	Mars'	"
(d)	1st, 2nd, 4th, 5th, 6th, 9th, 10th, 11th	"	Mercury's	"
(e)	1st, 2nd, 4th, 7th, 8th, 10th, 11th	"	Jupiter's	"
(f)	2nd, 5th, 6th, 12th	"	Venus'	"
(g)	3rd, 5th, 6th, 12th	"	Saturn's	"
(h)	1st, 2nd, 4th, 5th, 6th, 7th, 9th, 10th, 11th	"	the Ascendant	"

6. Place Marks or Points for Venus in the —

(a)	8th, 11th, 12th	houses	from the Sun's	house
(b)	1st, 2nd, 3rd, 4th, 5th, 8th, 9th, 11th, 12th	"	the Moon's	"
(c)	3rd, 5th, 6th, 9th, 11th, 12th	"	Mars'	"
(d)	3rd, 4th or 5th, 6th, 9th, 11th	"	Mercury's	"
(e)	5th, 8th, 9th, 10th, 11th	"	Jupiter's	"
(f)	1st, 2nd, 3rd, 4th, 5th, 8th, 9th, 10th, 11th	"	Venus'	"
(g)	3rd, 4th, 8th, 9th, 10th, 11th	"	Saturn's	"
(h)	1st, 2nd, 3rd, 4th, 5th, 8th, 9th, 11th	"	the Ascendant	"

7. Place Marks or Points for Saturn in the —

(a)	1st, 2nd, 4th, 7th, 8th, 10th, 11th	houses	from the Sun's	house
(b)	3rd, 6th, 11th	"	the Moon's	"
(c)	3rd, 5th, 6th, 10th, 11th, 12th	"	Mars'	"

(d)	6th, 8th, 9th, 10th, 11th, 12th	"	Mercury	"
(e)	5th, 6th, 11th, 12th	"	Jupiter	"
(f)	6th, 11th, 12th	"	Venus'	"
(g)	3rd, 5th, 6th, 11th	"	Saturn's	"
(h)	1st, 3rd, 4th, 6th, 10th, 11th	"	the Ascendant	"

8. Place Marks or Points in the *Sarvashtaka Vargas*

Total the number of marks of points in the Aries   House of each planet's *ashtakavarga* and place the entire total number in the Aries House of the *sarvashtaka varga* Horoscope and soon for every other House upto the Pisces House.

General Effects According to the Points in each House :

(1) If there are more than four points in any house, the planets give good results when passing through that house.

(2) If there are 5, 6 or 7 points in the house, the planets bless the natives with progressively more beneficial and fruitful results when passing through that house.

(3) If there are 1, 2 or 3 points only in the house, the planets will cause no good results when transiting through that house.

(4) If there are no points in the house, the planets cause diseases, dishonour and difficulties and tensions when passing through that house.

(5) If there are 4 points in the house, the planets give mixed results, both good and not good while transiting through that house.

(6) A planet with one point may cause diseases, misery, discomforts and make one wander.

(i) A planet with 2 points may produce mental agony, censure from government authorities and losses in business etc.

(ii) A planet with 3 points produces bodily deprivation, discomforts and mental uneasiness.

(iii) A planet with 4 points produces mixed pain, pleasure, expense and enhancement of income and increase of financial assets.

(iv) A planet with 5 points causes procurement of good clothes, luxuries, children, learning and wealth.

(v) A planet with 6 points produces a good personality, good character, wealth, and riches, victory in conflict and war, fame and strength.

(vi) A planet with 7 points produces honour, titles, horses, carriages and wealth.

(vii) A planet with 8 points produces glory distinction and other accompaniments, name and fame and distinction.

(7) A planet gives always good results in his own *varga,* in any house with 5 or more points and otherwise gives no good results.

(8) A planet is positively harmful while moving in a house with no points.

(9) All planets in their houses of exaltation, in friendly houses or other benefic houses and also in the *kendras* and *trikonas* produce perverse and inconvenient results if the houses they move in, contain less than four points.

(10) Planets in bad positions and in depression or inimical houses, give good results if they move in houses containing more than four points.

(11) If Saturn passes through a house with no points, he gives diseases, danger from enemies and troubles to the father and the other relations who are represented by the different planets.

Experience shows that the *sarvashtaka-varga* may be used as a confirmation of the results of every *bhava* in a horoscope, obtained while assessing the nature of a nativity according to the rules mentioned in the previous chapters. Where the number of points is great, that *bhava* is strong. But there is not much advantage in it, if the allied *bhavas* are not equally strong, e.g., the 11th house may get even as many as 50 points but if the 2nd and 9th houses do not get an equally good number and if the 6th, 8th and 12th houses get more, the results will be nil.

The Ascendant must get more points than any other *bhava*. The 6th, 8th and 12th *bhavas* must get less than those in the Ascendant while all other benefic houses must get more than what the evil houses get, but still less than the Ascendant, and the lord of the Ascendant should get more points in his own *ashtaka-varga* than any other planet in his individual *ashtaka-varga*.

This is an excellent condition showing that the native will be successful in life. The following rule may be adopted to decide whether a person will be able to save or not. The 2nd, 11th and 9th houses speak of wealth of some sort or other, and the total number of points in these houses must be greater than those in the 6th, 8th and 12th houses, for these houses speak of debts, misfortunes, etc.

There are so many other things that can be considered with the help of the *ashtaka-varga*, such as the direction which will be most helpful to the native, the longevity of a person, the three divisions of life, the father's and mother's death etc. The reader is requested to refer to other books where these have been treated elaborately. This is just to create interest.

22

DISEASES, AILMENTS AND AFFLICTIONS

This is a moot point, wherein a great amount of difficulty is experienced by an astrologer in deciding what the disease the native is suffering from, or is likely to suffer from, for the astrologer may not be an expert in medical science and as such, he may not be able to mention the name of the disease which the native is suffering, or is likely to suffer from. But the astrologer can find out the most vulnerable part of the human system and say that that is the portion of the body which is likely to be affected seriously whenever there is an opportunity.

The 6th house is mentioned as the house of disease etc., of course, not only from the Ascendant but from the Moon Ascendant and from the house wherein the lord of the Ascendant is placed. The 6th house is a house of disease and sickness, of servitude and obscurity, accidents and adversities.

The 6th house only shows whether the native is going to suffer from disease and whether his health is generally good or bad, or whether he is going to have some ailment which is more or less permanent with him, or the affliction is of a temporary nature. As has been stated elsewhere, if the lord of the Ascendant should be strong, at least stronger than the lord of the 6th house, of course, he will be able to overcome the ailment with more ease and comfort than the one who has the lord of the Ascendant weak and the lord of the 6th house strong in his horoscope. One has to see which particular house and its lord are weak or afflicted. In *kalapurusha anga* one can see Aries, the head and so on, until Pisces, the feet.

The same rule can be applied from the birth sign of an individual and the researcher will have to find out which particular house is weakened by the aspect of malefic planets or its lord being placed with malefics, and so on, just as any *bhava* is examined. The confirmation of this can be had from the Moon Ascendant, as also from that house which has the lord of the Ascendant situated in it.

For instance, suppposing one finds the 6th house very weak, in that it has the aspect of malefic planets and its lord is also weak. Therefore that house will be afflicted. That house, according to the Ascendant will indicate ailments around the intestinal portion and navel. One will have to decide that that particular portion of the physique is the most sensitive point in his body and that all diseases are likely to emanate from that house. Besides, he must also consider the humour of the planet which owns the 6th house and the humour of the planets which are aspecting the 6th house as well as its lord. A person may suffer from wind in the stomach or indigestion causing trouble in the intestines as well as near the navel. The excessive gas that is created by this process may also apparently make the native feel that he is having some trouble in his heart as well. It is just possible that the native may draw a conclusion, but the astrologer will have to get confirmation from the Moon Ascendant as well as the 6th house and from the house in which the lord of the ascendant is situated. Invariably, it can be seen in such cases that the 6th house from Aries is also afflicated in some form or the other. It is quite easy, astrologically, to find out the location of the disease but the native thought he was suffering from something else. In another case, it was advised from the natal chart that the native had some problem in his liver, whereas, the doctors thought it was trouble in the kidneys and there was an operation. The doctors assured him he would be alright. Three months later, the patient went to the doctors with a bloated stomach. It was then that doctors diagnosed the ailment as originating from the liver and the patient was subjected to another operation. So, one has to be very careful in predicting diseases and the weakest house in the horoscope will have to be carefully searched, for, according to the rules mentioned above and then a conclusion reached. This is true for all diseases, physical infirmities, ailments and accidents.

If Mars is weak in a horoscope, the native may suffer from want of enough bone marrow and if Mercury is weak, he may suffer from skin diseases, nervous complaints etc., meaning, thereby that the humour of each planet and the tendency of each sign of the Zodiac must be borne in mind.

Annexure

The Lord of the Ascendant must be strong. In his own house or in exaltation between benefics favourably placed from the ascendant and not associated or aspected by malefics, the Lord of the ascendant must be considered to be strong.

The Lord of Ascendant in 3rd, 6th, 8th or 12th house must be considered to be weak. Being aspected by malefics is an indication of weakness. Birth in *Suklapakshami* must be considered to be preferable to being born in *Krishnapakshami*. Especially for benefics *Krishnapakshami* is not good. The Lords of the *Kendras* must be strong and well placed. The Lord of the 8th house must not have malefic aspects. A benefic aspect will be really very good in giving long life.

1. If any planet or planets be strong at the time of the birth of a person in his Horoscope, the mental qualities represented by the said planets will be equally strong in the person, if the planets be weak, the corresponding mental qualities will also be weak, but in the case of Saturn alone, there is an exception and, that is, if Saturn be strong in the Horoscope, the misery represented by Saturn will be less but if Saturn be weak, the misery will be greater.

2. The different planets have particular characteristics :

   (a) The Sun is steadfast.
   (b) The Moon is wandering and unsteady.
   (c) Mars is violent.

(d) Mercury is mixture of various qualities.

(e) Jupiter is gentle.

(f) Venus is light or easy.

(g) Saturn is harsh.

3. Stars represent the body of a person thus :

   (a) *Hasta, Chittra* and *Swati* are placed in the head.

   (b) *Visakha, Anuradha* and *Jyeshta* are placed in the face.

   (c) *Mula* and *Purvashada* are placed in the neck.

   (d) *Uttarashada* and *Sravana* are placed in the shoulders.

   (e) *Dhanistha* and *Satabhisha* are placed in both hands.

   (f) *Purvabhadra, Uttarabhadra, Revati, Aswani* and *Bharani* are placed in the heart.

   (g) *Krittika* is placed in the navel.

   (h) *Rohini* is placed in private parts.

   (i) *Mrigasira, Arudra, Punarvasu, Pushyami, Aslesha* and *Makha* are placed in the knees.

   (j) *Pubba* and *Uttara* are placed in the feet.

4. If the 7th or 5th house is occupied by Saturn or Mars and is not aspected by other planets, the child will be given away in adoption.

5. Defects in the eyes are indicated :

   (a) If Leo is in the Ascendant and the Sun and the Moon occupy the Ascendant and are aspected by Mars or Saturn, the child is blind. But if benefics aspect the Ascendant, the child has some defect in the eye.

   (b) If the Moon or the Sun occupy the 12th house, the child is blind in the left eye, if it be the Moon and in the right eye, if it be the Sun.

6. Whichever of the following 7 planets is the strongest, death occurs in the period of such a planet :

   (a) The lord of the 8th house.

   (b) The planets in 8th house.

   (c) The planets aspecting 8th house.

(d) The lord of 22nd *Drekkana* from that of the Ascendant.

(e) The planet associated with the lord of 8th house.

(f) The lord of the 64th *Navamsa* from that occupied by the Moon.

(g) The greatest enemy of the lord of 8th house.

These seven planets are called *"Chidra Grashas."*

7. If the Lord of a major period is associated with a benefic planet, its period is good. If it is associated with both benefic and malefic and is neither weak nor strong, the results will be mixed.

8. (a) In the case of persons with a long life, death may occur in the 7th major-period of their lives.

   (b) In the case of persons with a short life span, death may occur in the 7th major-period of their lives.

   (c) In the case of persons with an average life span, death occurs in the 5th major-period of their lives.

9. If a malefic planet occupies the Ascendant, there will be disease, loss of wealth, the displeasure of the Government, trouble from enemies during its major-period of sub-period of a malefic planet. The results will be mixed during the sub-period of a benefic planet.

10. During the major period of the Lord of Ascendant of the sub-period of a malefic planet, there will be disease, death or loss of place. In the sub-period of Saturn there will be loss of money, enmity with relatives and friends.

11. Indications of a Defective Limb :

   (a) If Venus and the Sun occupy one of 7th, 9th and 5th houses, the person's spouse will have a defective limb.

   (b) If the Moon occupies the 10th house, Mars occupies the 7th house and Saturn occupies the 2nd house from the Sun, the person will have a defective limb.

   (c) If Mars occupies the 5th or 9th house or is aspected by a malefic, the person has a defective limb.

(d) If Saturn occupies 7th house and Mars is associated with Rahu or is weak, he has a defective limb.

(e) If the Moon occupies 10th house, Mars the 7th house and the Sun 2nd house, he loses his limb.

(f) If Mars occupies the 1st *Drekkana* of the Ascendant and be aspected by the Sun, the Moon and Saturn, the child will have no head.

(g) If Mars occupies 1st *Drekkana* of 5th house and be aspected by the Sun, the Moon and Saturn, the child will have no hands.

(h) If Mars occupies 1st *Drekkana* of 9th house and be aspected by the Sun, the Moon and Saturn, the child will have no legs.

12. The native will be deaf, dumb and insane :

(a) If malefic planets — the Sun, the Moon, Mars and Saturn — occupy 9th, 11th houses and are not aspected by benefics, he will be deaf.

(b) If Mars occupies 7th house, Jupiter occupies Ascendant or if Saturn occupies Ascendant and Mars occupies 5th, 7th or 9th house or if the waning Moon and Saturn occupy the 12th house, he will be insane or an idiot.

(c) If the Sun occupies the 1st house and Mars the 7th house, he will be insane.

(d) If Saturn occupies the 1st house and Mars a trine, he will have a maniacal wife.

(e) If one part of the Sagittarius Ascendant, or if the Sun and the Moon occupy the Ascendant, and a trine and if Jupiter occupies 3rd house or an angle, he is insane.

(f) If malefics occupy 9th, 11th 3rd, and 5th houses and are not aspected by benefics, he will be deaf.

(g) If all the three malefic planets — Saturn, Mars and the Sun — occupy the *Riksha Sandhis* or the last portion of any one of the houses of either the Cancer, Scorpio or Pisces he will be dumb. If only two malefics occupy in the above maniac, there will be very little speech, if only one malefic occupies such a portion of the chart there will be slow or stammering speech. In this rule the Moon must have a malefic aspect but if the Moon has a benefic aspect, the child will begin to speak later than usual.

13. Defects of the Eye are indicated when:

(a) If one of the 12th and 6th houses be occupied by the Sun and the other by the Moon, both the person and his wife will each have one eye.

(b) If the Sun, the Moon, Mars and Saturn occupy the 2nd, 6th, 8th, and 12th houses he becomes blind.

(c) If an eclipsed Sun occupies the Ascendant and if Saturn and Mars occupy the 5th and 9th houses, he loses his eyes.

(d) If the Sun occupies 5th or 9th house and is aspected by malefics he will have weak sight in the eyes.

(e) If the Ascendant be Leo, and the Sun and the Moon occupying it are aspected by Saturn or Mars, he will have no sight in the eyes.

(f) If the Moon occupies the 12th house, he will have the left eye hurt.

(g) If the Sun occupies the 12th house, the right eye will be hurt.

Note: If in (e), (f) & (g) benefics aspect the Sun and the Moon, the evil effects mentioned in (e), (f) & (g) will not happen.

(h) If the Ascendant be Leo and the Sun be in exaltation, he gets an eye disease.

(i) If the Ascendant be Libra and the Sun occupies it, he will be poor and blind at night.

(j) If the Ascendant be Cancer and the Sun occupies it, he will have inflamed eyes.

(k) If the Sun and the Moon occupy the 12th house jointly or separately, he loses his right or left eye, respectively.

(l) If malefics occupy the 6th and 8th houses, he loses his sight in the right eye, if the planet is in 8th house and left eye, if the planet be in the 6th house.

(m) If the Sun is associated with or aspected by Saturn or occupies the 10th or 7th house, he will not be the affected in his right eye. But if the Sun is associated with Rahu and Mars and the other conditions being same as above mentioned in rules (k) and (l), he will have his left eye affected.

(n) If malefics occupy the 6th, 8th and 12th houses and if the Sun and the Moon occupy the 12th house, he loses one of his eyes. If Saturn and the Moon associate with Mars and occupy 6th, 8th or 12th houses, he has no sight.

(o) If the Mars is the lord of 2nd house and if the Sun occupies the 8th house along with the Moon and if Saturn occupies the 6th, 8th, or 12th house, he will be blind. If Saturn and the Moon associate with Mars and occupy the 6th, 8th or 12th house, he has no sight.

(p) If the Moon occupies the 6th house, the Sun the 8th house, Saturn the 12th house and Mars the 2nd house, he will be blind.

(q) (i) If the lord of the 2nd house associated with the Lord of Ascendant occupies 6th, 8th or 12th house, he loses his sight.

 (ii) If the Lord of the 2nd house associates with Venus and the Moon and occupies the Ascendant, he will be the night blind. But if the lord of the 2nd house is exalted or is associated with a benefic, no such evil occurs.

(r) If the Moon or Ketu occupies the 12th house, Saturn occupies a trine, the Sun occupies the 7th or 8th house his eyes and teeth will be affected.

(s) If malefics occupy the 4th and 5th houses and if the Moon occupies 6th, 8th or houses, he will be blind. But if benefics occupy the said house, there will be no such result.

(t) If the Sun alone occupies the Ascendant and be aspected by Mars and the Sun, he will be blind in the right eye.

(u) If the Moon alone occupies Leo and be aspected by Mars and Saturn, he will be blind in the left eye.

14. Sudden wealth and sudden loss are indicated when :

(a) (1) If the Lord of 11th house occupies the 4th house and the Lord of 4th house occupies the 11th house. Or

(2) If Lord of Ascendant be strong and associated with Lord of the 4th house in the Ascendant or the 4th house and is associated with or aspected by a benefic, the person suddenly becomes wealthy.

(b) (i) If Lords of 2nd and 4th houses occupy 6th house and Lord of 6th house associates with Jupiter. Or

(ii) If Lords of the 2nd and 11th houses are depressed and malefics occupy 2nd house. Or

(iii) If Lords of 2nd and 4th houses associate with Lord of 8th house and during the major period of the Lord of the 2nd house. Or

(iv) If the Lord of 2nd house associates with Ketu and occupies 8th house, the person loses wealth suddenly.

15. Lung and Associated Disorders are :

(a) If the Moon occupies the *Navamsa* of Cancer or Scorpio and is associated with malefics, he will suffer from disease in the private parts.

(b) If the Lord of the 1st house occupies the 8th house and is associated with Rahu, he gets large testicles.

(c) If the Moon is associated with a malefic and occupies a house which is occupied by Lord of 8th house and Lord of 8th house is aspected by Rahu, he gets disease in private parts; if the 8th house is occupied by 3 or more malefics the same result occurs but if a benefic occupies 8th house, he will not get that disease.

(d) If Rahu occupies the Ascendant and associates with Saturn and Mars or if the Lord of the Ascendant occupies the 8th house and associates with Rahu or other malefics, or if Mars being Lord of the Ascendant occupies the Ascendant with association or aspect of a malefic, or if Saturn, Mars and Rahu all occupy Ascendant or if Lord of the *navamsa* house occupied by the Lord of the Ascendant associated with Rahu and Mars, or if the Lord of the *navamsa* house occupied by the Lord of 8th house associate with Rahu, there will be testicles complaint.

(e) If Moon is situated between Saturn and Mars and if the Sun occupies Capricorn he suffers from asthma, consumption, spleen complaint.

(f) If the Sun and the Moon occupy each other's house or *Navamsa* of the other, he suffers from consumption.

(g) If the Moon be together with Saturn and is aspected by Mars, he gets consumption.

(h) If the Sun occupies Ascendant and is aspected by Mars, he suffers from asthma and colic pain.

(i) If the Moon is placed between two malefics and Saturn occupies the 7th house, he suffers from comsumption, spleen complaints and boils.

(j) If Mercury and Mars occupy 6th house and be aspected by Venus and the Moon occupies malefic house, there will be consumption.

(k) If Rahu occupies 6th house, the Lord of the Ascendant 8th house and the Moon associates with or is aspected by a malefic, there will be consumption.

(l) If the Moon is hemmed between Saturn and Mars and the Sun is placed in Capricorn, there will be consumption.

(m) If the Moon occupies 8th house, Rahu 6th house or 8th house and Saturn 8th house from Rahu, there will be consumption.

(n) If the Moon associates with Mars or if Venus and Mars occupy the 6th house, or if Lord of the 8th house occupies the 6th house, or if the Lord of the 12th house occupies the 8th house and Lord of the 8th house occupies the 12th house, there will be diabetes.

(o) If Rahu or a malefic occupies Ascendant and Saturn occupies 8th house, he will have some ailment in the stomach.

(p) If the 5th or the 9th house be Scorpio, Cancer, Taurus or Capricorn and is either occupied or aspected by Saturn, he may be afflicted by leprosy.

(q) If Mars occupies the Ascendant and is aspected by both Saturn and the Sun, he may have to suffer from smallpox.

(r) If the Lord of the 3rd house is associated with Mercury he may be prone to throat infections or ailments.

(s) If the 3rd house is occupied by a malefic and is aspected by a malefic, he may get ear disorders or diseases.

16. Teeth and bald head :

(a) If malefic the Sun, the Moon, Mars and Saturn occupy 7th house and are not aspected by benefics, he will have deformed teeth.

(b) If the Ascendant be Taurus, Aries, or Sagittarius and if malefics aspect the Ascnedant, he will have ugly teeth.

(c) If the Ascendant be Aries, Taurus, Saggittarius, and is aspected by a malefic, he will have toothache.

(d) If malefics occupy the 7th house and are not aspected by benefics, he has irregular teeth.

(e) If Saturn and Rahu occupy the 2nd house and are associated with or be aspected by the Lord of Ascendant and the Moon is in depression, or if the Lord of the 8th house and Jupiter occupy the 8th house, and

Lord of Ascendant be in depression, there will be depression, diseases of the teeth.

(f) If one of the malefic houses, Aries, Leo, Capricorn, Aquarius, Sagittarius, or Scorpio be the Ascendant and if Ascendant be aspected by malefics, he will be bald headed.

17. How to verify the Ascendant :

(1) Generally the Ascendant will be the 5th or 9th house from the house containing the Lord of the house containing the Moon, or

(2) The Ascendant will be the 7th house or the 5th or 9th house from the Lord of the Moon house, or

(3) The Ascendant itself will be the Moon Ascendant, OR

(4) The Ascendant will be the 6th or the 9th house from the Moon Ascendant, or

(5) (a) Note the number of *Ghatikas* upto birth from the Sunrise,

(b) Halve the number of *Ghatikas* in (a)

(c) Add that half of the number of the star in which the Sun is situated that day.

(d) Divide the result in (c) by 27, if it is more than 27 and note the number which is the remainder, otherwise note the result.

(e) From the remainder count the star computing to that number from *Aswin*.

(f) Finally find the house corresponding to such a star found in.

(6) (a) Count the number of *Ghatikas* till the time of birth, from the Sun-rise.

(b) Multiply the said *Ghatikas* by 6 and note the product.

(c) Add to the product the number of the Tamil date of birth (the date according to the Solar month).

(d) Divide the total by 30 and note the quotient.

(e) Count that number from the next house to the house in which the Sun is situated at birth and that is the Ascendant at birth.

18. If in married partners, both of them start the same period, with the wife's period preceding the husband's, there will positively be misery, unhappiness and poverty even leading to struggle for their very existence or survival.

23

THE ROLE OF SATURN

Human life is the inter-play of joys and sorrows. While the joys of life and its comforts are represented in Astrology by the planet Jupiter, the sorrows, diseases and toils of life are represented in the birth chart by the planet Saturn. In this chapter, we will deal with the prominent traits and qualities of Saturn, which affect everyday life.

Saturn, being the farthest planet from the Sun, is devoid of the power of luminence. Saturn vibrates without the light on knowledge with least rhythms and frequency. Saturn's influence on the house of education, therefore, adversely affects education though it does not deny it altogether.

Inadequate education makes one selfish and poor in wealth. In fact "paucity" in all fields of human activity is denoted by this planet of dearth. Therefore, when Saturn conjoined with Rahu (who always acts similarly to Saturn) influences, by association or aspect, the factors for wealth, i.e., the second house, its lord and Jupiter (particularly in cases where Saturn is the lord of the 6th house—a house of "paucity" and "dearth"), it brings about dearth of wealth and makes the native rather poor.

Saturn represents hardships and labour in the native's career, influences the houses of wealth or their lords. Such a person has to toil much in life, though he may be engaged in a white-collared job.

The motion of Saturn is very slow. It takes about two and half years to traverse a distance of 30° which the Moon covers only in about two and a half days. Saturn thus symbolises "delay". Hence, if you find the influence of Saturn and Rahu on the factors of marriage, i.e., the 7th house, its lord and its significators (Venus for male nativities and Jupiter for female nativities) you can be sure that it is a case of delayed marriage. Marriage may even be denied altogether in case the malefic influence of these factors is great and the benefic influence absent.

Saturn is taken as on "Old" entity, person or thing. If, therefore, Saturn is found to influence the factors of marriage, i.e., the 7th house, its lord and its significator, in collaboration with the other "Old" planets, such as the Sun and Jupiter, the girl, if she marries, will marry a person much elder to her in age.

The slow motion of Saturn, however, makes it a desirable instrument for prologning longevity. In other words, a strong Saturn in the birth chart ensures fairly good longevity unless, the first and the 8th house of the horoscope and their lords are extremely weak and afflicted.

In Astrology, Satrun is considered as the sigificator for longevity. By being away from the *Satvic* atmosphere of the Sun, Saturn has less of culture. Its epithet *Manda* signifies its low level of culture and status. In the field of prediction, whenever we notice that a house has Saturn as its lord, and neither the house or its lord have on them any benefic influence, we may conclude that the result represented by the house involved is relatively low in status. For example, if in a male with a Leo the Ascendant, we find the Sun strong and well-aspected, we could infer for him a high status in life, but the native will be married to a girl belonging to a family very much lower in status particularly where Saturn is subjected to the influence of other malefic planets.

Saturn has been observed to be "Separative" in nature, that is it separates a native from the traits of the house etc., which it influences by association or by aspect. Such influence will be more pronounced, if it works in collaboration with other separative planets, Rahu and the Sun. For example, when Saturn and Rahu influence the 7th house, its lord and its significator, one is quite sure to get separated from his partner in life. If they influence the 10th house, its lord and the Sun, one loses his position. If they influence, by association or aspect, the 5th house and its lord, one has frequent abortions. If the influence falls on the 4th house and its lord, he will establish residence at a place far away from his place of birth.

Saturn is the significator of "Disease" as is Rahu. If both of them afflict a particular house, the limb represented by that house is diseased and even impaired. For example, in a Virgo nativity, Saturn as lord of the 6th house denotes diseases and if Rahu occupies the 7th house, in the horoscope, it will give trouble in the hips, 9th house, in the ears, 3rd house and 11th house etc.

Saturn is the lord of the sign numbers tenth and eleventh. Each of these signs represents the legs. Hence a weak and afflicted Saturn would cause some problem in the legs. For example, if someone has Aquarius as his Ascendant and Saturn is located in Leo in his birth chart with Rahu without the association or aspect of the benefic planets, the native gets much trouble in his legs and in cases where the malefic influence on Saturn is severe his legs are prone to cancer. Amongst the tissues, Saturn represents the "Nerves" and so does Rahu. If both influence by association or aspect the Ascendants and their lords, one gets his nerves impaired and suffer from a "Stroke or Paralysis" etc. Saturn located in the 11th house may indicate death by paralysis, if Rahu afflicts both the 8th house and its lord, Saturn gives tall stature and a slim body.

Saturn is a planet of philosophy and possesses much *viragya*, i.e., detachment. If Saturn and Rahu influence, by association or by aspect, the first and the fourth houses of the horoscope, on their lords and the Moon—the significator of mind — then the man possesses much *vairagya*.

Saturn behaves as a female planet though masculine by origin. For example, if in a Libra ascendant, Saturn is placed in Cancer in the 10th house, the person will have several daughters. If Saturn is placed with the Sun in the natal chart, the native must guard against heart ailments.

Saturn is the significator for property, particularly the barren or cultivable lands, with alluvial soil. Mars, too, stands for property, particularly constructed property, multi-storeyed flats etc. When both Saturn and Mars influence, by association or by aspect, the 4th house, the more the number of houses/ property, the native gets in life.

Saturn denotes dearth of sex, and the inability to enjoy sex fully. Like Saturn, Mercury too denotes "Impotence". When Saturn and Mercury act together on the factors denoting sex, i.e., on the 7th house, its lord and the significator and there is no other type of influence on the sex factors, the native becomes impotent.

Saturn denotes dead or decomposed matter such as coal , leather, stone, marble etc. When it is lord of the house of trade, i.e., the 7th house, it denotes trade in one of these articles. If Venus happens to occupy the sign of Saturn in the 7th house, the stone here is modified and refined by Venus into a precious gem or a jewel. Saturn is a retarding factor. Rahu, too, a retains restrictive nature. When Rahu or Saturn has its influence of the 12th house and its lord and when they cast the spell of their influence on the factors representing the body, they would send him to prison or to a strange distant place for settlement.

Saturn, the Sun and Rahu are planets for medicine and its analysis. When they influence the house of educaton, i.e., the 2nd house and its lord who is strong, they impart medical education to the native. When they influence the Ascendant and its lord, it infers that the subject will practise in the medical line. When both Mars and Saturn have their influence on the 2nd house and its lord, the nature of education becomes "technical" such as engineering. Saturn, lord of the 4th house is located in the 10th house, (as the 4th house is the *nadir* and the 10th one the *zenith*). The rise of a low planet from a very low position to the zenith signified by the 10th house gives the unusual rise.

Let us now analyse the role of Saturn in horoscopes with different Ascendants.

Aries Ascendant

Saturn becomes the lord of the 10th and the 11th houses. It primarily gives the beneficial results of the house of gains, i.e., the 11th house, if well placed.

Taurus Ascendant

In this case, Saturn is the lord of the 9th and 10th houses and as such acts as *yogakaraka*. Saturn is conducive to good income and immense riches, if well placed.

Gemini Ascendant

Saturn becomes the lord of the 8th and the 9th houses. Since its *Mool-Trikona* sign falls in the 9th house, it gives the results of the 9th house, i.e., of good luck in its major period and sub- period. Saturn is the significator of longevity. Here he will be one of the lords of the house of longevity (eighth). As such a strong and well-aspected Saturn makes the native long-lived. An afflicted Saturn, lord of the house of father and an afflicted Jupiter, the significator of father, of course, make the father of the native of moderate means.

Cancer Ascendant

Saturn becomes the lord of the 7th and the 8th houses. The 7th is an angular house and as such Saturn as lord ceases to be a malefic. But, it is at the same time, lord of the worst house in the horoscope: the 8th house. It gives bad results financially during its major-period and sub-period. Saturn can, however, give favourable results financially, provided the 8th house and Saturn are aspected and influenced by malefic planets only, and there is no influence on them of the benefics. In such a case, Saturn constitutes a *Vipareeta Raja-yoga*.

Leo Ascendant

Saturn is the lord of the 6th and the 7th houses of the horoscope. Here also Saturn ceases to be a malefic by virtue of the 7th *Kendra*. But, the simultaneous lordship of the bad house: 6th renders it a malefic planet functionally. Hence, Saturn in its major-period and sub-period gives adverse results financially.

Unless, Saturn is well-aspected or is otherwise under a benefic influence, the native marries a girl, much lower in status than himself.

Virgo Ascendant

Saturn becomes the lord of the 5th and the 6th houses. As the lord of a trine, Saturn is good financially, but as lord of the 6th house, it is bad. Hence, as a friend of the lord of the Ascendant, Saturn, on the whole, is slightly better in financial matters, in this case.

Libra Ascendant

As Saturn owns the fourth angle and the fifth trine, it becomes a *Yogakaraka* planet and gives very favourable financial results in its major-period and sub-period. This malefic becomes the very best of planets which is a unique feature.

Scorpio Ascendant

Saturn becomes the lord of the 3rd and the 4th houses of the horoscope. As lord of the 4th *Kendra*, Saturn becomes malefic. But the combined influence of Saturn and Mars on the 4th house and its lord generally confers land and built-up property on the native.

Sagittarius Ascendant

Saturn becomes the lord of the 2nd and 3rd houses of the horoscope. As lord of the 2nd house, Saturn has to give the results of the 3rd house, a bad house. Hence, in its major-period and sub-period, Saturn would give bad results financially, unless it is in an angle in a favourable position.

Capricorn Ascendant

Saturn assumes the lordship of the 1st and the 2nd houses of the horoscope. It gives very favourable financial results. If Saturn is weak, the educational aspects come into an adverse position.

Aquarius Ascendant

Saturn becomes the lord of the 1st and the 12th houses. The 1st house being both an angle and a trine, is one of the best houses, and as such Saturn in its major-period and sub-period will give very favourable financial results both with regard to Ascendant and the 12th house.

The influence of Jupiter, which is the significator of finances, besides being the lord of 2nd and 11th houses, on Saturn, would confer quite high status to the native. In fact, Jupiter's influence on any representative factor would boost the qualities of the factor. For the Aquarius Ascendant itself, if the 4th house and its lord Venus are influenced by Jupiter, the man possesses many conveyances and other comforts of life.

In the case of Pisces the Ascendant, Saturn is the owner c the 11th and 12th houses and is not good for the health of th native. But its influence over financial prosperity is fairly goo It bestows wealth and riches, in its periods [Major-Period an Sub-Period] if well placed or well aspected by benefics.

24

IMPORTANCE OF RAHU AND KETU IN HINDU ASTROLOGY

In Hindu astrology, considerable importance is attached to Rahu — the Dragon's Head and Ketu — the Dragon's Tail, the two nodes of the Moon. Physically non-existent, they are yet regarded and treated as full-fledged planets. Westerners do not believe in their aspects, but have done considerable research on tides, psyche of women and similar abstract things. They have realised the aspect of shadowy vibrations on the Moon's vibrations, which has a syondic period of 27 days. In the solar system, as such, these nodes have considerable significance for those belonging to the higher echelons of society as also on religion, philosopy and the occult.

The Moon's nodes as the cross-roads of cosmic influences were full of potency, and gave them the status of planets, in as much as their influence on human lives as well as the lives of nations concerned. The real character of the Hindu astrology can only be fathomed realistically, if one recognizes their impact on the true perspective, though they are mere shadows in calculation.

A knowledge· of Rahu and Ketu, however, could be ascertained with their relative position on Earth with respect to the latter's diurnal and annual motion with the Sun as the focus. Besides the Ascendant, or the particular point in the ecliptic, or its appearance and/or a part of it and the time at which it recurs also give knowledge of Rahu and Ketu. Astrologers in the East question their omission from nativity which would result in a severe handicap to the astrologer. The subtle relation between the Sun, the Moon and the Earth plays a large part in the unfoldment of consciousness of the individual. The ecliptic is the plane of the Earth's orbit around the Sun. Rahu and Ketu the nodal points at which they are coplanar or lie on one axis.

It is really astonishing to note mere points of intersection of the Earth and the Moon's nodes should be so strong that they impinge on human beings. It had been recognised that they produce unprecedented results, at times more than what the planets are supposed to do. Since Rahu and Ketu are in exact opposition, their effects should be analysed simultaneously.

Judging affairs, as evident, palpable movements and mundane affairs, as evident, that their apparent effects are rather the cursive writing of God in Heavens for our guidance?

Rahu is known as the Dragon's head and Ketu as the Dragon's tail, a significant clue to the nodes, for the head is a top, while the tail is end-on. The position of Rahu represents the patent qualities of the individual besides his actions during the present birth, whereas the position of Ketu indicates the qualities developed during the previous birth, besides the actions oriented to the individual in the present birth. Consequently, they are referred to as Cosmic planets. We could ascertain the native manifesting a spectrum of qualities represented by the sign containing Ketu, seeking to mould the qualities belonging to the sign in which Rahu is positioned. The manner in which they project is expressed by the sign and house in which they occupy and aspect the native.

A planet in conjunction with Rahu or Ketu has some special significance in relation to the things notified by the nodes. The native's position will deteriorate with age, if Rahu occupies the first half and Ketu the second half of the natal chart. And the native will prosper, if it is vice versa. The intensity of effects, however, will be subjected to certain modifications caused by the powers of the other planets on them.

A well-positioned Rahu or Ketu with beneficial connections/ aspects would raise the native to dizzy heights in his career. No other planet can be compared to the nodes as the afflicted nodes strike the native with AIDS, Cancer or Leprosy, make him crazy or chase him upto the mountainous forests or deep down the oceans, or to a place of unknown origin.

Hindu astrologers believe both the nodes are malefics. Rahu indicates mundane prosperity whereas Ketu motivates the spiritual vibrations to emancipate the native. They are also indicators of *Raja-yoga* depending upon the permutation and combination of planets in the native's chart. Whether a native is going through difficulties, miseries or happy and joyous days is only manifested by the role of the nodes.

Sages of yore have referred to Rahu as a diplomat and Ketu as a seer. They also believe that the Sun and the Moon are eclipsed by them, in short, the apparent Solar and Lunar eclipses on Earth. In short the spirit and the mind of the living beings on Earth, irrespective of which species it belonged to, is influenced by them. The nodes have a greater influence on the native's liberation or re-birth. Rahu and Ketu, within two degrees of the Ascendant, give an unusual type of personality and a very distinctive appearance.

Rahu has the combined influence of Venus and Jupiter. When the native starts learning with attainment of added skills, under the influence of Jupiter or Venus, as the case may be, he begins to orient with vocational guidance under the influence of Mars or Saturn, in getting a suitable job, depending upon his family/educational background. Rahu is exalted in Gemini, the ruler in Virgo, harmony in Libra, fallen in Sagittarius, detrimental and in disharmony in Aries.

Ketu has the influence of Mars conjoint Saturn. When the native learns the disciplinary influence that the Saturn/Mars connotation exerts over his Ketu, he will be meeting with his destiny. Ketu is exalted in Sagittarius, the ruler in Pisces, in harmony with Aries, fallen in Gemini, detrimental in Virgo, in disharmony with Libra.

Rahu is feminine. It is represented in gem by Agate or Lapis lazuli. Rahu rules over three asterisms—Aries, *Swati* and *Satabhisha*, the lunar orbital points or stars with magnitude of 13 deg 20 min. They fall in the signs of Gemini, Libra and Aquarius ruled by Mercury, Venus (rules pleasure) and Saturn (on misery). Consequently, Rahu is to enhance these if well aspected. He holds sway over Air, on the principle of the five elements. Incidently, it may be noted that these signs, indirectly ruled by Rahu, from the airy triplicity. Rahu guards the paternal grand father, while Ketu the maternal grandmother. Rahu's period is for 18 years and Ketu's for 7 years in *Vimshottari* period system of compartmentalisation of human span of life.

Ketu is a eunuch by physique. Its gem is Turquoise. Ketu rules *Aswini, Magha* and *Moola*, is ruled by Mars, the Sun and Jupiter in Aries, Leo and Sagittarius signs. Mars rules kinship or brothers, the Sun, the spirit or soul and Jupiter on the fleshy part of the body.

HOW RAHU AND KETU AFFECT OUR DESTINIES

Rahu and Ketu are shadowy planets, i.e., imaginary points of intersection in the path of other planets. In Hindu Astrology, they are generally considered to be malignant and people dread them. Rahu (the dragon's head) and Ketu (the dragon's tail) affect all sectors of life depending upon their placement in the natal chart. Rahu, for example, if placed in the Ascendant, gives a good physique and personality whereas Ketu's placement in the 1st house of the natal chart makes the native handsome, bold, daring and pleasant.

Rahu

Rahu gives the following effects depending upon its placement in the 12 houses of a birth chart.

In the first house, Rahu bestows the native with good personality and strong physique. It makes him obstinate and crazy. In the airy signs, it gives better results than in earth or fiery signs.

In the second house, it causes interruptions in academic career. It also causes denial of assistance and help from Government agencies. It may also cause eye and dental ailments.

In the third house, Rahu strains relations with younger brothers and sisters, bestows the native with sharp intellect, ready wit and long life.

In the fourth house, it causes setbacks and obstacles in the academic career but motivates the native to acquire a high proficiency in foreign languages. It causes strains in his mother's health, and wellbeing, plural marriage and benefits through foreigners, foreign countries, and foreign lands. It also adversely affects the native's health in childhood.

In the fifth house, it delays the first issue, causes some problems pertaining to pregnancies, enhances the possibility of the native getting a twin and causes distractions and losses due to games of chance, speculation, horse-racing and gambling.

In the sixth house, it will display aggressiveness in dealing with his numerous adversaries. He will be tough and rough in these matters. He may have many opponents. He may be prone to dumbness. He should be cautious not only of his adversaries but also the so-called friends and hidden inimical forces.

In the seventh house, Rahu causes delay in marriage and strains in marital life, it could lead to marital discords and also plural marriage. It is recommended with regard to matters pertaining to spouse or family, to ascertain its influence with a view to keep tensions under check.

In the eighth house, Rahu leads to higher expenditure: higher liabilities. The longevity factor comes under adverse stars; possible loss of life partner: interest in religion, philosophy and spiritualism. It could also cause prolonged illness.

In the ninth huose, Rahu may cause delays and difficulties in getting inheritance: instability in professional career, many changes in jobs: possible loss of children: higher attainments for some but after bitter struggle and sustained efforts. It makes him popular but involves him in litigation.

In the tenth house, Rahu leads to high position in a short span of time, immense earnings and wealth: political connections and a rise in politics : honours and awards. It brings beneficial changes and improvements after 48 years.

In the eleventh house, Rahu causes immense riches : gains through the opposite sex; association with persons of doubtful integrity; ill health.

In the twelfth house, Rahu may lead to possible loss of a limb; losses and higher expenditure; gains through foreign connections.

Ketu

Ketu has the following effects depending upon its placement in different houses of the natal chart.

In the first house, Ketu blesses the native with a pleasing personality, regular manners and easy acceptability in social circles.

In the second house, Ketu adversely affects the educational prospects of the native. It causes delay in marriage.

Ketu in the third house, denies younger brothers, but bestows — intellectual capabilities. It also favours religious bent of mind.

In the fourth house, Ketu causes struggle in early part of life, many changes of residence, problems/irritants with motor vehicles, idle gossip etc. It also affects the health of his mother.

In the fifth house, Ketu leads to deficient progeny, pilgrimage, devoid of children, non-enjoyment of the parental property, plural marriage etc.

In the sixth house, Ketu may lead to destruction/annihilation of all enemies.

When Ketu is placed *in the seventh house*, the natives are strongly advised to marry late, otherwise marital discord is very likely.

In the eighth house, Ketu may cause dangers in life and also affect the longevity of the person. It could also cause mental disorders.

In the ninth house, Ketu leads to misunderstanding with the father, but enhances spiritual interests.

In the tenth house, Ketu stimulates in the natives' spiritual interests, makes them scholars, philosophers, but may tend to cause separation from parents.

In the eleventh house, Ketu may make the native a scholar, philosopher. He will have less help and gain from the elder brother, sister and business partners, but it is conducive to accrual of wealth, stimulation and development of intellectual talents. The natives are prone to deafness.

In the twelfth house, Ketu indicates long overseas journeys and the possibility of settlement abroad.

25

ASPECTS OF RAHU AND KETU

Ketu rules the asterisms *Aswini* (Aries), *Makha* (Leo) and *Moola* (Sagittarius) corresponding to Mars (courage), the Sun (soul) and Jupiter (wisdom) respectively with regard to their lordships.

Consequently, Ketu in Aries (and Scorpio), Leo and Saggitarius (and Pisces) should nomally be expected to give good results, unless other factors come into account. In other signs and asterisms, Ketu might yield good results, or if the sign or asterism in which Ketu is the Ascendant Lord or *Yogakarakam*, excellent results could be predicted. It will be noticed that when Ketu is not in one of the friendly signs, the house it occupies should preferably be an *Upachaya* house.

If a native has a Leo Ascendant and Gemini the Moon Ascendant, with Ketu in Taurus in the asterism of the Sun (*Kritika*), Ketu conjoins Mars and Venus in the 10th house from Ascendant and 12th house from the Moon Ascendant, but the Mars-Venus conjunction as Lords of 9th and 10th house does not confer *Raja-yoga*, because Mars as Lord of the 9th house. is malefic and Venus as lord of the 3rd house is inauspicious. Moreover, Ketu does not do as well in 10th house as Rahu lacks positional strength.

Another native has a Cancer Ascendant and Libra, the Moon Ascendant and Ketu in Leo in the 11th house from the Moon Ascendant and in the Sun's asterism (*Uttaraphalguni*). The Sun as lord of the second house is good for the native with

Cancer Ascendant. Although, here it is placed in the 12th house from the Ascendant, but in the asterism of *Yogakaraka* Mars, yet debilitated in Libra in the *Navamsa* had remarkable achievements in Ketu's major-period, Venus sub-period in Ketu's major-period, Jupiter sub-period and in Venus major-period, Venus is well placed in the 9th house from the Moon ascendant, in the asterism of Jupiter and in the 10th house from the Moon. Jupiter, exalted, in the Ascendant aspects the 9th (luck, dharma), the 5th (government) and the 2nd house from the Moon ascendant, which makes him a good orator.

Another notable personality had Ketu in Taurus in the Sun's asterism (*Krittika*) in the 7th house from the Scorpio Ascendant and third from Pisces the Moon Ascendant. This native was running the Sun's major-period and Mercury's sub-period. Both the Sun and Mercury were in the 2nd house from Ascendant and in Ketu's asterism. Ketu was placed in the 7th house from Ascendant in the Sun's asterism. This was an un-usual exchange between the 2nd and 7th houses, leading to the violent end due to the malefic influence of Ketu.

Another native had a Taurus Ascendant and Gemini the Moon Ascendant. He had Ketu in the 8th house from Ascendant 7th house from the Moon Ascendant in the Sun's asterism (*Uttarashadha*) in association with Mars, lord of the 7th house from Ascendant, the Moon in the 2nd house from the Ascendant with Rahu. His wife and he met with the tragic end, in an air crash far from home.

He was running Ketu's major-period, the Moon's sub-period, was in the asterism of Rahu in the asterism of Jupiter, a malefic one for both Ascendants and Jupiter was in the second house from the Moon Ascendant. With a Virgo Ascendant, Mercury in the 10th house from the Ascendant and Ketu in the eleventh in the asterism of Mercury, the native could hardly be discouraged from his path of marked success. Mercury as the lord of the 1st and 10th houses bestows *Yoga* for the house with Virgo Ascendant.

Another distinguished native has Leo Ascendant and Gemini the Moon Ascendant. He barely got elected to a high public office in Mercury's major period, Rahu's sub-period.

Mercury is a malefic for a Leo Ascendant, and is in the 6th house from the Moon Ascendant, Rahu in *Kritika* in the 10th house from Ascendant and 12th from the Moon Ascendant was not conducive to fulfilment of his higher aims. In Ketu major-period, Venus sub-period, he was re-elected to a high office by a comfortable margin. Ketu in Scorpio in the 6th house, an *Upachaya* house from the Moon Ascendant, gave the results of sign, more than the asterism of Saturn. Venus, well placed in the 5th house from Ascendant, is aspected by Jupiter in Libra in the *Navamsa*, and conferred *Yoga* from his Moon Ascendant.

A native with Scorpio Ascendant and a Libra Moon Ascendant, Ketu in Capricorn in the 3rd house from Ascendant in the asterism of Mars, the Lord of Ascendant, was nominated to a high judicial post. He was later confirmed and assumed his high office. Both events occurred in the Ketu major period and Venus' sub-period. His Venus in Leo is in the asterism of Ketu. He was again nominated after three months of acrimonious and divisive debate because of his very conservative views. He was confirmed and took the oath of office in Venus's major Rahu's sub-period. Rahu in Cancer is in the 10th house from the Moon Ascendant, but 9th house from the Ascendant and neither Cancer nor Mercury's asterism were helpful. Ketu in Capricorn, sign owned by Saturn, which is a *Yogakaraka* for his Moon Ascendant and Ketu in the asterism of Mars, the Lord of Ascendant, were powerful during the period.

Another distinguished personality with creative genius, had a Gemini Ascendant and a Cancer the Moon Ascendant with Ketu in Pisces in the 10th house from the Ascendant, aspected by Jupiter and in the asterism of Mercury, Lord of the Ascendant, Ketu is *Vargottama* in the *Navamsa* chart. He was quite successful in his life. An academician involved in active politics, became Prime Minister of an East European country at the commencement of Ketu's major period. He displayed exemplary courage and high organisational and managerial skills. The Ketu major period and Rahu sub-period (or vice-versa) is nearly always marked by untoward happenings and struggle, because full impact of the Ketu-Rahu nodal axis is brought to bear on the native.

Another notable personality in a European country had a Leo Ascendant and Libra the Moon Ascendant in Aquarius aspected by Mars and in Jupiter's asterism. Rahu in Leo with Mars is aspected by Saturn and in the asterism of Venus. He ruled the country as a powerful dictator without any Parliament, but the referendum yielded a landslide victory for the opposition, unseating him. He refused to abdicate, but was forced to leave the country and spent the rest of his life in exile. He was then passing through Ketu's major and Rahu's sub-period.

The last Emperor of a mid European power, had a Virgo Ascendant and Cancer the Moon Ascendant, Ketu in the 5th house in Capricorn has the aspect of both Mars and Saturn. Rahu in Cancer in the 11th house is with Mars, Saturn, Mercury and the Moon. In the *Navamsa*, Ketu and Saturn exchange signs from these in the natal chart and Ketu is with Mars. He became Emperor in Ketu's major period and Venus' sub-period. Venus is debilitated in Virgo and as ruler of the second as well as the 9th house and the Moon Ascendant, proved death inflicting (*maraka*).

The native was deposed by the Parliament and forced into exile. He was then under the influence of Ketu's major period and Rahu's sub-period. He had his end in Saturn's major-period.

A native with a Gemini Ascendant and Pisces the Moon Ascendant had Ketu in Libra in the 5th house and Rahu in Venus' asterism. In the *Navamsa* chart, Ketu in the 2nd house in Aries is aspected by Saturn, while Rahu is in the 8th house in Libra with Jupiter. Thus, Ketu and Rahu are in signs opposite to those in the natal chart. In the natal chart, Ketu in Libra gives the results of Venus in the seventh, Ketu is also in the asterism of Jupiter, lord of 7th house. In the *Navamsa* chart, Venus is again in the seventh, but debilitated and aspected by Mars, lord of the 2nd house, where Ketu is in Mars sign. In the natal chart, Rahu is in Aries in the sign of Mars and Mars is in the 7th house from the Moon Ascendant. Rahu is also in the asterism of Venus positioned in the 7th house. He was involved in the murder of his parents, sister and brothers, and was sentenced to death.

26

INTERPRETATION OF RAJA YOGA

Almost all classical works on Astrology are unanimous regarding the formation of *Raja-yoga*. According to Yayana and others, three or four malefic planets in their exaltation make the king cruel. Benefic planets in exaltation make the king virtuous and if the planets in exaltation which go to raise him to kingship be both malefic and benefic, he will be of mixed nature. Jeevasarma is of the view that malefics in exaltation do not bestow royalty on the person born under their auspices, he will be wealthy and at the same time cruel and quarrelsome. According to Varahamihira, three or more planets occupying their exaltation or their own signs shall be at the same time, trine to one another, the persons born under them become kings if they belong to a royal family. If there are five or more such planets, those born in ordinary families may become kings. Those having such planets but less than five will be possessed of wealth, position, name and fame, but not be kings.

When Saturn is in the Aquarius ascendant and four planets occupy their exaltation signs, an emperor is born. When Aries occupied by Mercury is the rising sign, and Jupiter is in the exaltation sign, a ruler of men comes into existence.

If the Moon occupies the rising sign Taurus and the Moon occupies *vargottama* or *pushkarma*, the person born is a king. When the full Moon aspected by benefic planets is in the 10th *bhava*, a ruler of the Earth has his birth under the *yoga*. When the

Moon in conjunction with Jupiter and Venus occupies Sagittarius, Mercury is in the Ascendant, Mars in Virgo and Saturn occupying the fourth *bhava* is in Capricorn, the person born will be a mighty king held in high regard by all other kings.

The native at whose birth Mercury, the Moon, Mars, Jupiter and Saturn occupy Virgo, Pisces, Gemini, Sagittarius and Capricorn respectively will become a king. Another *yoga* leading to kingly fortune is when the full Moon with abundant strength occupies the Pisces Ascendant and when Mars and Saturn are in Capricorn and Aquarius respectively.

Note : — In the first half of this *yoga*, the rising sign must be Capricorn, the 2nd part is clear.

The person at whose birth the rising sign Capricorn is occupied by Mars, and Cancer by the Moon becomes a king. Again when Mars, the Sun and Jupiter occupy respectively Capricorn, Aries and Aquarius, the person born is a king.

If the full the Moon in conjunction with a planet other than the lord of the Ascendant be aspected by Venus, Mercury and Jupiter, the person born will be a King. Again, if Jupiter, Venus and Mars occupy *Vargottamamsa* and malefic planets be not in angular houses, the person born under this *yoga* becomes a ruler of men.

When all the planets occupy *shershodaya* signs and when the Moon occupying Cancer is aspected by benefic planets, the person born is a king. Again when the lord of the rising sign occupies the 9th or the 10th *bhava* and when the Moon is in the ascendant, the person born will be a ruler of the Earth.

The Sun has traversed the first half of Sagittarius, the Moon is just there, Saturn possessed of much power is in the Ascendant, and Mars is in the exaltation sign. If this be the planetary position at the time of native's birth, he will grow into such a mighty Emperor that his enemies, overwhelmed by his fiery valour, will do homage to him from afar, regarding him with awe, giving up all idea of measuring their strength with him in battle.

When the lord of the Ascendant occupies an *upachaya* place in respect to the Moon, when the benefic planets occupying angular positions are in benefic *Navamsas,* and when malefic planets have no strength at all, the person born will be a king equal in might to *Indra* (the Immortal ruler).

If the Sun, the Moon, Mercury and Venus are in the 10th house the *bhava* occupying the friendly *Navamsa* in a sign which is not owned by an enemy and where they neither become invisible nor develop, a great King in whose royal progress, the dust is laid by the dropping from elephants composing his train. (This *yoga* is applicable only to persons born in a royal family).

If, at the birth, Mars occupy in strength the exaltation sign and be aspected by the Sun, the Moon and Jupiter, that person, though low born will become an illustrious ruler of men, capable of protecting the whole Earth.

The person at whose birth Mercury is in Virgo Ascendant, Jupiter and the Moon in the 7th house, Venus in the 10th house and Mars and Saturn in the 5th house rules the Earth in good health and without any hindrances.

Jupiter occupying the 2nd *bhava* in conjunction with Venus at the birth of a person will make him a lord of the Earth capable of vanquishing all enemies.

The person at whose birth, the lord of the first *bhava* is in an angle, the lord of the 10th house in the 4th, the lord of the 9th *bhava* in the 11th, such a person will become a king and he will be blessed with a long life.

If, at a native's birth the Sun and Mercury occupy the 4th *bhava,* Saturn and the Moon, the 10th house and Mars the 1st, the person born will undoubtedly become a king.

Even a low, born man becomes a king if at his birth the Sun occupies in the rising sign Leo a *Navamsa* other than what belongs to Venus, and if Mercury be in Virgo.

27

IMPORTANCE OF *PARIVARTANAN*
YOGAS IN ASTROLOGY

Astrology is a part of Hindu culture and philosophy and is held in the highest reverence by one and all. Human needs and aspirations are the basis for interest in astrology. In prosperity or adversity, in every walk of life people desire to know how the future will help them.

One of the ancient Astrologers, a sage by the name PARASARA who lived about 1500 B.C. made a special study of astrology in relation to health, disease and death. He deals with several other aspects of astrology viz., *Raja-yogas*, *Arishtayogas*, *Dhanyogas*, *Ayuryogas* etc., including *Nabhasayogas* and the like.

These *Yogas* are very important to assess the values of a Horoscope. *Yogas* tend to reveal the degree of wealth, fame, rank, position, adversaries, ill health, death and other misfortunes, one is supposed to face within the present life based on the past deeds. All *Yogas* are combinations of planets but in different detail. In this chapter, *Parivartana yoga* has been dealt with in detail.

The *Parivartana* phenomenon manifests in a planetary constellational exchange between two planets. The first planet in his own sub-period will give the results of the second planet and the second in his sub-period in the major-period of the first will yield the results of it. Besides, in a planetary *Parivartana yoga,* one planet will delegate his power of lordship involved in the *Parivartana yoga* to the other. And in a constellational *Parivartana yoga,* if the *Dustana* lords (malefics) are involved, they will produce *Vipareeta Raja-yoga.*

By the Interchange *Yoga* or the mutual exchange relationship, both the planets possess the properties of the other house and express their respective ownership through the medium of the other. Every planet has two houses or rather the rulership of the two *Bhavas.* Due to this Interchange *Yoga,* the effects are restricted only between the two *Bhavas* whose respective lords have mutually exchanged their places and not in other *Bhavas.*

Interchange between two benefic *bhava* lords would give benefic effects. If the interchange is between a benefic *bhava* lord and a malefic *bhava* lord, then the result would be sometimes good and sometimes unpleasant. But if both the *bhava* lords are malefic, the interchange effects would also be malefic. But all the same, being a *Raja-yoga* though of opposite nature, some silver lining could be expected.

Counting from the *lagna* or the ascendant, there are twelve *bhavas* (houses) and for the Interchange *Yoga,* we need *bhavas* at a time. Therefore by combinations we get 66 Interchange *Yogas* which are related with the twelfth, eight and sixth lords and these constitute *Dainya Yoga.* Those Interchange *Yogas,* which are related with the third lord, constitute *Khala Yoga,* and those Interchange *Yoga* which are related with the *bhava* lords other than the third, the sixth, the eighth, the twelfth lords, are known to be *Maha Yogas.*

Dainya Yoga

(a) An interchange of the twelfth lord with any of the following lords: Ascendant, the second, the third, the fourth, the fifth, the sixth, the eight, the tenth, or the eleventh — a total of eleven *yogas.*

(b) An interchange of the eighth lord with any of the following lords: Ascendant, the second, the third, the fourth, the fifth, the sixth, the eighth, the tenth, or the eleven — a total of ten *Yogas.*

(c)   An interchange of the third lord with any of the following lords: the Ascendant, the second, the fourth, the fifth, the seventh, the ninth, the tenth and the eleventh — a total of eight *Yogas*.

Maha *Yogas*

(d)   An interchange of the Ascendant lord with any of the following lords: the second, the fourth, the fifth, the seventh, the ninth, the tenth and the eleventh — a total of seven *Yogas*.

(e)   An interchange of the second lord with any of the following lords: the fourth, the fifth, the seventh, the ninth, the tenth and the eleventh — a total of six *Yogas*.

(f)   The fourth lord interchanging with any of the following lords: the fifth, the seventh, the ninth, the tenth and the eleventh — a total of five *Yogas*.

(g)   Interchange if the fifth lord with any of the following lords: the seventh, the ninth, the tenth and the eleventh — a total of four *Yogas*.

(h)   Interchange of the seventh lord with any of the following lords: the ninth, the tenth and the eleventh — a total of three *Yogas*.

(i)   Interchange of the ninth lord with any of the following lords: the tenth and the eleventh — a total of two *Yogas*.

(j)   Interchange between the tenth and the eleventh lords — a total of one *Yoga*.

Total Maha *Yoga* = 28.

Therefore, there are *Dainya Yoga* = 30.

Khala Yoga = 8.

Maha Yoga = 28 whose total is 66.

Counting from the Ascendant, there are twelve *Bhavas* in twelve signs.

According to the above rule, there can be 18 interchange *yogas*.

These are given as follows:

Mutual Exchange *Yogas*

1.   Between the Ascendant Lord and the Fourth Lord:

    (a)   The Ascendant Lord in the second and the Fourth Lord in the third.

    (b)   The Ascendant Lord in the sixth and the Fourth Lord in the eleventh.

    (c)   The Ascendant Lord in the tenth and the Fourth Lord in the seventh.

2. Between the Ascendant Lord and the Seventh Lord:

    (a)   The Ascendant Lord in the third and the Seventh Lord in the fifth.

    (b)   The Ascendant Lord in the eleventh and the Seventh Lord in the ninth.

3. Between the Ascendant Lord and the Tenth Lord:

    (a)   The Ascendant Lord in the fourth and the Tenth Lord in the seventh.

    (b)   The Ascendant Lord in the eighth and the Tenth Lord in the third.

    (c)   The Ascendant Lord in the twelfth and the Tenth Lord in the eleventh.

4. Between the Second Lord and the Fifth Lord:

    (a)   The Second Lord in the third and the Fifth Lord in the fourth.

    (b)   The Second Lord in the seventh and the Fifth Lord in the twelfth.

    (c)   The Second Lord in the eleventh and the Fifth Lord in the eighth.

5. Between the Second Lord and the Eighth Lord:

    (a)   The Second Lord and the Eighth Lord in the eighth.

    (b)   The Second Lord in the twelfth and the Eighth Lord in the tenth.

6. Between the Second Lord and the Eleventh Lord:

    (a)   The Second Lord in the fifth and the Eleventh Lord in the eighth.

    (b)   The Second Lord in the ninth and the Eleventh Lord in the fourth.

(c)   The Second Lord in the first and the Eleventh Lord in the twelfth.

7.   Between the Third Lord and the Ninth Lord:

(a)   The Third Lord in the fourth and the Sixth Lord in the fifth.

(b)   The Third Lord in the eighth and the Sixth Lord in the fourth.

(c)   The Third Lord in the twelfth and the Sixth Lord in the ninth.

8.   Between the Third Lord and the Ninth Lord:

(a)   The Third Lord in the Fifth and the Ninth Lord in the seventh.

(b)   The Third Lord in the first and the Ninth Lord in the eleventh.

9.   Between the Third Lord and the Twenth Lord:

(a)   The Third Lord in the tenth and the Twelfth Lord in the fifth.

(b)   The Third Lord in the second and the Twelfth Lord in the fifth.

(c)   The Third Lord in the second and the Twelfth Lord in the first.

10.   Between the Fourth Lord and the Seventh Lord:

(a)   The Fourth Lord in the fifth and the Seventh Lord in the sixth.

(b)   The Fourth Lord in the ninth and Seventh Lord in the second.

(c)   The Fourth Lord in the first and the Seventh Lord in the tenth.

11.   Between the Fourth Lord and the Tenth Lord:

(a)   The Fourth Lord in the sixth and the Tenth Lord in the eighth.

(b)   The Fourth Lord in the second and the Tenth Lord in the twelfth.

12. Between the Fifth Lord and the Eighth Lord:

   (a) The Fifth Lord in the sixth and the Eighth Lord in the seventh.
   (b) The Fifth Lord in the tenth and the Eighth Lord in the third.
   (c) The Fifth Lord in the tenth and the Eighth Lord in the eleventh.

13. Between the Fifth Lord and the Eleventh Lord:

   (a) The Fifth Lord and the Eleventh Lord in the ninth.
   (b) The Fifth Lord and the Eleventh Lord in the tenth.

14. Between the Sixth Lord and the Ninth Lord:

   (a) The Sixth Lord in the seventh and the Ninth Lord in the eighth.
   (b) The Sixth Lord in the eleventh and the Ninth Lord in the fourth.
   (c) The Sixth Lord in the third and the Ninth Lord in the twelfth.

15. Between the Sixth Lord and the Twelfth Lord:

   (a) The Sixth Lord in the eighth and the Twelfth Lord in the tenth.
   (b) The Sixth Lord in the fourth and the Twelfth Lord in the second.

16. Between the Seventh Lord and the Tenth Lord:

   (a) The Seventh Lord in the eighth and the Tenth Lord in the ninth.
   (b) The Seventh Lord in the twelfth and the Tenth Lord in the fifth.
   (c) The Seventh Lord in the fourth and the Tenth Lord in the first.

17. Between the Eighth Lord and the Eleventh Lord:

   (a) The Eighth Lord in the ninth and the Eleventh Lord in the tenth.
   (b) The Eighth Lord in the first and the Eleventh Lord in the sixth.

(c)   The Eighth Lord in the fifth and the Eleventh Lord in the second.

18.   Between the Ninth Lord and the Twelfth Lord:

(a)   The Ninth Lord in the tenth and the Twelfth Lord in the eleventh.

(b)   The Ninth Lord in the second and the Twelfth Lord in the seventh.

(c)   The Ninth Lord in the sixth and the Twelfth Lord in the third.

The lords of the benefic *Bhavas*, wherever they are placed enhance the properties of that *Bhava*, the lords of the evil *bhavas* cause the opposite, i.e., destroy certain properties of that *bhava* where they are placed. If the lords of the good *bhava* are related in Interchange *Yoga* then both the *bhavas* enhance the power of any particular beneficial effect. On the other hand, if the lords of the evil *bhavas* are inter-related then both the *bhavas* lose that power of any particular adverse effect. Eventually, the loss of evil effects of a *bhava* bring some good in the midst of adversity and after some untoward happenings.

If the lord of a good *bhava* is related in Interchange *Yoga* with the lord of an evil *bhava* then it destroys the effects of the good *bhava* but increases the qualities of the evil *bhava*. The fruit of all the above mentioned Interchange *Yogas* are — A natural benefic planet according to the type of Ascendant could be the lord of a good *bhava* and also an evil *bhava*. Similarly, a natural malefic planet, according to the type of ascendant, could also be the lord of both the good and evil *bhavas*. Therefore, according to the Ascendant, the following effects will exhibit their evil and good characteristics.

Results

Persons born in *Dainya Yoga* naturally are unwise, act in haste, are thoughtless in dealing with intricate matters and not warm and enthusiastic in their relations with others. They are often inclined to commit questionable acts. They will suffer at the hands of their enemies and speak harshly. They do not have

balance of mind. There will be impediments to successful execut-
tion of all their plans and undertakings.

People born with *Khala Yoga* at one time or the other could
go astray while at other times, they are gentle in speech and
manners. Sometimes, they may regain prosperity while at other
times, they may have to face distress, poverty, misery, hardship
etc.

People with *Maha Yoga* are most fortunate and wealthy.
They are well-dressed and wear expensive dresses and
ornaments. They will receive valuable gifts and souvenirs from
influential friends or people in authority. They command vehicles
and wealth and are also blessed with good children.

Let us study the following charts :

Chart—I

Aries Mars : Taurus Ketu; Virgo Moon and Saturn; Libra Jupiter;
Scorpio Dragon's head; Sagittarius Ascendant; Scoricorn Saturn,
Mercury and Venus.

The ascendant is Sagittarius, the lords of the second and
tenth houses, i.e., Saturn and Mercury exchanged houses forming
a *Maha Yoga*. Here, the significant factor is that Mercury should
be treated as the lord of the 10th house only rather than the 7th
even though he has the ownership of that house. Similarly, Saturn
should be treated as lord of the 2nd and not as lord of the 3rd
house.

The ascendant is Sagittarius, the lords of the 2nd and 10th
houses, i.e., Saturn and Mercury exchanged houses forming a
Maha Yoga. Here, the significant factor is that Merucry should
be treated as the lord of the 10th house only rather than the 7th
house even though he has the ownership of that house. Similarly,
Saturn whould be treated as lord of the 2nd and not as lord of
the 3rd house.

If Merucry is treated as lord of 7th house, he will be a
badhaka and would not have helped the native to retain the
position which he had gained in life. Whatever results the 7th
house gave him were given by Mars, lord of the 5th house

aspecting Jupiter who in turn transferred the cumulative effects to the 7th house resulting in the native concentrating on the welfare of mankind and the alleviation of human suffering. Similarly, the 3rd house being aspected by Jupiter bestowed good result, setting aside the ownership of Saturn.

Chart—II

Aries-Jupiter; Cancer-Saturn; Leo-Ketu; Libra-Ascendant; Scorpio-Mars; Capricorn-Moon; Aquarius-Mercury and Rahu; Pisces-Saturn and Venus.

The native was born in the Libra Ascendant. There is an exchange of lords of 4th and 10th houses, i.e., the Moon and Saturn. Saturn is fully benefic for this native being lord of the angle and trine and his stay in the 10th house came to his advantage in relation to *karma*. Saturn powerfully aspects the 7th house. So marriage was denied to the native. Even though Saturn happens to be the lord of the 5th house, he did not help much towards material gains/prosperity since it functioned purely as the lord of 4th house. The 5th house occupied by Mercury and Rahu, aspected by Mars, so the native is a renowned scholar with logical acumen, *upasana* and enterprise in Treatise on *Mantras,* and has high social esteem and philosophical outlook on life.

Chart—III

Aries Ketu; Leo, Ascendant; Libra, Rahu; Scorpio Mars and Venus; Sagittarius Mercury; Capricorn Sun; Aquarius Jupiter, Pisces Moon and Saturn.

The native was born in Leo Ascendant with Jupiter in the seventh house. The disposition of Jupiter-Saturn is occupying the eighth house belonging to Jupiter. Thus there is a exchange of lords of seventh and eighth house. Had it been the mutual exchange of lords seventh eight lords that would have conferred an auspicious yoga and would have been highly favourable. The native lost his father in the major period of Saturn, since Saturn happens to be in twelfth sign to ninth *bhava* of Saturn governing the father. This reveals the lordship of sixth *bhava* of Saturn was not functional. It is clearly seen that in mutual exchange, the planets appear to lose the ownership of their houses. When Saturn exchanges with Mercury or Jupiter, the planets are equally strong. But when the planet exchanges with the Moon, the latter obviously loses his strength for conferring good and benefic results.

Chart—IV

Scorpio Jupiter; Gemini Ketu; Cancer Ascendant and Saturn; Leo Mars; Scorpio Rashi-Sun and Mercury; Sagittarius, Venus and Rahu; Capricorn Moon.

This native was born in Cancer Ascendant with its lord occuying the 7th house of Saturn. Saturn occupies the Ascendant *bhava*. Hence there is exchange of the lords of the 1st and 7th houses. The second lord the Sun has exchanged places with 11th lord Venus. As a result the houses 10, 9, 4 and 8 have lost their ownerships. The houses 2, 5, 6, 7, 11 and the Ascendant have owners. The ownerless 10th house has the aspect of the seventh lord, Saturn who is a pure benefic by single ownership, having lost the eighth *bhava*. The 4th house has become weak since Venus is purely the lord of the 11th house resulting in depriving her of her mother. The 8th house lost its ownership as aspected by Mars lead to the early death of her husband, since the 9th house is equally ownerless.

So during Saturn's major and Venus sub period, the native had many worries resulting in massive afflictions to a certain extent. The exchange with the Moon made Saturn stronger but he being a natural malefic had caused her assassination in Rahu's sub period.

The native was born as one of the children of an officer of a Government department. Mercury is the lord of the Ascendant in the neutralization of the debilitation effect. But 1st, 5th and 9th lords are in 10th house and the tenth lord is in the Ascendant. So, the chart could be considered to be strong enough, even for international fame. But, the aspect of Mars, lord of 6th and 11th, on 10th, the combination and on the house lord Jupiter in the Ascendant is not healthy. But it is unable to specify the *yoga*, though it reduces the phase of success and reputation and in the major period of Mars, his rise was checked. The native was an intelligent Civil Service official had a penchant for music and belatedly elevated from a District Judgeship as a High Court Judge only in the major period of Rahu. It eventually caused his death too as such, since Mars aspects Rahu.

28

EFFICACY OF GEMS

Many people doubt whether gems can help solve human problems. The reason for this thinking is quite obvious. Precious and good quality gems are expensive. To set them in a gold ring is even more expensive. Therefore, anyone who wishes to invest such huge sums in gems would like to know if they can really help advance one's prosperity, health, business interests etc.

The Need for Gems

The planetary positions at birth can give good or adverse results either during their major period and sub-period or transit periods. Sometimes they give results throughout life like when there is a *Gajakesari Yoga* or *Nabasa, Daridra Yoga* etc.

Suppose a native has an adverse *Yoga* like the ninth lord in the 6th or 12th house then whatever he may do, it may end in loss or failure. A student may have the fourth lord in a bad house, then his education will not be so smooth. One has a weak Ascendant lord or a cruel planet in the Ascendant. So he may suffer ill-health most of the time. In such situations it is necessary to counteract the weak planets by the right and proper use of Gems through correct astrological advice.

Types of Gems

Gems are of two types, precious and semi-precious. Precious gems naturally cost more. Semi-precious gems are not so costly and one can easily afford them. In *Brihat Parasara Hora Sastra* the remedial measures like donation of cow, gold etc., at the end of *Mrityunjaya Japa Sivasahasranama* etc., have been recommended. Gems are quite handy to those who cannot afford to give away in charity expensive items like cows and gold. A rich person can use diamonds, rubies and star sapphires. While an ordinary person can use white coral or white zircon with the same results. The result will not depend on whether the gem is costly or not, but entirely on whether it is for a good lord or not based on the Ascendant. The gem purely based on the sign will not be so effective because hundreds of persons are born on the same day when the Moon will be more or less in the same sign. The Ascendant on the other hand will change every four minutes.

However, the weight of the gems should be more than three carats (carat = 200 miligrams). A diamond should be atleast one half carat. In a *Navaratna* set, the gems may be smaller in size, with the original diamond or zircon.

The Appropriate Gemstones

The most difficult task is to choose the right gems. One can follow the *parasari* system and prescribe a gem for a good lord only, i.e., the first, second, fourth, fifth, seventh, ninth, and tenth lord or for a planet in the 11th house of financial and business prosperity. But sometimes we have to choose a gem for a bad lord also like the third lord. If the third lord is combust or in debility one lacks courage. The longevity could get affected. For certain Ascendants, for example, for Virgo, Saturn becomes the fifth and sixth lord.

For Gemini, Saturn becomes the eighth and ninth lord, for Pisces Ascendant, Venus is the Lord of 3rd and 8th houses. Such planets when in debilitation signs or combust can cause inauspicious results.

Sometimes two inimical planets become weak. For a native, the Sun in Libra and Saturn in Aries or both Mercury and the Moon combust become weak. In such cases prescription of an appropriate gemstone becomes difficult. In such a situation, it is advisable to prescribe the *Navaratna* set so that all planets will become neutral and give one more gem for a good lord like ascendant lord, the ninth lord or the fifth lord so that the benefic results will get accentuated. Whenever a gemstone for a bad lord is necessary then it is safe to give the *Navaratna* as a balancing factor. For best results, the native may be asked to read *Ashtottara* [108 times] for a planet who is in a bad place or bad lord. Say a native has Rahu *Ashtottara* can reduce his malefic effect with a gem of a native for the Ascendant lord or the ninth lord. In the case of *Kalasarpa yogas* (where all planets are within Rahu-Ketu axis), a *Navaratna* ring is better than a single gemstone ring.

In the case of a native who was getting leucodermic patches, he was having a Rahu major period and could not get cured for long. In such a case the following three gems proved effective:

(1)   Mercury who is debilitated and the ninth lord.
(2)   Venus, Ascendant lord.
(3)   Saturn, the *yogakaraka*.

In the case of another native, in whose birth chart, the Moon and Jupiter were combust, for both of which he was prescribed gems. This improved his financial status within a short period.

Another native was without a job for long. He was recommended a gem for ninth lord Mars (but in 8th). He wore gems at the time of going for an interview. He was selected against stiff competition from amongst several others.

Another native was having Rahu's transit and facing problems in his marital life, profession, health and finances. In this case, gems for Jupiter, the second and fifth lord, were suggested. Within a year, his problems disappeared and his life became smooth and pleasant.

As the saying "prevention is better than cure" goes, natives should wear appropriate gems as early as possible so that they can prevent bad results or atleast the intensity of adverse results could be minimized.

It is hoped that people will take advantage of gems therapy and use gems as a preventive measure. Sometimes it is necessary to prescribe more than 2 or 3 gems. Normally beneficial results can be expected within a few months of the use of right type of gemstone.

Planet	Precious Gems	Semi-precious Gems
Sun	Ruby	Star Ruby, Garnet
Moon	Pearl	Moonstone
Mars	Red Coral	Red Coral, Garnet
Jupiter	Yellow Sapphire	Golden Topaz
Mercury	Emerald	Onyx
Venus	Diamond, White Sapphire	White Zircon, White Coral
Saturn	Blue Sapphire	Amethyst
Rahu [Dragon's head]	Gomedha	Gomedha
Ketu [Dragon's tail]	Cat's Eye	Cat's Eye

For more detailed advice, readers are requested to refer to the author's book titled **"Gems Therapy"** published by *Sagar Publications*, 72, Janpath, Ved Mansion, New Delhi-110001. [Tel : 3320648].

29

MATERIAL AND PROFESSIONAL ADVANCEMENT

The term 'promotion' is used in a broad sense to include all sorts of advancements in service and professional life from initial job entry, increased pay and responsibility to switching over to a better job or expansion of commerical ventures and the signs of eminence in social and political life. The 10th house, its lord, which gives indication about professional advancement, has to be analysed for a correct appraisal of its strengths/weaknesses to throw light on this vital aspect of life. Besides this house, the strength and weakness of 2nd and 11th houses should also be considered simultaneously.

These parameters in a natal chart help us to determine the extent of the successes and failures in one's life in all our gainful economic activity and business ventures. All planets gain optimum potency in the 10th house. Jupiter and Mercury, being the natural significators, give good results when they occupy the zenith of a birth chart. Saturn in the 10th house can raise a native to dizzy heights of success and good fortune through dint of hard labour. Even Venus and the Moon, though being devoid of directional strength in that house, can bless a native with a stable and fruitful career and lot of power and affluence. All planets transiting through the meridian of chart accentuate the positive cosmic influences. It is possible to make accurate forecasts about promotions in career, provided the relevant birth chart is properly analysed keeping the 10th house and its lord at the centre because once the horoscope is analysed thoroughly from all relevant angles, it is possible to assess the extent to which the tenth lord either directly or indirectly has been able to rejuvenate the birth chart for benefiting the native in his professional career at the opportune moment.

Take for instance the tenth house. When a planet occupies the 10th house, the tenth lord becomes automatically its sign dispositor. As result, the planet in its own major-period in the sub-period of the 10th is very likely to give result of the tenth *bhava* provided such major-periods and sub-period lords are friendly to each other and the sub-period lord is congenially placed from the major-period lord.

Otherwise, there may be some results but such results may be untoward in the form of setbacks in career etc. Several variants of this simple rule could be traced. Thus a planet in the tenth *bhava* in the sub-period of friendly planet conjoined with the tenth lord may give similar results as mentioned above or the sub-period of a friendly planet in the 10th house etc.

30

INAUSPICIOUS PLACEMENT OF MARS — MARS *DOSH*

Mars *Dosh* or *Angaraka Dosha* as it is called, is said to be present in a Natal Chart when Mars is placed in 1st, 2nd, 4th, 7th, 8th 12th houses. This adverse propensity is also called *Manglik Dosh* in some parts of India. 1st house indicates self, 2nd house family (*kutumb*), 4th for family comforts, 7th for spouse, 8th for longevity and death of an individual whereas 12th house represents pleasures of bed, sleeping comforts, foreign connections, etc. So in the presence of Mars in any of the houses, Mars being a natural malefic is termed as *Manglik Dosh*. Mars being a fiery planet, when badly placed or disposed, his fiery qualities destroy the domestic harmony, culminating in widowhood/separation/divorce.

For this reason, unless aspected by Jupiter, Mars could play havoc in one's life (both love life and domestic bliss). So if Mars be placed identically in both charts, while matching the charts for marriage, the marital life could be estimated to be long and uninterrupted, otherwise the person not having *Manglik Dosh* may either face risk of life, or suffer through separation or marital discord.

Through marital discord, some astrologers have made this *Dosh* so fearful that the common man is very much afraid even to hear the name of this *dosh*, whereas there are certain exceptions not popularly known but if applied by a competent astrologer will be of great help, use and relief to the common man. Such exceptions render this *dosh* null and void. These exceptions should be applied to remove misunderstandings and fears from minds of all. Above all, the *Dosh* should be checked from the Mars position from those of the natal Moon, Venus and Ascendant. The Moon stands for mind and emotions, Venus for love life and spouse/wife and the Mars for the husband, Venus too stands for sex, sexual pleasure, music, dance, ornaments, conveyance and luxuries etc. So if Venus be comfortably placed in the birth charts, Mars in the 1st, 2nd, 4th, 7th, 8th or 12th house from the Ascendant, the Moon and Venus if Mars is weak, strong and strongest respectively will play the mischief.

There is no Mars *dosh*, if Mars is weak, aspected by, or in conjunction with malefics, devoid of strength on account of combustion or a defeat in the planetary war. For the native born in *mrgairas dhanistha* and *chitra* constellations, the Mars *dosh* is not effective. Mars placed in Aries, Leo, Scorpio is not considered to be covered by the *Manglik dosh*.

The Sun and the Moon can adversely affect marital life if they occupy 7th house in a male chart and 8th house in a female chart, Rahu and Ketu can act to detriment as a rule only when such a 7th or 8th house happens to be owned by a naturally malefic planet. Saturn, on the one hand, could cause troubles but, on the other hand, he will give a philosophic outlook to the native concerned and thus help to mitigate the rigours of the adverse *yoga* of Mars. It may be noted that even the greatest misfortune cannot affect one unless one really feels oneself to have been affected by it. Perhaps, this peculiar nature of Saturn could have weighed more as against its disdvantages in determining his role in making a marrried life happy or otherwise.

Mars on the contrary, affects more as its aspects are on 4th, 7th and 8th houses from its natal placement, which are adverse houses. So Mars is often more dreaded than other planets in marital life which no doubt is an important sector of one's life. Mars in the case of a native is placed in the 8th house in association with the Moon causing so-called Mars *dosh*. Yet the native had a long and happy innings of marital life. The lord of the 7th house, the Sun occupies the 10th house. In spite of its being in the state of infancy, it gets strength because of placement in an angular house. The significator for wife, Venus, in this case is combust and the 7th house receives the aspect of Jupiter. The aspect of Jupiter to the 7th house is quite wide. The weakness of the significator and the lord of the 7th house have caused some amount of health problems to the spouse of the native but the presence of Mars *dosh* has not affected the marital bliss of the native as Mars is not a functional malefic in this case. Also in the case of his spouse, malefic planets like Saturn and Rahu are placed in the 4th and 7th houses, viz., *Manglik* houses, which off-set the adverse cosmic influences of Mars.

Mars presence in the first house (also the Ascendent) gives rise to the so-called Mars *dosh*. The native in this case continued to be blessed with a happy married life in spite of the fact that lord of the 7th house and the significator for wife was a bit weak. Mars is functional benefic and has close conjunction with the middle point of the house. The sub-periods of weak planets when such planets are not severally afflicted by functional malefics, Rahu and Ketu do not end the significations ruled by them. However, such weak planets, could cause some tensions. Afflicting planets are functional malefics, Rahu and Ketu.

Mars *dosh* is also caused by placement of Mars in the 12th house. Mars is a functional benefic in this case. The native has been blessed with the happy company of his spouse in spite of the fact that the 7th house does not contian a *Moolatrikona* sign and its significations are not under particular focus. The significator for the spouse is placed in the 6th house, the lord of the 7th house or the significator for spouse do not suffer any affliction. The 7th house in another case does not contain a *Maoolatrikona* sign. The 7th lord is placed in the 2nd house while the significator for wife is placed in the 12th house, the house of losses, expenditure etc. The placement of Venus in the 12th house causes some amount of financial strains and higher expenditure but the marital life of the native was quite smooth and uninterrupted in spite of presence of the adverse Mars. Rather, Mars is a functional benefic for the native and the significations of Mars have contributed considerably to the native's rise in life.

In another case the Mars *dosh* is also caused due to placement of Mars in the 12th house along with Venus. The association of Rahu with the 7th house is close in this case. The lord of the 7th house does not suffer from affliction. The 7th house receives close aspect of the 12th lord, the Moon. The impact of the affliction of the Moon is always feeble due to the fast movement of the luminary. The marital life of the native has been quite smooth and pleasant. The concept of Mars *dosh* has played a significant role in the lives of many persons in our society by delaying their marriage and/or denying them the spouse which would have proved more fortunate for them.

The afflicting planets, even if it be Jupiter, when forming exact/close conjunction with the houses pertaining to marital affairs, the lord and significator of the 7th house, can cause an adverse impact believed to be caused by the inauspicious Mars *dosh*.

The effective remedial measures for such affliction are to propitiate the afflicting planets and strengthening the weak ones representing marital bliss in an auspicious time. For a correct appraisal of the extent of marital happiness for a native, it is necessary to investigate not only the strength or otherwise of the 7th house, pertaining to vital sectors of life and happiness, *viz.*, finances and family happiness (2nd house) and financial gains and business prosperity (11th house), for without the requisite financial support, life in the present-day world is very difficult.

31

BEAUTY, LOVE AND MARRIAGE

The 7th and 8th houses of a female's horoscope reveal her marital happiness, the qualities of the husband, and the period of married life. The 1st house of the horoscope reveals the complexion of the body, general features including the attractivities of the eyes, the facial expressions, beauty of the hair, the softness of the body etc., which go to add to the beauty and personal charm of a lady. These also include grace, tenderness, gait, her peculiar physical and mental charm.

In India, in the last decade or so, there has been a revolution in the thinking process of the fairer sex. More and more women are taking up professional careers and are fearlessly interacting with men, whether at office or in social circles. The sectors which were hitherto the monopoly of men have been invaded by the fairer sex, who are making their mark in every walk of life. Divorce and re-marriage are also becoming very common. Nearly 35% of the horoscopes of ladies which were examined by the writer during 1992-93 had problems in their marital life. These were the horoscopes of the working ladies, who had made a mark in their respective professional fields and moved ahead in life but the only negative factor was that their 7th angle of marital happiness was under some sort of affliction.

In general female/natives born in an odd sign (Masculine sign) with the Moon also in an odd sign, would normally lack modesty, grace etc. (The odd signs are Aries, Gemini, Leo, Libra,

Sagittarius, Aquarius). She would be a strong, masculine woman and specially if this happens in strong malefic Ascendant such as Leo, without the benefic aspects. In such cases, she is advised to take up a professional career, rather than suffer through the rigours of marital discord.

If either one of the two — the Ascendant and the Moon Ascendant — be an odd sign and the other, an even sign, (feminine sign), the rigours of marital dicord would be somewhat tolerable and the couple can maintain their marital ties, in spite of periodical separations which may be for professional or business reasons. But if both the Ascendant and the Moon Ascendant be even signs, (faminine signs). (The even signs are Taurus, Cancer, Virgo, Scorpio, Capricorn, Pisces). The female native would be truly feminine retaining all the charm and attraction of the fairer sex which will become far greater if there is the benefic aspect of some other planets.

Venus is the significator of love and affection, wealth, comforts, ornaments, passions and pleasures. And if Venus be placed in the 1st house, she would be able to magnetise others with her charm and beauty. She would be intense in love affairs and have passions of a very high order.

If, however, there are more than one malefic plants in the Ascendant, the native may not care much for the marital life or husband but will be more devoted to her professional career and may have numerous love affairs/attachments.

If the Ascendant and the Moon are in odd signs and receive the aspect of malefics, the lady would be outgoing, bold, courageous and would interact and mix freely with the opposite sex.

If the 7th house (or the setting *Navamsa*) belongs to benefic planet, the famale native will have an impressive personality and slim hips. If the Moon is placed in a sign ruled by Saturn, she will be very outgoing and assert her personality and will not be averse to having sexual pleasures and will cross all barriers of age, caste and creed with ease.

The placement of Venus in 4th, 5th, 7th, 10th and 11th houses of her natal chart, would also enhance her social image and make her skilful in amorous sports and make her fond of music, fine arts, ornaments and good colourful and attractive dresses.

Mars and Venus conjunction in the 5th house from the Ascendant makes a female native more dynamic, pleasant, lovable and romantic. It makes her beautiful with extra feminine qualities, versatility and sex appeal. Mars, Venus and the Moon conjoined similarly in the 5th angle of the birth chart make a female native modest, sweet and highly feminine, with beauty being amply and highly exhibited. The combination of Mars/Mercury/Venus makes a lady more sexually active. Such a native can easily seduce the opposite sex in seconds. Natives having Mars/Mercury in the 3rd angle of their horoscope having no benefic influences could have doubtful intentions and their manoeuvres should be watched. These two planets could make the natives best administrators, surgeons, senior executives and managers. Venus/Mercury/the Moon in dual houses (Pisces, Gemini, Virgo and Sagittarius) or in the seventh angle of natal chart makes a native unealistic in her intentions and dealings with the opposite sex and she might sail in rough seas in her marital/personal life.

32

JUPITER, THE GREAT BENEFACTOR

While analysing a natal chart, the following factors are to be essentially considered for understanding a planet like the great Jupiter — his mood and functioning and its subtle influence is felt on human beings.

(a)   Natural assigned portfolios,
(b)   Functional duties,
(c)   Strength,
(d)   Major and sub-periods, and
(e)   Transits of planets over natal position.

No planet is so greatly eulogised in astrological parlance as Jupiter. Savants of astrology have also accepted him as a benefic planet. He is thought to be the greatest, the wisest, the finest and the most august member of our Solar system, excluding, of course, the Sun, which is beyond comparison. He earns high commendation for the nature of the portfolios assigned to him and his dominant role in blessing the natives with all that is best in life.

Jupiter is the only planet which represents spiritual excellence as well as human traits. He affects us more forcefully at all levels of our existence vis-a-vis the physical, the mental and the spiritual, than any other planet. Without his divine blessings, it is difficult to lead a comfortable cosy life and be bestowed with status and recognition.

A benefic and strong Jupiter is a great asset in a chart. He is thus a significator of wisdom, prosperity, wealth, good conduct, religious fervour, reverence for the elders, *Sastras*, interest in the occult, law and justice, pilgrimage, teaching, truth, morality, philanthropy, charitable disposition, joviality, expansion, abundance optimism, the company of the learned analytical ability, solemnisation of religious ceremonies, especially wedding, progeny, creative genius, compassion, sense. It controls liver, adipose tissue, circulation of blood in the arteries, fat in human body, thighs and feet. He also signifies some important houses of a natal chart, e.g., the 2nd, the 5th, the 9th, the 10th and the 11th.

Jupiter is basically a *Satvik* (noble-minded) planet. Being so, he gives the native a strong aversion towards baser motives and evil ways.

A look at his significant role reveals the fact that a benefic and well placed Jupiter is in no way against the usually sought material prosperity and worldly attainments. Jupiter rarely puts the natives to misery.

No doubt, Jupiter is the main propeller for a native's achievements but this does not mean that he "relegates the importance of the material welfare and worldly achievement to an unimportant place." This is an incorrect education.

A benefic and well placed Jupiter does take the native towards divine and spiritual interests, but he doesnot do so at the cost of making his life unworthy of living. He blesses us with strong will power and the ability giving us a proper, right direction and follow a harmonious path. There is no compulsion from his side to renounce this world. He restrains us from getting entrapped in the unscrupulous manoeuvres. He lends a certain refinement to keep us away from any activity which belies human dignity and moral values. He enhances our zest to live, lending an added impetus to life and help one and all with a certain zeal and devotion to do good to others.

He doesn't make us disinterested in life, rather he activates the urge for knowledge, wisdom, travels, and action. It is he who alone encourages us to discharge our social responsibilities in a decent and honourable manner and clear our debts, which the *Sastras* speak of. In a nutshell, he is not against our fruitful life on this planet, Earth.

The Jupiterian influence has been found to be providing providential assistance to the natives when efforts fail to show to the desired effects. But it doesn't come to all of us. When Jupiter is placed in the 10th house in his own sign, *viz.*, Sagittarius or Pisces, or rules this house and also aspects it, he can grant his special benevolence and smiles on several occasions.

On the other hand, a weak or an afflicted Jupiter is a drawback. In such a case, the native may lack the urge for divine excellence and finer humane traits. His mind becomes somewhat polluted, and his soul is stifled. To him, the ends are more important than the means. He is not repentant of his misdemeanour. Selfishness, self-centredness and lust for money and power alone dominate his mind. Legal disputes trouble him. He needs to have self-control. He may tend to be harsh, cruel extravagant, over-optimistic, entertaining false hopes and liking cheap popularity. Children could cause him a lot of anxiety. He could commit wrong deeds knowingly and face their consequences for a long time.

He is slave to his abnormal sexual urges. He may be an athlete by nature. He may revile God, religion and places of worship. He tends to ignore his social obligations. He rerely behaves in a dignified manner. He could be a drag on human dignity and honour. His life could lack finesse and grace.

A weak and afflicted Jupiter when associated with the 6th house, its lord and significator, Saturn (in case of ailments), or with Mars, Rahu and Ketu also makes the native suffer physically and undergo prolonged illnesses. The possibility of this kind of affliction is more during his sub-period, provided he has also established some contact with the Ascendant, or its lord, or the Sun or the Moon, as they govern our general health and vitality.

The native's ailments may be due to liver disorders, pleurisy, flatulence, abscesses, blood poisoning, adiposity, diabetes, eczema, skin troubles arising out of poor circulation of blood, leprosy, tumours, jaundice, cerebral congestion.

Jupiter rules two signs of the Zodiac-Sagittarius and Pisces having different traits.

Sagittarius is an enterprising and fiery sign. It inclines the natives towards philosophy, occult studies, science, religion, a good personality, conventional views, sympathy, honesty, hatred towards none, fondness for liberty and external show, freedom from hypocrisy and well disciplined life. It is also a sign of social obligations and responsibilities.

Pisces is a watery sign, somewhat mystical, but with a great sense of morality, based on purity and high principles. It rules religiosity, stoicism, corpulence, rigidity in social customs and traditions, orthodox views, restlessness, frugality, dependence and fair dealings.

Jupiter feels equally convenient when placed in either of these two houses. When he occpuies Sagittarius, he has comparatively more strength to make headway in worldly affairs so that his social and family responsibilities are executed decently. Therein lies his spiritual gratification. When Jupiter is in Pisces, the native is seen engaged in making offerings and homage to God Almighty and places his full confidence in him. From there, he discharges his responsibilities towards his family, society and country. He progresses spiritually, more than he does in mundane affairs. He will have no problem of money and finances till his end. But he should not indulge in risky ventures particularly in the middle part of his life, i.e., between 41-45 years.

When the Ascendant lord, the Moon (ruling our thoughts, emotions and reactions) and Mercury (ruling over intelligence and discrimination) are placed in Jupiter's sign, they get coloured in their traits, though not totally, and then the native is observed having them reflected in his versatile personality. But there should be no adverse influences on them, otherwise they are wiped out to a great extent.

Jupiter is exalted in the 5° of Cancer, owned by the Moon. Jupiter's fundamental nature harmonises with the results allotted to the 4th house of the natal chart, such as mother, domestic peace, general happiness, education and comforts (house, property, real estate vehicles and articles of luxury). A mother is man's first teacher. He learns the sense of love, sacrifice, kindness, tolerance etc., from his mother. And this is what a benefic Jupiter has to give to the native when he is placed in the Moon's sign in the natural Zodiac, the signs and the *bhavas* are identical.

A planet in exaltation may not enjoy a sound footing, as he has to depned on his depositor's, i.e., the lord of the house where the planet is placed), strength to be of any real advantage to the native. The Moon is certainly a weak depositor for the Deva Guru.

For a Sagittarius Ascendant, Jupiter claim to be exalted becomes bleak, as he has to lie in the 8th *bhava*. The Pisces Ascendant is that way luckier, as Jupiter occupies the 5th *bhava*. Despite all this, it is not harmful to have an exalted Jupiter, irrespective of its placement.

If Jupiter, as Lord of Ascendant is in the eighth house it confers *Raja-yoga*, e.g., name, fame, wealth and immense happiness. Jupiter is consequently debilitated in the 5° of Capricorn, an earthly sign. Saturn rules over Capricorn. Capricorn is the 10th sign (*bhava*) of the Zodiac, governing business, status, profession, position and prestige. Jupiter's basic nature does not suit this sign much. But its placement in this sign accentuates wordly affairs, and the native has a dedicated approach and believes in nothing but hard work. It is not, on the whole, a happy sign for him to be in. He loses much of his glory in this sign.

Jupiter's *Moolatrikona* sign is Sagittarius (0° -10°). Frankly speaking, the *Moolatrikona* position of a planet (i.e., position sign owned by it) does not serve any real purpose, except that it looks fascinating to mention it in astrological parlance. It is difficult to say why part of *Moola Nakshatra* is not included in Jupiter's *Moolatrikona* segment. Ketu interacts with Jupiter when he is in Sagittarius upto 13°-20° of it. Ketu helps Jupiter half-way-only in religious/spiritual matters.

As regards Jupiter's placement in other signs, it may be clarified that he does modify and boost their respective traits. For example, Aries is the fiery, headstrong and forceful sign, and its lord is Mars who is Jupiter's ally. Jupiter checks its rash and erratic characteristics. The sign occupied by him also influences him in some way or the other. The same sign, Aries, makes him more dynamic, energetic and dashing, with a lot of initiative and drive.

It is indeed strange that Jupiter, too, gets combust when it moves backwards or forwards of the Sun. Some learned astrologers are not quite optimistic about a combust Jupiter, and think him to be a powerless planet. It is a debatable point that all that it denotes or signifies as a significator is destroyed wholly or partially, depending upon its proximity to the Sun. This view is not wholly convincing as empirical facts go against it. Combustion is, no doubt, a technical flaw in a planet, but it does not make him totally ineffective. Most of its significations are not nullified. Such a Jupiter generally fails.

The significations likely to be affected adversely are to be sorted out carefully, taking into account the *bhavas* which also rule them. Jupiter remains retrograde for a period of 120 days. He generally tends to become retrograde when in the 5th *bhava* from the Sun and resumes direct motion on entering the 9th *bhava*. Sarvartha Chintamani states that the ruling period of retrograde Jupiter behaves oddly, particularly during his major sub-periods, causing uncertainties about all that he happens to govern in the natal charts, besides his own *karakatwas*. Results expected of him, even if he is strong when jundged by the other methods, may or may not take place. Some delays are also likely. All these factors are due to his slow movement.

Another view held is that the position of a retrograde planet in a house or a sign is intended to indicate its basic characteristics, that is, whether the planet is functioning as benefic or malefic whilst its location for the previous house (its aspects) should also be considered backward.

What are the functional aspects of a planet. It may be stated that a planet should not be considered as benefic or malefic simply on the basis of his ruling this or that *bhava* In a birth chart no house of chart is totally inauspicious whether it be the 8th or the 9th in addition to the planets owning the 6th, the 8th and the 12th houses could cause only the normal obstacles, provided they are strong unafflicted, occupy their own *bhavas*. It is the affliction or weakness of the planet under consideration which matters most. There is need to make a slight deviation from this view while judging the lordship of the 6th, 8th and 12th *bhavas*, as when they rule, both good and inauspicious significations get accentuated, whereas the inauspicious ones get subdued.

When Jupiter rules any of the *bhavas*, the 6th, 8th, and 12th *bhavas*, as they rule both the good and inauspicious significations. If their lords are strong-unafflicted, their positive significations get accentuated, whereas the inauspicious ones get subdued. When Jupiter rules any of these *bhavas*, 6th, 8th, and 12th, and is also weak-afflicted, the adverse influence caused by him during his major sub-periods is comparatively much less than that produced if the Sun, Mars, Saturn, Rahu and Ketu were their rulers. The jolts given by Jupiter are bearable because of his inherent benefic and benevolent nature.